GODDESS ACTIVISM

CAMERON MONTGOMERY

Cover: Remixed by Studio Dreamshare, www.studiodreamshare.com. Samples courtesy of The Riahi Brothers, Arash T. Riahi, Arman T. Riahi, at www.everyday rebellion.net, the glorious *vinok* crown handmade by Nataliya Martynets at Etsy shop **NeedleworkUkraine**, and FEMEN Women's Movement's Flickr account for the image *Azarov Pursued by Bloody Tits 'Krovosisi'*. Special thanks to the incredible Moujan Taher for her picture "I'd rather be a rebel not a slave", and the quote for the back cover of the book.

Copyright 2017 by Cameron Montgomery
Copyleft 🄯 2017 Studio Dreamshare
First edition 2017
All rights flexible upon request and attribution.
For information about permissions to reproduce selections from this book, or to contact the author, write to studiodreamshare@gmail.com.
@StudioDreamshare
www.StudioDreamshare.com
ISBN: 978-0-9959557-1-4

ACKNOWLEDGEMENTS

I am indebted to the University of Ottawa for generously supporting my research in so many ways. Thank you to my cohort of PhD students in whom I found friends for life. Thank you to Naomi Goldenberg, my PhD supervisor, whose brilliance and mentorship guided me through the doctorate journey. My heartfelt thanks to Emma Anderson, Marie-Françoise Guédon, Heather Eaton, and Craig Martin for their encouragement and feedback. Thank you to all of the brave artists in the book who generously gave me permission to share their stories and photos.

CONTENTS

INTRODUCTION 1
    Overview of the Book 4
    Methodology 5

CHAPTER ONE: UKRAINE AND THE BIRTH OF FEMEN 9
    A Note on Ukrainian Paganism 9
    Contemporary Ukraine 17
    Femen Goes International 47
    Amina Sboui 51
    The Ukrainian Revolution of Dignity: Maidan 62

CHAPTER TWO: BEYONCÉ FEMINISM. FEMEN. AND SEXTREMISM 73
    Critics of Femen 73
    Femen in Canada 93
    Femen in Iran 101

CHAPTER THREE: THE GODDESS AND ACTIVISM 105

God the Father 105
Feminist Theology 112
Why Women Need the Goddess 115

CHAPTER FOUR: BETWEEN CALIPH AND REPUBLIC IN TURKEY AND THE GÜLEN MOVEMENT 120
Gezi Park 120
The Gülen Movement 132

CHAPTER FIVE: RELIGION AND PROTEST IN A POSTSECULAR AGE 141
The Religion/Secular Binary 141
Naomi Goldenberg: Theory of Vestigial States 148
Re-orientations of Identity 159
Supernational Entities and Subjugated Knowledges 163

CONCLUDING STATEMENT 172

INTRODUCTION

This book is a feminist theological presentation of the ethnographic research I collected for my PhD thesis at the University of Ottawa. Dissertations are notoriously dry—and mine was no exception, I'm afraid—so I wanted to create a version journalistic and vibrant enough that I would actually want my family and friends to read it. This is my attempt at presenting my work in a way that preserves its academic integrity, but at the same time allows me to speak my mind as a curious scholar and artist in the heartfelt manner of a conversation.

Here it is: what I was doing from 2013-2016. I hope you enjoy my first significant contribution to knowledge and research. Thank you for your support.

Why Femen?

I vaguely followed Femen on the internet from 2009-2012, but they first truly piqued my interest as a scholar of religion in 2012, when Egyptian Femen activist Aliaa El Mahdy wrote "Sharia is not a constitution" on her bare breasts, held a Qur'an over her naked vagina with Femen activists standing to her left and right holding a Bible and a Torah over theirs.

Bad girls, I thought.

Screen capture from the film *Everyday Rebellion* by The Riahi Brothers—Arash T. Riahi and Arman T. Riahi—at www.everydayrebellion.net.

Then I noticed the comments. People disproportionately hated these women—and it was not only men heaping them with scorn, but other women too. They were called satanic witch sluts, and people were publically wishing that they would die in a fire, get ovarian cancer, or get raped to death. What was going on here? I was fascinated.

Not only did I find what they were doing with their bodies incredibly artful and bold and brave (a.k.a. *awesome*) but I had never seen anyone ever openly challenge organized religion that way. It was, in a word, revolutionary. After toying with several possible projects for my PhD—something to do with Quakers, a critical history of women freethinkers, a feminist analysis of the Ghent Altarpiece—I ultimately decided I had to study Femen, admittedly because I am irresistibly drawn to underdogs. Craig Martin, the external examiner of my dissertation, said to me after my defense: "Femen is a constellation of things people hate." (i.e. Autonomous poor women publically protesting against religion).

People who hate women especially hate Femen. What surprised me though, when I dug deeper, looking for academic analyses of the group, was that a surprising number of feminist bloggers did not like Femen either.

Why?
I was very confused.

This book aims to tell the story of this group of courageous and outrageous women, providing the context and depth that you simply don't get in flashy headlines which aim to incite reaction. I have included as many photos as legally possible because this group is quintessentially iconic, and it would be impossible to share the story of Femen without a visual catalogue of their protests.

Women know that everything we do with our bodies is a political statement. You shave your armpits? Political statement. You don't shave your armpits? Political statement. You wear something on your head? Political statement. You wear nothing on your head? Political statement. What you eat, where you stand, whether or not you are smiling, all of your health choices, everything to do with your sexuality—these things are political statements whether you intend them to be or not.

As the great Carol Hanisch wrote, "the personal is political".

There is no 'personal' space where men have private beliefs about whether or not a god wants them to beat their wives, or a god wants them to stop all women everywhere from using birth control. That is political, in every sense of the word—and for women, it's intimately personal, every time. It's not your religion or your faith, it is your political orientation and your political crusade to control women's bodies.

As an ethnographer, I listen to a lot of stories. To really listen to, and then make sense of these stories, I found it impossible to separate the 'religious' from the 'secular'. These are abstract terms that are meaningless in practice. For feminist scholars of Religious Studies, the tools of analysis are fairly clumsy: for example 'faith' and 'worship' are terms that get used a lot, but these words have fundamentally different gendered meanings, do they not? And yet they get defined in the traditionalist frameworks, like Ninian Smart's, to give one of many examples, as static, neutral terms. If your experience of worship is your brother reciting the *kaddish* at your father's funeral, while you listen from behind a screen, then your experience of, and thus the foundation of, your perspective on worship is different. What gets protected for a man by the Freedom of Religion clause in the Canadian Charter of Rights and Freedoms is different than what gets protected for a woman.

In my research, I needed to provide a case for analysis alongside Femen to test my theories about popular understandings of religion and the state. In 2014, through a series of synchronicitous circumstances, I ended up in Turkey with the Gülen Movement, the group accused of orchestrating the coup against the Turkish government in 2016. I felt that this ethnographic research needed to be recorded and so I used it as my comparative case in my dissertation. Although this book will be much lighter on theory than my dissertation was, I have kept the Gülen Movement research piece and I have tried to make my analysis of the state as accessible as possible.

The people I talk about in this book are loved by some and hated by others, and each and every one has risked their social capital and all of their access to a 'normal' 'safe' life, for what they believe in. There is something about the rawness of this work that I think can touch everyone who is able to see beyond the politics of the day. These people were not sponsored by election petitions or corporate campaigns, but stood in the street, whether in Gezi Park in Turkey, Maidan Square in Ukraine, or Notre Dame in France, with their own bodies, hoping to be seen and understood.

I have tremendous respect for the work of the people I have met, engaged with, or studied through this research, and I am so happy to share their stories in this book.

OVERVIEW OF THE BOOK

Here is a road map of where we are going:

Chapter One, Ukraine and the Birth of Femen, jumps into the history of the movement called Femen, from their roots in Ukraine, to their activist diaspora internationally.

Chapter Two is called Beyoncé Feminism, Femen, and Sextremism. I was surprised to discover that side-by-side with the misogynists, some bloggers thought of Femen as disgusting white colonizing pretty girls performing for the male gaze. This chapter tackles some of the recent shifts and developments in feminist movements.

Chapter Three, The Goddess and Activism, is my analysis of Goddess iconography in Femen actions through the lens of feminist theology. I tie the movement to the work of brilliant feminists like Starhawk, Mary Daly, Aysha Hidayatullah, Maryam Namazie, and others.

Chapter Four examines the Gezi Park Protests and the Gülen Movement in Turkey. Recent events in Turkey have been under-reported and widely misunderstood, in ways similar to Ukraine and Femen.

Chapter Five is my analysis of this ethnographic work through theory I find particularly relevant, most notably Naomi Goldenberg's Theory of Vestigial States.

METHODOLOGY

Any ethnographic work is incomplete without an explanation of methodology. First it is important to mention that although I have Ukrainian ancestry, I myself was born and raised in Canada. My reflections on Ukrainian history and current events are told here through the lens of a multicultural Canadian fantasizing about Ukrainian art and culture.

The empirical domain of this work is composed of text and image-based narratives shared online by leaders and practitioners of Femen and Native Faith, and observations of the Gezi Park protesters and the Gülen Movement. What began as a fascination with the artistry of the planned actions themselves and then with the public reactions to these actions transformed into documentation and research. I 'followed' Femen International on the social media platform Facebook immediately, and subsequently Femen France, Femen Sverige (Sweden), Femen Australia, Femen Canada, and the group Feminists Against Femen. More recently, as chapters were established, I followed Femen Kurdistan, Femen Nederland, Femen Iran, Femen Polska, and Femen Taiwan. There are many other chapters around the world, but the ones listed above have a coordinated social media presence on Facebook. Other groups, like Femen Egypt, send their updates via the Femen International website, www.femen.org, an online source I also regularly frequent.

I follow several chapters on Twitter. I follow Femen France leader Inna Shevchenko on Twitter and I subscribe to talks and debates that she participates in on YouTube and Vimeo. I have watched a plethora of Femen filmed productions, from amateur YouTube videos to professionally produced documentaries available on Netflix. I have conversed with Femen members and Gezi Park protesters in person and online.

My information gathered on the contemporary Nativist Movement is culled from my membership in Facebook groups and my subscriptions to personal blogs of Ukrainian pagans. I selected the groups based on my personal interest in gender and women's issues. I avoided groups which appeared to be overly masculine-presenting to focus more closely on my interest in feminist theology. In this book I have excluded much of the data on Ukrainian paganism included in my dissertation because there was simply too much material to incorporate without extensive analysis that was beyond the scope of this book.

My empirical data is comprised predominantly of images with accompanying text—'taglines'. I have also collected stories and sound and video bytes of interest to my research. In particular, I use several first person narrative style articles from the Femen website in my thesis.

    I have included pictures and screen captures in the book. Some of these images were taken by professional artists and journalists, and others by amateur friends and family supporting the movements. Some images presented in my dissertation under 'fair use' do not appear in this book due to the copyright restrictions of this book as a commercial product. Studio Dreamshare, the small press producing this work, presents this edition under a copyleft license, in the spirit of many of the activists in this book. Copyleft means that readers are encouraged to share this work without feeling afraid of copyright infringement—in other words, I, the author, encourage you to scan, share, print etc. what you want from this book. All that I ask is that you let me know about it and offer attribution.

    I curated these images with the intentions of Femen activists themselves in mind, so any covered nipples were censored by media channels, not by myself or by Femen. Another goal of my assemblage of this catalogue was to convey the story of Femen visually as followers of their online presence would experience them. All data I have shared in the book are in the public domain or represent my own firsthand accounts. (Since releasing my dissertation, some of the material—stories and photos from blogs—has been removed from the internet, most notably from websites in Belarus.)

    My information on the Gezi Park protests was first limited to Twitter and Facebook trends, because conventional media dissemination was blocked by the Turkish government. While in Turkey I was able to learn a great deal more about the movement on the streets, in bars, shops, restaurants and cafés—over time my ability to look for the right information online improved. Similarly, my knowledge of the Gülen Movement began through living and travelling with members in 2014, and this background equipped me with insight on their various names and organizations to properly further research their activities.

    I am interested in the popular culture of the growing class of people who are unpropertied, educated, young, poor, and childless. These people often do not attend church or temple services, do not participate in the census due to their unpredictable housing and employment conditions, and do not identify as 'religious'. Their digital lives are often more colourful than their embodied lives. I chose this method of research, monitoring these digital communities, because it reveals aspects of the 'lived religion' of this demographic that is not revealed by other research means.

My methodological goal in assembling a digital ethnography was observation, to help me understand and explain, particularly in the case of Femen, the development over time of these movements. Some aspects of protest (and religion) have changed radically in the digital age, and I wanted to highlight this in the book.

I narrowed the focus of my research to the sites of correspondence of 'religion', political commentary, and feminism/social justice. What I have noticed is not that these fields of interest intersect, but that they are not separate. The general ethos and character of each of these groups differ between communities, but politics, religion and feminism are integral and interconnected aspects of group participation. The undifferentiated overlapping of posts about religion, politics and feminism is important to my work and worthy of investigation because it exemplifies my hypothesis that the top-down secular/religious binary approaches obscure the nature of these groups. In Turkey, the Gezi networks are as likely to talk about feminism, unions, Ramadan, or Kurdish repression as they are to talk about environmentalism. The 'elective affinities' cross the boundaries of gender, race, religion, or other conventional identity categories.

Femen activists stage actions against Ukrainian political scandals, Catholic Church scandals, Orthodox Church misogyny, economic interference in Ukraine by Russian President Vladmir Putin, Religious Freedom legislation which persecutes gay people, and a number of other causes which defy 'religious' and 'secular' categorization. It is through these online communities, and irl (in-real-life) communities mobilized through digital networks as case studies that it becomes clear that contemporary theories of religion need to address notions of governance beyond the religious/secular binary to get at the changing ways we think about religion globally.

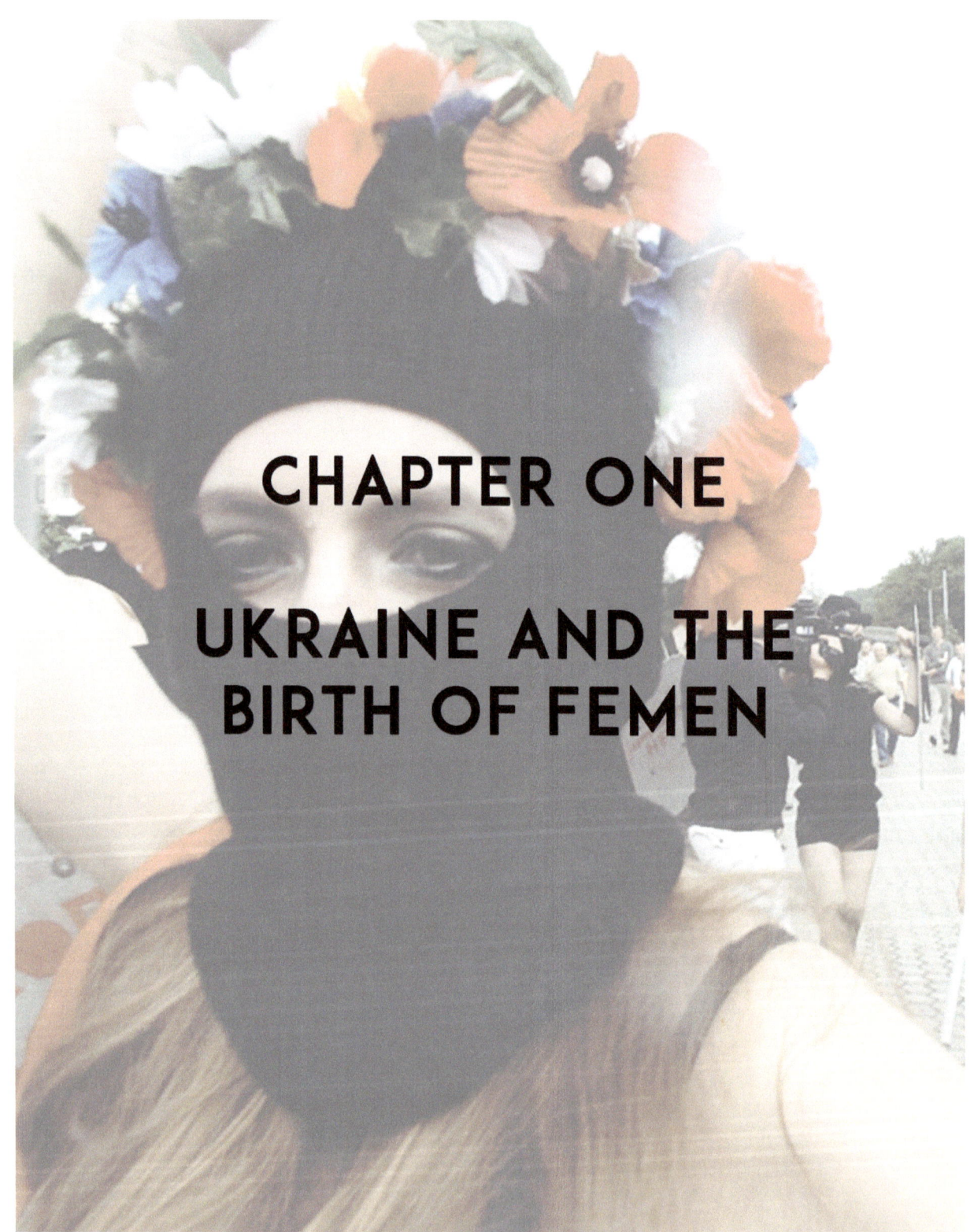

CHAPTER ONE

UKRAINE AND THE BIRTH OF FEMEN

CHAPTER ONE

UKRAINE AND THE BIRTH OF FEMEN

Power and violence are opposites; where the one rules absolutely, the other is absent. Violence appears where power is in jeopardy, but left to its own course it ends in power's disappearance.
—Hannah Arendt, *On Violence*
(Arendt 1970: 56)

A NOTE ON UKRAINIAN PAGANISM

Before I go into the contemporary politics of Ukraine, I want to discuss paganism. As someone born and raised in Canada, I am acutely aware of the intensely patriarchal heritage of Roman Victorian Christianity on mainstream contemporary culture. The territories now called Canada were colonized by the British and French just after a period of mass extermination of pagans by Christian groups in Europe, so the kind of Christianity brought over by early European colonists in Canada was entirely centred on male iconography. 'Neopaganism' for white Canadians often means a modern movement incorporating female deities that draws inspiration from a combination of ancient (pagan) extinct traditions from European immigrant homelands. This is not the case in Ukraine, a region which has a long continuous history of earth worship and female deities who have always been difficult to suppress. My research constantly reminded me of this fact and I urge the reader to keep it in mind when thinking about Ukrainian history.

Ukraine's government tourism website defines paganism as "all religions other than Christianity, Judaism, and Mohammedanism".[1] In keeping with this framing, the word "**testamenter**" is sometimes used to describe "Christianity, Judaism, and Mohammedanism", referencing the shared history, shared mythological lineage, and systemic similarities of these traditions. Christianity, Judaism and Islam are traditions of conversion which have clear historical entry points in Ukraine. Paganism refers to indigenous traditions which have been practiced in the region since ancient times.

'Neopagan' is not an accurate word to describe Ukrainians and pan-Slavic pagan movement adherents. Ridnoviry, Native Faith, Nativism, Native Ukrainian National Faith, Rodism, The Union of Indigenous Ukrainian Faithful, Religion of the Ancestors, and Native Faith Movement are terms used by these communities. The prefix "Neo-" in 'Neopaganism' makes no sense because it implies a discontinuity between pre-Christian practice and contemporary practice. Both popular and academic discourses on paganism influenced by the North American colonial context discredit indigenous movements with this language, particularly in comparison to the language used to describe testamenters. For example, Lyubitseva describes these movements as: "a 'return' of some Ukrainians to ancient religious roots, promoting actually paganism (Native Ukrainian National Faith), rituals of which are reconstructed".[2] In the same article quoted above, the author writes that "[t]he oldest Christian shrines of Ukraine are located in Crimea. They are presented by cave complexes, which, despite the difficult course of historical events, revived and continue to perform their sacred function".[3] The 'difficult course of historical events' refers to Soviet repressions of non-Russian Orthodox Christian citizens. There is no mention of the 'difficult course of historical events' of Christian persecution of Slavic pagans. There is also no mention of the pre-Christian usage of the cave complexes.[4] The language used to describe non-ROC Christians is soft and complimentary, while the language used to describe Ridnovirs is sceptical and dismissive. There is no doubt in the tone of the article that the Christian caves have revived their sacred function, but the pagan practices are dubious modern guesses. This is typical phrasing in studies of religion written from either an evangelical or a North American perspective and any study of non-testamenter traditions should account for it.

In contemporary Ukraine, there is no clear distinction between what is Christian and what is pagan, because both groups have adopted many of each other's practices. Native Faith Movements have a pre-Christian calendar which traces holidays and special occasions through the seasonal cycle, on a lunar calendar beginning around March.[5] Many Ukrainian Christians celebrate these holidays as well, sometimes with Christian names and sometimes not. For example, erecting a coniferous tree and decorating it with lights during the winter solstice is an ancient Slavic tradition adopted and practiced by many contemporary Christians. There are many Ukrainian villages where, in the past as well as today, it is difficult to classify practices as Christian or pagan. The fusion was named **dvoriyya (Double Faith)** by frustrated Christian leaders in the fifteenth century, and is still called this today. Hagstone, a blogging community for pagans and heathens, defines this community as a distinct tradition:

> [T]here is Double Faith (Dvoje Vierie, or Dve Viere) – a syncretic Slavic religion that arose as a result of forceful conversions that survives in traditional culture in the villages. It combines Orthodox and Catholic practices with heathen ones, syncretizing old gods with Christian saints and blending heathen stories into Christian folklore.
> (Sanna 2016)

As Christianity spread in the 11-16th centuries, more churches were dedicated to Mary than any other Christian figure; according to Boris Rybakov, this was because Eastern Europeans, who almost universally worshipped female goddesses alongside male ones, sought to modify Christianity's lack of female representation.[6] Some churches displayed the goddess holding a baby girl in her lap, both representing Mary and Jesus, and the mother and daughter deities Lada and Lélia.[7] The mother of Mary was also emphasized in Eastern Europe more than Western Europe because of the indigenous significance of grandmothers in Ukrainian culture.[8] It was in Ukraine that the feast day celebrating The Intercession of Mary began in the 12th century. The first Christian church in Ukraine was dedicated to "Our Most Holy Lady Theotokos".[9] The Eastern Orthodox churches call Mary 'Theotokos', or 'Dei Genetrix', literally meaning the creator of God, or female parent of God. This reflects the Great Schism of 1054 between the Roman Catholic tradition, whose leaders chose to focus on the otherworldly creation of Jesus, and the Eastern Church, whose leaders preferred to emphasize his humanity.

Ukraine's famous ancient wooden churches, like Rizdva Bohorodytsi (Birth of the Mother of God), are dedicated to aspects of Mary's life and feature murals of wealthy female patrons or leaders.[10] Churches with later murals from the eighteenth and nineteenth centuries feature men exclusively.

Protective amulets were a popular Slavic pre-Christian accessory.[11] From the eleventh to sixteenth centuries, amulets were prevalent that featured Christian saints, such as Mary, on the outside. On the inside, against the wearer's skin, was a snake goddess. The exterior Christian symbolism appeased the Christian elites, and the snake goddess on the inside protected the wearer.

Gold dvoriyya amulet from the 11th century. Found in Chernigov, 1821. Image courtesy of the State Russian Museum.

Gold dvoriyya amulet from the 12th century. Found in Smolensk, 1886. Image courtesy of the State Russian Museum.

Amulet from the Late 12th century carved in Jasper. Discovered in 1890 at the Sacristy of the Nativity Monastery, Suzdal. Image courtesy of the State Historical Museum.

While the Christian movement spread north into Ukraine from the Middle East by the Eastern Orthodox Church, the message that was intriguing to pagans was its notion of afterlife. The business of everyday life was regulated by the old ways:

> From a perspective of a Slavic peasant, Christianity must have not been seen as the replacement of old Slavic mythology, but rather an addition to it. Christianity may have offered a hope of salvation, and of blissful afterlife in the next world, but for survival in this world, for yearly harvest and protection of cattle, the old religious system with its fertility rites, its protective deities, and its household spirits was taken to be also necessary. This was a problem the Christian church never really solved.

(Panayiv 2016)

Boris Rybakov, the pre-eminent Russian scholar of Slavic pagan history, writes that in his examination of the literature he did not notice a distinct shift between a pagan time and a Christian time. He noticed a new focus on afterlife, but that the character of public revels and festivals, dress, and songs did not significantly change. Over several centuries, the imagery of mermaids (snake goddess), the tree of life, the horned goddess, and griffins were replaced by the imagery of the life of Jesus.

Left: Ukrainian Lullaby, featuring examples of indigenous imagery.

Right: Classic example of Ukrainian embroidery featuring the goddess Mokosh.

Photograph of Marppa Martiskainen embroidering a classic goddess design in Karelia in the 1920s. Image courtesy of Elder Mountain Dreaming.

Women in the contemporary Native Faith Movement often wear crowns of flowers in their hair during festivals in the spring and summer. This is an ode to Mokosh, the horned goddess of harvest and fertility often depicted in ancient and contemporary Ukrainian embroidery.

Ridnoviry makes space for the worship of female gods, absent in the church of the god called God. The crown of flowers is also emblematic of the rural lifestyle of a Ukrainian peasant, the people brutally persecuted by Stalin's program of starvation. This is why the activists of the iconic Ukrainian protest group, Femen, wear crowns of flowers in their hair.

Left: Postcard of a Ukrainian woman, 1916. Right: Alexandra Shevchenko of Femen.

CONTEMPORARY UKRAINE

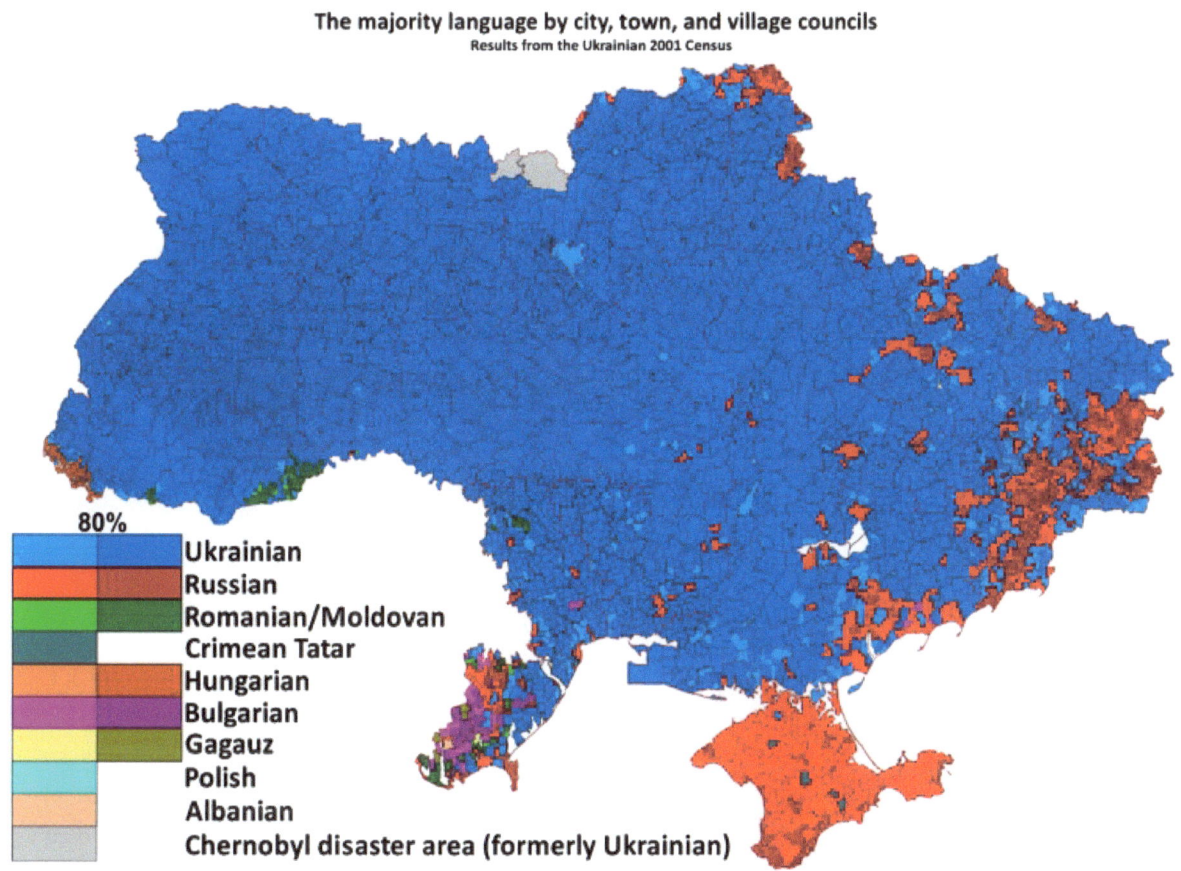

Map of majority languages spoken in Ukraine. Image courtesy of the Ukrainian 2001 Census.

Ukraine is a country on the brink of war and revolution. Since gaining sovereignty as a nation in 1991, Ukraine has held democratic elections, overthrown a corrupt oligarch in the Orange Revolution, carried out a census, implemented an independent currency, and ousted a corrupt oligarch in the revolution of the Maidan. Ukraine has also been invaded and continues to be occupied by Russian armed forces. Her sovereignty may be short-lived.

The latest major protest in Ukraine was the 2014 Ukrainian Revolution of Dignity. Hundreds of thousands of protesters camped out in the central square of Kiev. State forces violently engaged the protest. The reasons were many and complicated, and this section will explain the historical circumstances that ultimately resulted in the events at Maidan.

Intrigued by footage and plays of the protests, author and film critic Peter Pomerantsev travelled to an encampment to take in the revolutionary setting in person. He writes:

> When I first arrived in Maidan a few months after the violence had ended, the square was still a tent city surrounded by barricades of tires, car parts and furniture (as if the very fabric of the city had risen up and rebelled). The dregs of the Maidanistas were still living in the tents, refusing to leave. Wandering among them I found a crucible of utopias: Cossacks dreaming of a return to the Hetmanate; "liquid democrats" inventing ways to vote and then unvote for parliamentarians as with "likes" on Facebook; ethno-pagan nationalists searching for pure Ukrainian chromosomes; libertarians, anarchists, neo-fascists and Christian socialists.

(Pomerantsev 2015)

The Maidanistas, named for the Maidan Nezalezhnosti—Independence Square, the central square of Ukraine's capital city of Kiev—are only the latest Ukrainians struggling to maintain a border with Russia in what Adrian Karatnycky says has been a pseudodemocracy since independence.[12] Self-governance in former colonial territories is often a bitter struggle to establish sovereignties free of corruption and chaos in their early stages. This has been the case for Ukraine throughout the 20th century.

At the end of the nineteenth century, the Russian Empire's military expenditures outpaced her investment in infrastructure and the economy fell hard. The Tsarist government disseminated propaganda to keep up popular support for the war efforts, but support waned. By 1917, over a million Russian soldiers had died fighting on the massive 1,600 kilometres-long Western front in the Second Fatherland War—the war that is called World War One by westerners. All productivity was channeled into the war effort; metal and chemical manufacturing increased while food production dropped by 22 percent and the cost of food doubled and tripled during the war.[13] Peasants were funneled into the cities to work in industrial factories, living an average of twenty people in a room as men were shipped off to the war front. The women grew increasingly frustrated as the war laboured on and on with no end in sight and they were forced to produce weapons instead of food. Urban factory workers as well as soldiers slowly starved to death over food shortages. Tsuyoshi Hasegawa writes:

> Resentment is felt worse in large families, where children are starving in the most literal sense of the word, and where no other words are heard except,

"Peace, immediate peace, peace at all costs." And these mothers, exhausted from standing endlessly at the tail of queues, and having suffered so much in watching their half-starving and sick children, are perhaps much closer to a revolution than [members of the Duma], and of course, they are much more dangerous...
(Hasegawa 1981: 201)

People with a history of civil disobedience and dangerous revolutionary ideas were forbidden to work in factories or as soldiers. By 1917, due to crippling numbers of casualties, these dissidents had to be sent to fill the depleting ranks. At the war front, they took up leadership positions in organizing an anti-war movement. This lack of support both from home and the front meant that no matter what Tsar Nicholas II wanted Russia to do, the war was ultimately unsustainable.

Several general strikes took place in January and February of 1917. On February 23—March 8 of the Gregorian calendar—the socialist holiday proposed by Clara Zetkin in 1910 called International Women's Day, women textile workers held illegal meetings in the morning. In the afternoon they left their seats on the factory line and marched to local metalworking factories demanding that the men join them. According to Édourd Burdzhalov, the police reported that over 75 000 people went on strike that day. He shared a firsthand account by one of the workers at the Noble Machine Construction Factory:

On the morning of February 23 one could hear women's voices in the lane which the windows of our department overlooked: "Down with the war! Down with high prices! Down with hunger! Bread for the workers!" Myself and several comrades were at the windows in a flash…. The gates of No. 1 Bol'shaya Sampsion'evskaya Manufaktura were wide open. Masses of women workers filled the lane, and their mood was militant. Those who caught sight of us began to wave their arms, shouting: "Come out! Quit work!" Snowballs flew through the window. We decided to join the demonstration...
(Burdzhalov 1987: 107)

This event is called the February Revolution. In days all manufacturing in St. Petersburg ceased. Tsar Nicholas II sent a telegram from the Western Front ordering the military garrison to open fire on the protesters. These soldiers refused their orders, some firing on their commanding officers, and many joined the strike. Nicholas Romanov abdicated the throne March 2 (Gregorian March 15).

After a brief rule by provisional government, the Soviets—workers' councils who had been stirring since 1905—and the Bolshevik party established the Russian

Soviet Federative Socialist Republic. This new government was led by Vladmir Lenin. The Bolsheviks signed the Treaty of Brest-Litovsk with Germany to end Russian involvement in World War One. This chaos precipitated declarations of independence from Imperial Russia by the outer territories of the empire, like Belarus, Latvia, Georgia, Estonia, Azerbaijan, Finland, Armenia, and Lithuania; Ukraine declared in 1918, establishing the Ukrainian People's Republic. There was widespread civil war within the UPR and Russia reconquered most of it in 1921. A western portion, including the major city of Lvov, joined independent Poland.[14]

Lenin died in 1924. His successor, Joseph Stalin, implemented a theory of "Socialism in One Country", introducing the First Five-Year Plan. The policy most significant to Ukraine was the introduction of *kolkhoz*, or collective farming. Stalin's economic policy was a dismal failure and between 1932-1933 millions of farmers—*kulaks*—were worked and then starved to death. Children born in 1933 in Ukraine had a life expectancy of seven years.[15]

I will not include photos of actual Ukrainian peasants during this time out of respect for the dead, but here is an artistic rendering by Nina Marchenko, a survivor. If you wish to be very sad, feel free to research 'Holodomor' for yourself. *The Road of Sorrow,* Marchenko 2000.

In 1937, Stalin launched a purge of intellectuals in the borderland republics of the Soviet Union, including Ukrainian territory under Soviet control. He built a network of prison camps in the most remote and inhospitable regions of Russia where torture, grueling labour, unsanitary living conditions, and starvation were endemic. These camps are most remembered through Aleksandr Solzhenitsyn's 1973 book, *The Gulag Archipelago.*

The effects of the Holodomor—'death by hunger' in Ukrainian—and the destruction of their artists, great thinkers and community leaders, is not to be understated. Much of the most significant cultural preservation for generations took place in Canada and the United States, where large Ukrainian populations had emigrated in 1918, and in the communities of ethnic Ukrainians in Poland. Soviet Ukraine was a devastated wasteland of death and destruction, scarred by genocide and starvation. Timothy Snyder writes:

> The good people died first… Those who gave food to others died. Those who refused to eat corpses died […] parents who resisted cannibalism died before their children did. Ukraine in 1933 was full of orphans, and sometimes people took them in. Yet without food there was little that even the kindest of strangers could do for such children. The boys and girls lay about on sheets and blankets, eating their own excrement, waiting for death.
>
> In one village in the Kharkiv region, several women did their best to look after children. As one of them recalled, they formed "something like an orphanage… The children had bulging stomachs, they were covered in wounds, in scabs; their bodies were bursting. We took them outside, we put them on sheets, and they moaned. One day the children suddenly fell silent, we turned around to see what was happening, and they were eating the smallest child, little Petrus. They were tearing strips from him and eating them. And Petrus was doing the same, he was tearing strips from himself and eating them, he ate as much as he could. The other children put their lips to his wounds and drank his blood. We took the child away from the hungry mouths and we cried."

(Snyder 2010: 50)

Countless such stories surface today; under the Soviet regime, until the 1980s, the use of the word 'hunger' in history books in Ukraine was forbidden.[16]

In 1941, the Ukrainian territory was invaded from the west by Germany. The remaining peasants resisted, but were occupied until 1944. Almost 7 million Ukrainians were killed, including 1.5 million Jewish Ukrainians. In 1944, the Tatar community in Crimea was deported to the Siberian gulag by Stalin, and Russian-speaking peasants were established in their homes in time to harvest the crops. When Germany unconditionally surrendered in 1945, the Allies declared victory in World War II, and the Soviet Union regained control of Ukraine.[17]

Between 1933 and 1945, 14 million people, not including soldiers on active duty, were killed between Nazi Germany and Soviet Russia in the region known as 'the bloodlands'—Poland, Ukraine, Belarus, and the Baltic States. As Snyder reports, "most were women, children, and the aged; none were bearing weapons, many had been stripped of their possessions, even their clothes".[18]

After the Allies delivered Ukraine back to the Soviets, a resistance movement in the 1950s and 1960s developed. The resistance was met with "the biggest wave of political repressions of the post-Stalin period. According to the KGB, from 1954 to 1959, 183 'nationalist and anti-Soviet groups' in Ukraine were eliminated".[19]

The Ukrainian Diaspora abroad played a large role in publishing and distributing Ukrainian books, poetry, art, and cultural mythology and folklore during the repressions. In 1970 an anonymous bulletin began circulating in Ukraine, the Ukrainsky Visnyk ('Ukrainian Herald'), whose issues appeared at different times by different publishers until 1990.[20] The Herald told the stories of political prisoners and repressions, missing persons, incarcerations of activists in psychiatric hospitals, as well as stories of the Holodomor, Ukrainian history, and artistic writings. Dissidents met in Russian prisons and shared their stories with one another, organizing actions within labour camps. Family members and visitors of the prisoners smuggled out secret writings and sent them to the diaspora in North America and elsewhere to be published.[21] International pressure by human rights organizations resulted in the release of many of these dissidents in the late 1980s, and when they returned to Ukraine they motivated Ukrainian student uprisings and formed organizations like the Ukrainian People's Movement for Restructuring. This period also marked the rise of Native Faith movements, or Ukrainian Neo-paganism movements.[22]

Pagan festivals, rituals and gatherings had been brutally repressed under the Soviet regime because the Soviets understood the connection between 'religious' movements and ethnic nationalism.

After a rock concert in 1986, 300 Latvian youth marched down Lenin Avenue calling for an end to Soviet oversight and an independent Latvia. In 1987, 5000 people gathered to lay flowers to commemorate the forced deportation of Latvians to ethnically cleansed regions, a history officially denied by the Soviet Union. After that, police blockaded the main square on significant holidays to prevent demonstrations, but on these days thousands of Latvians lined the streets in silent protest. Similar non-violent protests followed in all of the Baltic States.

In 1989, an estimated 2 million people in Estonia, Latvia and Lithuania held hands in a peaceful chain across 600 kilometers, called the Chain of Freedom, calling for the independence of their states from the Soviet Union.[23]

Students in Kazakhstan rioted in 1986; several were killed by police and many more were detained. Some were sent to labour camps and others, from one hundred to several hundred, were summarily executed. It is difficult to say how many.[24]

That year marked the Chernobyl disaster in Ukraine. A reactor at the nuclear power plant exploded, killing over ten thousand people and causing intergenerational health damage for millions more. In 1988, a rally commemorating the Chernobyl disaster turned into a nationalist protest. Ukrainians gathered illegally that year to celebrate one thousand years since the 'Baptism of Kiev' by Volodymyr the Great, the ruler of the ancient Ukrainian kingdom of Kievan Rus'. Ukrainian Catholics held secret services in the forest. Catholicism was especially suspicious to the Soviets because of their allegiance to a foreign authority, the Pope. Tens of thousands of Ukrainians held rallies in 1988, protesting the government and celebrating the Kievan Rus' millennium. These services were led by political dissidents, Ukrainian Catholic and Greek bishops, and students, and they were violently suppressed by state officials. Protesters then held rallies focussed on 'ecological issues', and these drew tens of thousands of demonstrators. Protesters in Ukraine and Belarus demanded better cleanup of the Chernobyl disaster and aid for people living in the contaminated zones. While these ecologically focussed rallies appeared less politically threatening at the outset than rallies led by churches, the discursive language of religion quickly became embedded in the action as Native Faith Movements connected environmental concerns with pagan earth worshipping. In *Nova Religio*, Adrian Ivakiv describes this movement as "the fusion of environmentalism and nationalism" phrased in the language of religion.[25] Parallels can be drawn here to the Water Protectors movement of indigenous peoples in North America.

The character of protest in Soviet Ukraine was slightly different than the movements taking place in the more westerly states. Rudnytsky argues (1987) that Ukrainian society lacked the intellectual class to articulate a political theory of independence. He describes the writings of Ukrainian dissidents as "lower and narrower" than those of revolutionaries in the Baltic States and in Russia.[26] Rudnytsky identifies that the shift from peasants and working-class factory workers to newly educated youth played a role in the demographics of the protesters. He writes:

> This state of affairs reflects the general provincialism of contemporary Ukraine's cultural life: the lack of contacts with the outside world, the insufficient knowledge of foreign languages, and the limited access to non-Soviet books. Furthermore, because of continual purges directed primarily against elite elements of Ukrainian society, present-day Ukraine's intelligentsia is sociologically very young and hence culturally immature. In examining the family backgrounds of Ukrainian dissidents, one finds in most cases that they are first-generation intellectuals. This causes a cultural handicap that even gifted individuals find difficult to overcome.
> (Rudnytsky 1987)

Rudnytsky's comments ring particularly true in hindsight when looking at the effects of the internet on contemporary Ukrainian dissent. Protesters are now able to communicate and rally with movement political leaders without relying on the influence of Ukraine's religious leaders as they did in the late 20th century. They also have access to a wealth of historical information online, including histories written in other countries and other languages translated easily online.

Patricia Monaghan notes that the rural elements of Ukrainian paganism that survived centuries of Christian domination were those practiced by peasants. Historians suggest that wealthy nobles in the ancient Ukrainian Caucasus were associated with a male trinity; this reflects the close mythological relationship with Vedism and the Brahma-Vishnu-Shiva trinity reserved for the elite caste in the Indus valley. Ukrainian[a] peasants were associated with a multitude of local spirits and goddesses. In the early days of Christian encounter in Ukraine, Slavic male deities were combined in the thunder god Perun, one aspect of the pagan trinity, and monotheism became the marker of elite status in post-conversion Ukraine. In the nineteenth and twentieth century purges of the elites of Ukrainian society, only the peasant practices remained, and still constitute a majority (if not all) of pagan or double-faith practices today.[27]

Contemporary Ukrainian babas celebrating masnytsya, an end-of-winter festival welcoming the sun by burning a goddess effigy and burying her ashes to fertilize the fields.

---

[a] The term 'Ukrainian' is used here for regional specificity, but keep in mind that the contemporary nation of Ukraine was federated by an Act of Independence in 1991, so using the term 'Ukrainian peasants' to refer to ancient people is technically anachronistic.
The name 'Ukraine' means 'borderlands'. 'The Ukraine' (*the borderlands*) was the way that Moscovites would refer to the rural, primarily nomadic region to the west of Moscow after the fall of 'Kievan Rus', the ancient proto-Ukrainian state centred around the ancient city that is also modern Ukraine's capital city, Kylv.
Steinmetz, Katy. "Ukraine, Not the Ukraine: The Significance of Three Little Letters." *Time Magazine Online*. (March 5 2014. Retrieved at: http://time.com/12597/the-ukraine-or-ukraine/)

Ukraine's wooden churches in service of ancient indigenous gods.

February 26, 1989, as many as thirty thousand people participated in a service commemorating the Ukrainian intellectual, artist and poet Taras Shevchenko, and unauthorized *molebens*—public rituals practiced by Old Believers—took place. Protests and marches around the country were staged by the Ukrainian Greek Catholic Church, the Ukrainian Autocephalous Orthodox Church, the Marian Society *Myloserdia*, and other groups that had been forbidden since the 1930s.[28] In September 1989, the mass graves of Ukrainians killed by the Soviets were exhumed. Parishes that were officially Russian Orthodox declared that they were now Ukrainian Orthodox. Communities in Western Ukraine converted to Ukrainian Greek Catholicism, and Pope John Paul II began asserting authority over the new Catholic communities and applying international pressure on General Secretary Mikhail Gorbachev, the leader of the Soviet Union. Alexei Krindatch explains how the jurisdiction of the Moscow Patriarchate was severely reduced by the Ukrainian independence movement:

In Russia… with the exception of a few scattered areas with a predominantly Islamic population… the Russian Orthodox Church (ROC) [has] de facto the status of something like a state church. In Ukraine, however, the religious, ethnic and political features of particular Ukrainian *oblasti* and even *raiony* determine in equal part where a particular church will flourish. The political changes in post-soviet Ukraine and the aspirations for a new national independent Ukrainian Orthodox Church initiated by a significant number of Ukrainian Orthodox clergy and supported by the new Ukrainian political elite have caused splits and schisms in what was until 1990 the Ukrainian Exarchate of the Russian Orthodox Church, uniting all Orthodox parishes and dioceses in Ukraine. By the autumn of 1993 three rival Orthodox churches had formed, hostile to one another and competing for the souls of Ukraine's inhabitants. These are the Ukrainian Orthodox Church -Moscow Patriarchate (UOC-MP), which remains under the jurisdiction of the ROC, the Ukrainian Orthodox Church -Kiev Patriarchate (UOC-KP) and the Ukrainian Orthodox Autocephalous Church (UOAC). The latter two both claim to be the bearers of a distinctive ethnic Ukrainian Orthodox tradition, and try to outdo each other in efforts to explore the idea of 'one state-one church'.
(Krindatch 2003: 38)

In 1990, the local governments in the Soviet Republics of Lithuania, Moldova, Armenia, Georgia, Estonia and Latvia collectively refused to pay taxes to the Soviet Union. That year, the Ukrainian Autocephalous Orthodox Church (UAOC) declared independence from the Russian Orthodox Church and the Moscow Patriarchate, and Patriarch Mstyslav I 'of Kiev and all Ukraine' (Stepan Ivanovych Skrypnyk) returned from exile in Canada and the United States after 46 years to lead the movement. More Russian Orthodox parishes defected, and Patriarch Mstyslav I attended and lead nationalist rallies.[29b]

In 1944, the Soviet Union had deported, imprisoned or executed the entire Tatar population on the Crimean peninsula and resettled Russian-speaking peoples there. In the 1980s, the surviving Tatars who had been resettled to Siberia returned in waves to the Crimea and established a Tatar parliament to work within a future independent Ukraine.

---

[b] See Michał Wawrzonek's book *Religion and Politics in Ukraine: The Orthodox and Greek Catholic Churches as Elements of Ukraine's Political System* for a more in-depth explanation of how deeply imbedded church institutions are in the foundations of the modern Ukrainian nation-state.

Ukraine held a national referendum in 1991 and voted 90% in favour of sovereignty, adopting an Act of Independence. Leonid Kravchuk was elected the first President of Ukraine. Belarus, Ukraine, and Russia signed an agreement, the Belavezha Accords, dissolving the Soviet Union and forming the Commonwealth of Independent States (CIS).

Leonid Kuchma, known for election rigging, corruption scandals, pro-Russian politics, and shutting down independent media, was elected in 1994. In 1996, Ukraine adopted a constitution, becoming a semi-presidential republic, and implemented an independent currency, the hryvna. As with any newly sovereign state, Ukraine suffered from growing pains. Inflation, economic turmoil, high crime rates, and corruption plagued the state.

Although the economy somewhat stabilized by the late 1990s, corruption is embedded in Ukraine's new government system. Karatnycky writes that during the Kuchma years, "[w]ide-ranging privatization enabled government insiders and cronies to buy state enterprises at bargain-basement prices. Steel mills, today worth several billion dollars, were bought for a few million. Regional energy companies fell prey to the same forces".[30] For example, Kuchma sold Ukraine's most lucrative steel mill to a family member for much less than the variety of offers by other investors. The tax system also promotes little oversight for the oligarchs buying up public works, and anyone challenging Kuchma's politics was forced out of business. Ukraine's major industries are run by different wealthy and influential families who support the conservative agenda. Karatnycky's explanation of contemporary Ukraine's system of oligarchs is helpful:

> Under Ukraine's constitution, local government officials are not elected but appointed by the president, who allowed oligarchic groups to create local enclaves headed by their allies. In the Zakarpattya (Transcarpathia) region, local and central government officials enabled one oligarchic consortium to amass vast fortunes from the lumber industry by stripping the forests of their trees. Now, parts of this once richly forested mountain region have been dangerously depleted, compounding the problems caused by deforestation in the Soviet era. Over time, several Ukrainian oligarchic clans became dominant in the young nation. Medvedchuk, who became presidential chief of staff in December 2002, represented the Kiev clan, which controlled regional energy and timber companies and invested in broadcast media. The Dnipropetrovsk clan, which invested in the energy pipeline industries, included Viktor Pinchuk, now Kuchma's son-in-law. A powerful group from the eastern coal-mining Donbass

region included metallurgy baron Rinat Akhmetov, the postcommunist world's second wealthiest man, with a net worth of $3.5 billion. Each interest group established its own political party in parliament. The Kiev clan ran the Social Democratic Party of Ukraine (United). The Donetsk oligarchs created the Party of Regions, the ranks of which included a local governor who later became prime minister: Yanukovich. The Dnipropetrovsk group created and backed the Labor Party. And the influence did not stop there. The oligarchs owned or controlled their own national broadcast media and local and national newspapers. Each was capable of massively funding political campaigns in the emerging pseudodemocratic system.
(Karatnycky 2005: 40)

In 2001, the European Union called for an inquiry into the disappearance of investigative journalist Georgiy Gongadze; it was later determined that he was strangled and beheaded by President Leonid Kuchma by his own admission in tapes secretly recorded by Kuchma's former bodyguard.[31] The tapes revealed other crimes, such as electoral fraud, and in 2003, tens of thousands of protesters rallied in the streets demanding his resignation. Kuchma promptly announced that his successor would be Viktor Yanukovych.

Yanukovych ran against several candidates, most notably Viktor Yushchenko, a socialist with a great deal of popular democratic support. Yanukovych and his powerful backers went to great lengths to take the election, including preventing Yushchenko's plane from landing before major political rallies, running him off the road in his car, and falsifying ballots. Yushchenko was almost killed by dioxin poisoning during the campaign, leaving his face brutally scarred. University students rallying against Yanukovych were threatened with eviction from residence in the middle of winter, and "monitors discovered that pens had been filled with disappearing ink, so that ballots would appear blank after they were cast" in areas where Yushchenko had the most support.[32] In spite of these setbacks, Yushchenko appeared to be handily winning the election until exit polls announced in the last hour that Yanukovych had won by 2.5%.

The morning after the election, hundreds of thousands of Ukrainians marched to Kiev's Independence Square wearing orange, the colour of Yushchenko's campaign, in what is popularly called the Orange Revolution. Adrian Karatnycky attributes the sparking of the 2004 Revolution to the coming of age of the first generation of internet-using post-Soviet youth, and the dissemination of independent media and information by digital means.[33] However, there were people of all ages in the streets. A retired coal miner from Eastern Ukraine describes his reasons for joining the protest:

> He went to a polling station and saw the lists of voters, and he discovered that lots of his deceased colleagues from the coalmine were on this list as actual voters (this was a widespread election fraud technology dubbed "the dead souls": deceased people were included into voting lists and later "their" ballots were marked with the "right" candidate). He said he exclaimed: "This is voting from hell, the underworld!"
> (Snyder and Zhurzhenko 2014)

Even producers, reporters, and editors went on strike after the election, sick of many years of the censorship of television networks and other traditional media. Surrounded by supporters, Yushchenko declared himself president, holding a public 'swearing in' ceremony that was recorded and quickly went viral. In the video, he called on the military to endorse him. The bold move paid off—Yanukovych ordered the troops to attack the protesters, but there was widespread disagreement among military personnel. The cabinet, besieged by demonstrators, panicked and voted to declare the poll invalid. The Supreme Court annulled the fraudulent election, followed by new elections. Yushchenko handily won, supervised by more international observers that any election in history. A plot by Russian gangsters to blow up a one-kilometer wide area in central Kiev to kill Yushchenko's leadership team was foiled.[34] Many high-ranking government officials were found to be complicit in the many schemes to control the elections. Yushchenko's government, widely supported by dissidents and revolutionaries, accepted the pro-democratic recommendations by the international election overseers, like more elected and less appointed positions, and promises to reduce government corruption. Yushchenko's government cancelled the sale of the Kriorizhstal steel mill, and re-auctioned it for six times what it sold for previously. Other dubious sales were investigated and re-sold, and the dividends were re-invested in the budget. Despite economic strain, Yushchenko was able to offer more public services without increasing taxes, and this gained him even more public popularity.[c]

---

[c] Yushchenko tapped into the nationalist discourse, branding himself the Ukrainian candidate opposed to the Russian-controlled Yanukovych. When the Patriarch of the Russian Orthodox Church came to

Inna Shevchenko, a young teenager from an impoverished home in Kherson on the Black Sea, watched the Orange Revolution on television. "'I was just a girl then, but for the first time I understood that we could have democracy in our country.' She followed the proliferation of talk shows that pitted politicians against journalists, who 'looked more intelligent, so I wanted to be one'".[35] Several years later, she enrolled in journalism at Taras Shevchenko National University of Kyiv. A successful intellectual and a star of student politics, she graduated with honours and landed a job in the press bureau of the Mayor of Kiev, in a climate hostile to women.

In 2006, Yushchenko lost the presidential election to Viktor Yanukovych. The economic crisis of 2008 hit Ukraine hard, and hit women harder. In her report, "The Impact of the Crisis on Women in Eastern Europe," Ewa Charkiewcz notes that people with less job security are the first to be unemployed, and this largely means women (2010). Ukraine is the largest country in Europe, with the largest number of people living in poverty. While inflation skyrocketed and life expectancies dropped, Ukraine's shadow economy thrived, organized by a network of big-business oligarchs sheltering money in Cyprus.[36] Young women in university saw their classmates faced with difficult decisions; Oksana Shachko describes being propositioned for sex every day.[37]

Shachko, a quiet, intellectual artist, was raised by a mother working many jobs to support her children and an alcoholic father, driven to depression by the collapsing economy after the fall of the Soviet Union. From a young age, she was fascinated by iconography and wanted to join a convent. She took art classes, painting beautiful Byzantine icons of Mary and the saints. Her family staged an intervention, and she did not join the convent.[38] She began to study continental philosophy, dialectics, and metaphysics. Shachko was inspired by her mother. Mrs. Shachko called herself 'stupid' and 'weak', and yet she was the one who held their family together in the face of economic turmoil. Oksana read Simone de Beauvoir, and a love of knowledge and exploration of the human condition replaced her fascination with heaven. Shachko became sick of the denigration of women; she saw that her mother was strong. She grew weary of the constant demands for sex for money on the streets, and the reports of violent rapes

---

visit Ukraine to celebrate the 1020 year anniversary of the Baptism of Kiev, he responded by having the National Bank of Ukraine release a "Rebirth of Christian Spirituality in Ukraine" series of coins featuring the Ukrainian Orthodox Church. "Christianization of Kievan Rus Commemorative Coins." *National Bank of Ukraine*. (Accessed April 20 2014. Posted 2008)

and murders of the women who said no. Shachko and two of her childhood friends from their hometown of Khmelnytskyi in Western Ukraine, Anna Hutsol and Alexandra Shevchenko, began staging public protests against sex tourism and sex slavery in Ukraine.

In this image photographer Dmitry Kostyukov, Femen activist Yana Zhdanova, and three childhood friends (the three women on the right) from their hometown of Khmelnytskyi in Western Ukraine, Oksana Shachko, Anna Hutsol and Alexandra Shevchenko, stand outside the district court building in Kiev after their hearing. They allege that they were kidnapped, beaten and held by Ukraine's security service "to prevent protests during a visit to Kiev by President Vladimir V. Putin of Russia and Patriarch Kirill I of the Russian Orthodox Church".[39] The police say that they were spotted randomly by police committing "petty hooliganism". They were fined fifteen to twenty dollars each and released after Putin and Kirill left Kiev.[40]

Shachko said:
The Femen Movement developed out of our first campaign: 'Ukraine is not a Brothel.' We started out activities in Kiev, we wanted to express our anger and combat Ukraine's reputation in Europe and around the world as a brothel, that all Ukrainians are prostitutes. Ukrainian women got that reputation after the USSR fell apart. The factories closed, the job went, and there was just crisis and

poverty. A lot of women and young girls went to Europe to sell themselves like fresh meat or some kind of product.
(*Je Suis Femen,* 2014: 13:31)

In April 2009, Alexandra Shevchenko attended the book signing of Oles Buzina, writer of *Ladies, Back to the Harems*, known for "his open stance against the right for a woman to say no to sex".[41] She threw a cream pie at him.

In August 2009, Shachko and her friends marched in a Ukrainian Independence Day rally; Shachko attended topless. The group instantly garnered widespread attention as images of Shachko's bare chest saturated social media.

Ukrainian Independence Day rally in August 2009, where Oksana Shachko marches topless for the first time.

The group attracted many more members, and suddenly they had a brand—beautiful women styled as traditional Ukrainian peasants. The crown of flowers refers to an old Ukrainian saying: 'Gola, bossa i ou vinkou,' which means 'without clothes, without shoes, but with a crown of flowers in her hair'.[42] Anna Hutsol explained to Russian magazine *Ogoniok* in 2010 that to her this meant that a young girl may live in poverty, but she is cheerful and full of life, and will not let life beat her.[43] It also references the *kulak* peasants murdered and oppressed throughout Stalin's reign in the twentieth century. Her breasts are uncovered, and Femen's twist is that they are proclaiming a political message.

"A wedding photo from the Carpathian mountains, circa 1930s." (@third_roosters 2016)

Contemporary Ukrainian native dress. This is wedding wear; the Femen *vinoks* are casual festival wear. Photo by artist *Treti Pivni,* @third_roosters.

Inna Shevchenko, working in the Mayor's press office, felt increasingly restricted in her work, allowed only to publish positive reports about the government.⁴⁴ She was impressed by Femen activists and she reached out to them via vKontakte, the Slavic equivalent of the social networking site Facebook. Initially she was against the topless tactic, but she was soon converted and she enlisted her breasts for the cause. Shevchenko describes the beginning of her involvement with Femen: "We started to meet and talk, at first just primitive talks about how we were fed up being harassed by guys on the street. It's not like overnight you decide to become an activist. Life takes you there".⁴⁵

Inna Shevchenko joins the movement.

Experienced protester Viktor Sviatsky, as well as Jenia Kraizman joined their team. This was a turning point—a strategy was coordinated, t-shirts were printed, a logo was styled and the movement was branded. From this moment onwards, Femen was not focused on drawing supporters to rallies in the traditional form of protest; now they staged carefully planned actions, which they filmed and photographed for dissemination on social media.

Femen creates a logo, sealing their international brand. (Femen.org)

Top: Staged action. Photo courtesy of artist Camilla Lobo.

Bottom: Femen activists prepare for a rally called "Day of Wrath", organized by Christians and neo-fascists protesting the French government's proposal to legalize gay marriage. After this photo was taken, they marched down to the rally bleating and herding the "extreme right sheeps". Photo courtesy of artist Jacob Khrist.

Shevchenko says "it's more important to have five cameras at the action than fifty people around, because behind each of the cameras are a million minds, who at night are sitting at home having dinner, and they will see what women are doing, and the next day they will join".[46]

Shevchenko lost her job in the Mayor's office before she ever protested topless. When an entirely male cabinet was appointed in Ukraine in 2010, the women "dressed up as men, then took off their suits to reveal women's clothing".[47] This was the action that Inna was fired for. In an interview with *The Atlantic*, she describes her radical awakening:

> **"My consciousness was not raised by a blow from heaven or by a single event. It came gradually. My anger grew, starting from the day the press office fired me for my activism, not for any work-related reason. The more we demonstrated, and the more I saw how the police tried to stop us, the angrier I became. In each protest I went out to shout about what I couldn't stand anymore".[48]**

The reactions to the protests became more intense. Femen members received death threats and got their teeth knocked out. Shachko broke both of her arms.

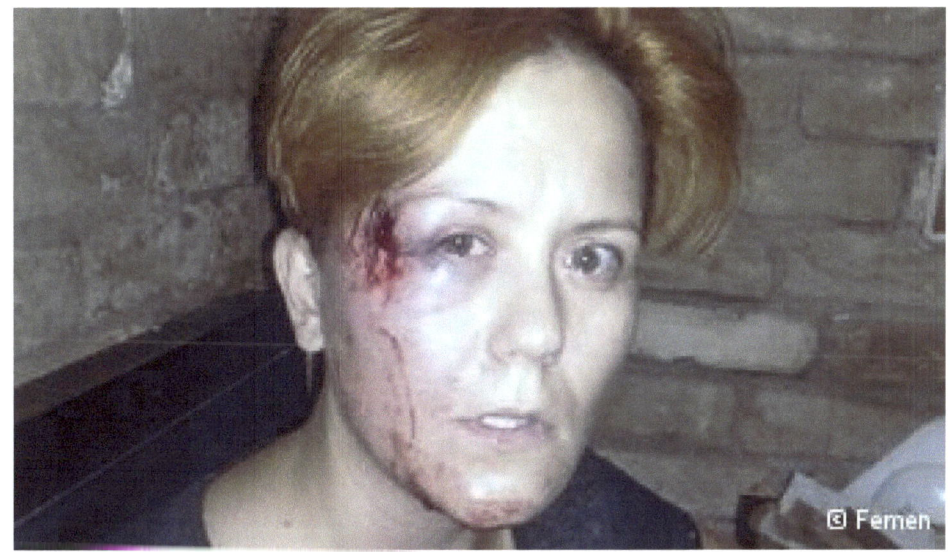

Femen's Anna Hutsol is beaten by Ukraine's police.

Top: Members of the public reacting violently to a Femen action. Photo courtesy of Alexander Nemenov.

Bottom: Sasha (Alexandra Shevchenko) tussling with police at a protest.

In December 2011, Femen members Inna Shevchenko, Oxana Shachko and Alexandra Nemchinova traveled to Belarus, the post-Soviet dictatorship on Ukraine's northern border. In December of 2010, Alexander Lukashenko was announced President after another rigged election, marking his seventeenth consecutive year as ruler. Approximately 50 000 Belarusians gathered for a mass protest in Minsk, resulting in over 700 arrests and prison sentences. One year later, opponents of the regime tried to stage a vigil, carrying posters with the faces of missing persons detained in last year's protest. Femen joined them, holding posters saying 'Freedom to political prisoners'. Over thirty women and men carrying portraits were snatched away by plainclothes government agents.[49]

Protest in Belarus.

After leaving the rally, Shevchenko, Shachko, and Nemchinova were grabbed off the street, forced into vans with blacked out windows, and blindfolded. They were taken far into the woods, beaten, stripped of all of their clothing and possessions, and doused with oil. They heard jeers, felt knives pressed to their faces. Their blindfolds were removed, and the men were holding torches, threatening to burn them alive. They shaved Nemchinova's head, poured green paint on Shevchenko, and cut Shachko and Shevchenko's hair off with knives.

43

After twenty four hours, the men left, and the girls, 21 and 22 years old, were left to wander the Belarusian outback in the winter, naked. They found a small village called Beki and called the Ukrainian embassy.

Inna Shevchenko was later asked by a journalist if she is scared while protesting. She responded:

> It would be silly to say we're not, but the fear of everything around us is bigger than the fear of being beaten up […] In my head I resigned myself to the idea that I would die that day [in Belarus]. That changed completely the way I understand myself, the world and my activity, my thoughts, goals and vision. You check yourself and understand what really matters. After that situation I have only one real fear – to be imbecilic and passive. Losing teeth can be fixed.
>
> (Carmen Gray 2014)

Without the Femen action in solidarity at the Minsk protest, there would have been little to no coverage in the European media. Femen's life-threatening demonstration resulted in the first significant international media spotlight on human rights abuses in Belarus.

Femen group members regularly face public abuse; they are detained by police, and assaulted on the street by body-policing citizens who do not approve of their toplessness. Oksana Shachko's apartment was ransacked and her art destroyed, an experience which was disheartening. She cites the case of Oksana Makar as a source of continued resolve in her activist work.[50]

On International Women's Day, 2012, Oksana Makar, 18, Yevhen Krasnoschek, 23, and Artem Pohocyana, 22, went to a friend's house. This friend was Maksym Prisyazhnyuk, 24, a young and wealthy lawyer from a powerful political family. Oksana was beaten, violently raped, strangled with cable, and lit on fire. Her body was found in the pit of a nearby construction site the next morning. She was wrapped in a blanket, "which at the time of her discovery had been on fire for hours, causing irreparable lung damage".[51] Implausibly, Oksana was still alive; she was able to tell police what happened to her and who did it. Her feet and one of her arms were amputated. Prisyazhnyuk, the lawyer, and Pohocyana, who had a rich father, were immediately released from police custody. The case would likely have ended there, but Makar's mother made a video in the hospital, coaxing her daughter to "wave the stump that was her right arm to the camera, and persist[ed] in getting her to repeat, 'I'll live while I'm alive,'" in visible agony.[52] She posted the 1:19 minute video clip on YouTube. Femen responded by staging an action on the roof of the general prosecutor's office, topless and chanting "death for sadists". Old Ukrainian women rallied around them, crying for the tortured Makar. When the police showed up to arrest the protesters, Ukrainian grandmothers told them "unhand those girls, shame on you, what are you doing" and the police, embarrassed, let them run away.[53] The protest led to public outcry and international media attention which forced President Yanukovych to order the general prosecutor to intervene in the case. The suspects were re-arrested and charged with attempted murder. "I'm scared to walk through the streets," said Makar's best friend, visiting her grave.[54]

Memorial graphic for Oksana Makar—"We remember… we love"—who was beaten, raped and lit on fire.

Femen protest at the general prosecutor's office provoking justice for Oksana Makar.

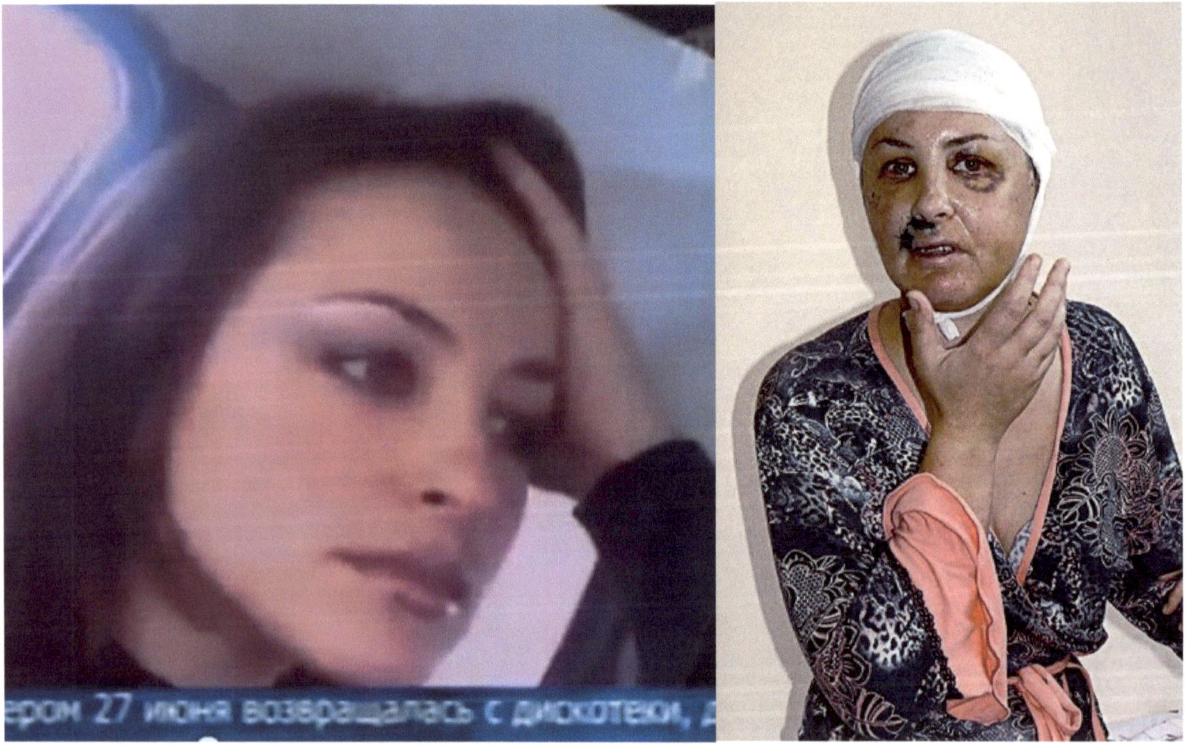

Iryna Krashkova of Vradiyivka, before and after a brutal gang rape.

In 2013, 29-year-old Iryna Krashkova was pulled into a car by two men, who drove her to a remote forested area. All three beat and raped her, leaving her to die. She survived, and named her assailants, but only two were taken into custody. The other was a police officer with political family connections. The case was similar to others, and appeared almost identical to the 2011 murder of 15-year-old Alina Porkul, who was also raped and had her eyes beaten, but she was thrown into a pond and did not survive. After Krashkova's survival, the townspeople of Vradiyivka took matters into their own hands; hundreds of locals stormed the police office demanding the arrest of the accused officer.[55]

Jeremy Maccaud and Genaro Bardy describe the Femen activists as "pioneers of the revolution".[56] In an interview with Anna Hutsol, in exile in Switzerland, she describes how at first people saw their protests as overreactions and bad behaviour, but their audacious derision of political corruption provided the impetus to the young people of Kyiv in the Maidan to join the critique. Since the beginning, Femen have been the Valkyric harbingers of the radicalization of Ukraine. According to Yevhen Solonyna and Inna Kuznetsova, "Ukraine has long been pregnant with revolution".[57]

Inna Shevchenko says of the topless tactic: "No one is ready to listen to women. They only want to [look at our bodies]. That's why we tell them, look at me; but now, I'm not smiling, I'm not trying to please you… I'm trying to make you scared. […] This nudity is aggressive. They are not used to seeing aggressive nudity, nudity that can attack, that [is] not promoting yogurt…".[58]

FEMEN GOES INTERNATIONAL

Until this point, Femen actions were aggressive, but not illegal. In 2012, Inna Shevchenko cut down a wooden monumental cross in central Kiev with a chainsaw to protest the jailing of the Russian punk band Pussy Riot. This was the opportunity that police were waiting for. Shevchenko alleges that 20 police officers swarmed her apartment building, and she jumped from a window and fled to the Polish border. She contacted the Riahi brothers, Austrian-Iranian filmmakers who had reached out to Femen in the past to collaborate. They arrived the next day, and instantly bonded with Shevchenko; she said that they were not just "director[s] wanting to make a cool film; they understand politically, since they're Iranian and also fled their country".[59] They helped her seek political asylum in France, and worked with her on a film project called *Everyday Rebellion.* She was happy with the film, because it "shows that the first step was taken – that the revolution is starting. People may think that sounds a little romantic but I do believe that with all these rebellions all over the world, you see people care about each other and the situation. There's a moment in the film when we're screaming, 'Freedom to political prisoners,' and then it moves to Iran and they are screaming the same in Farsi, and you think, 'This is it, we're living in the same world and we want the same for it'".[60]

"In Gay We Trust".

"Holy Sperm" protest in Paris.

"Pope No More" in Paris.

Shevchenko opened a training headquarters in Paris, which attracted a new cohort of volunteers. She launched an online shop to raise money for demonstrations, and people donated money to Femen.org. She received support from all over the world. Shevchenko quickly became close friends with the journalists and artists at Charlie Hebdo. They got together to commiserate over the constant death threats that they received by the same groups, particularly Christian neo-Nazis and Islamists.[d] The artists collaborated with Femen on several issues, including their Women's Day issue. Jeffrey Tayler interviewed Editor-in-chief Gérard Biard and the Charlie Hebdo team, writing:

> Bespectacled and gentle, he likened Femen to the original "eco warriors," and told me their tactics (baring breasts among them) recall those once deployed by the radical 1960s Mouvement de la Libération de la Femme. What first drew his attention to the group? "Femen picks its targets very carefully -- religious places, centers of political and social power and the patriarchy, the places embodying what they're struggling against."
>
> Luz presented Shevchenko with the drawings he had just finished. She was not pleased.
>
> "Why do you show us standing this way? Femen stands straight, holding posters high… We are more ugly, I don't want us to look sweet. We never look sweet." She summed up her advice for revisions: "More scandal! More violence!"
>
> [Hebdo artist] Javel laughed, adding, "One of us is going to be killed. That will be a big scandal!"
>
> (Tayler 2013)

This conversation, of course, took place before the January 2015 shooting at Charlie Hebdo by some of the radicalized fundamentalists who had been threatening their lives for years. Shevchenko mourned the loss of her friends, writing, "[d]o we really need to have 12 dead journalists to admit they were free thinkers?... Our modern society is a coward that is turning away from everyone who bravely denounces the truth in a non-violent creative way like Charlie Hebdo."[61] This event marked a shift in Femen actions toward issues of freedom of speech. Shevchenko writes: "[e]ven in modern times and even within 'secular' states, the universal law of freedom of speech does not guarantee us the right to criticise religion. In reality, to criticise or to mock religion is

---

[d] The ideological complicity of these groups is reminiscent of reactions to the second-wave Feminist Movement. Toni Head, for example, writes that when she attended the International Women's Year Florida Conference in 1975, "Mormons, Baptists, and various fundamentalist religious groups were there in force, joined with the American Nazi Party, John Birch Society, and Ku Klux Klan to try and subvert the conference."
Stone, Merlin. "The Great Goddess." *Heresies: A Feminist Publication on Art and Politics*. (New York: Heresies Collective Inc., vol. 2 no. 1: 1978) p. 16.

neither allowed, nor safe. But, as long as blasphemy remains dangerous, there will be a need to commit it."⁶²

AMINA SBOUI

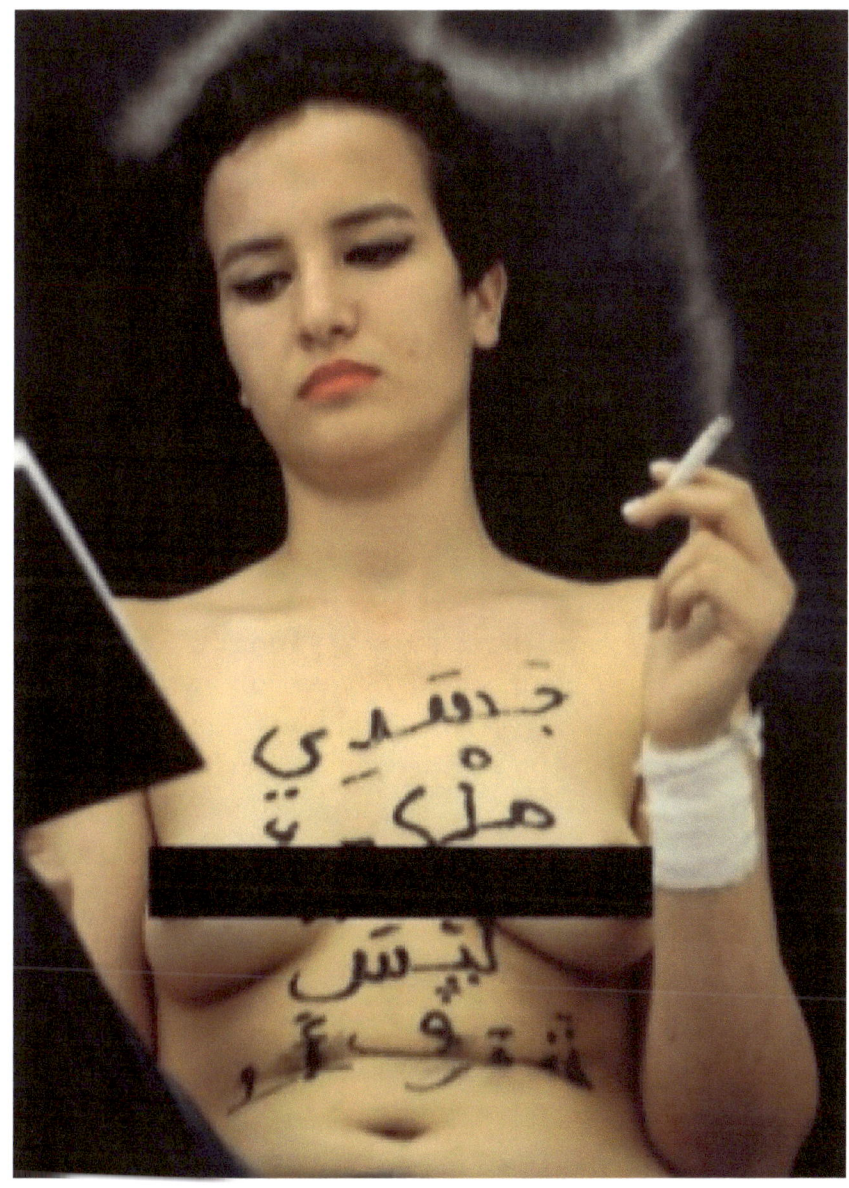

Amina Sboui: "My body belongs to me and is not the source of any man's honor."

Amina Sboui committed one such dangerous blasphemy.

On 8 March 2013, from her grandparents' house in the Tunisian capital, an 18-year-old activist called Amina Sboui uploaded a photograph to Facebook, took a deep breath, and hit "post".

The photo showed Amina reclining on a leather sofa, reading a book and smoking a cigarette. She wore red lipstick and black eyeliner. She was naked from the waist up, and across her torso was a message written in Arabic: My body belongs to me; it is not the source of anyone's honour.

As she watched the comments stack up beneath the picture – almost a thousand in the first hour – Amina began to panic. She had anticipated the abuse, the misogyny, even the death threats. What she hadn't considered was something that now looked inevitable: her mother was going to find out.

("The Return of a Topless Rebel" 2013)

Amina uploaded the photo because she was inspired by the Femen actions she saw on social media. Feminist blogger Céline Trèfle of BlaqSwans writes that "when Amina writes on her chest 'my body is nobody's honour' she asserts her refusal to submit to her father or brothers, and asserts her sovereignty over her own body, as a free individual. Through that action, she doesn't promote nudity, but tests women's freedom".[63]

Femen International 'shared' the image on their Facebook page. Amina received a fatwa and death threats from public figures in Tunisia. Then she disappeared. Shevchenko writes:

> When she was kidnapped, we started an international campaign to support Amina. We called women all over the world to send their pictures in the style of Amina's topless picture. To write a message: "Free Amina." To support her. During this campaign we got more than 1,000 pictures from many countries, including Arab countries. There were a few women who wore hijabs but they did it topless, to support Amina… we started to

scream as much as we could, once we asked for international support, the world started to make noise about it. And this is what saved her.[...] We have only one protection: the media world and spreading information. If we kept silent about Amina, she would not have been set free. After we made noise that she got kidnapped, her family let her go. They didn't want to give her her passport and documents, so we started to push publicly and they gave her all her documents. So Amina was free after that.

(Larsson 2013)

Amina's mother had taken her to a rural exorcist, where she was heavily dosed with medications, locked in a house, and virginity tested. After her release, Amina later wrote 'Femen' on the wall of a cemetery. She was arrested by police. Several Femen activists traveled to Tunisia to protest Amina's arrest, and they too were arrested. Femen chapters around the world staged protests, some of which were criticized for being racist, along with criticism from radical clerics calling for Amina to be lashed and stoned.[64] Tunisian politician Maya Jribi stated that Amina set women in Tunisia back.[65]

The Facebook group "Feminists Against Femen" was made. Despite her detractors, Amina has the public support of many Muslim feminists in Tunisia, and her father declared that he is proud of his daughter's bravery in standing up for her convictions.[66] In his book *Power, Surveillance, and Culture in YouTube™'s Digital Sphere*, Matthew Crick discusses the YouTube video "Amina Tyler for Tunisia women's rights, inspiring women Arab Spring".[67] The video has over a million views, with an active debate in the comment section about Amina's role in triggering the Arab spring.

Safia Lebdi, the Arab-French eco-feminist and Regional Councillor for Ile-de-France, organized a Free Amina demonstration in Paris, commenting that "[w]e Arab women are oppressed by our families and religion, and it all begins with us, in our own families, in our communities, and in society in general".[68] [e] She invited the Ukrainian Femen refugees who had just arrived in Paris to participate.

The Amina Sboui event was an international test of intersectional feminist discourse. On one hand, it was a testament to feminist intercultural solidarity, and on the other hand, some of the imagery produced was

---

[e] Lebdi organized a 23-city national women's march in 1998, founded the group 'Ni putes ni soumises', and is the president of 'les insoumises'. She is an anti-capitalist filmmaker who is a fierce advocate of Syrian refugees and Arab women living under religious law.

uncomfortable, shocking, and 'politically incorrect'. One image in particular, a white woman on her knees in prayer wearing a beard and towel turban with the words "Viva topless jihad" scrawled on her breasts, received a great deal of negative backlash, and turned many people against the group Femen as a whole. Many bloggers felt that the image reinforced orientalist negative stereotypes about Arabs or Arab culture in general, rather than targeting specific patriarchal Muslim beliefs protected by the category of 'religion'. The image generated many assumptions about race and culture. Although the image was created by Arab and Ukrainian women, it was shared and coded as Western imperialism. There was no language in intersectional feminist theory to address or understand colonized subjects in developing nations who are white, or non-white privileged secularists. Indeed, apprehension and distrust of Westerners is alive and well in Ukraine, a Eurasian country where Western invaders committed a genocide in the region in recent history, so the characterization of the image as "Western imperialism" is ironic.

Femen International was unapologetic about the ambiguous message, and indeed reinforced the message that Femen would not be apologetic about anything.

The image that confounded and offended many.

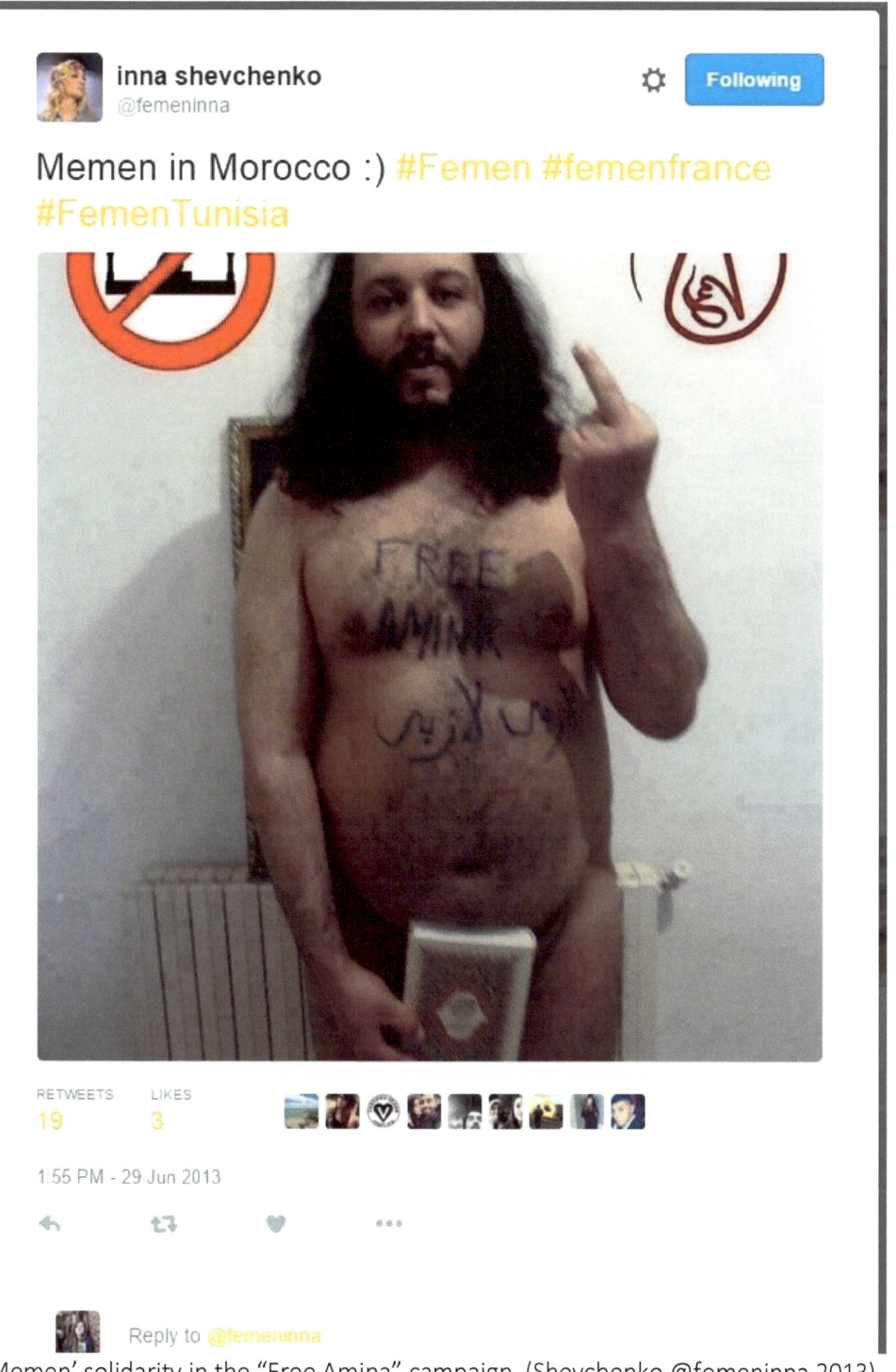

'Memen' solidarity in the "Free Amina" campaign. (Shevchenko @femeninna 2013)

After several months in prison, Amina Sboui and the other protesters were released, and Sboui distanced herself from Femen, planning to start her own Muslim feminist magazine. She wrote an autobiography of her experiences called *My Body Belongs To Me*. In the book:

> Amina stressed the point that she had been trying to get across in the original photograph – that when the female body is seen as the repository of a family's honour or the source of its shame, it immediately becomes a possession that must be owned and guarded by men. The male demand for female modesty, she argued, is implicitly backed by the threat of violence. So-called "honour killings", still endemic across North Africa and the Middle East, are just the most extreme manifestation of this threat.
>
> (Adamson 2015)

Iranian public intellectual and ex-Muslim Maryam Namazie was interviewed about the Amina Sboui situation while Amina was in prison. "Many people say the topless fight is a western idea for western ideal and it's not relevant for the Muslim world. What do you think about it?" a journalist asked her.[69] This was her response:

> This reminds me of a slogan shouted by Iranian women protesting compulsory veiling after the Islamic movement suppressed the 1979 Iranian revolution. It was "Women's rights are neither East nor West but universal". […] Plus there is no "Muslim world". There are as many differences of opinion in Tunisia as there are in Britain and France. Amina represents one strand; the Islamists another. She has much support not just in the west but in Tunisia, Iran and elsewhere. Her fight is also ours.
>
> (Maryam Namazie 2013)

Inna Shevchenko notes that female nudity is used by advertisers to sell things in Ukraine; it is used by the fashion industry and the sex industry, but never by women themselves. She believes that the message of Femen is that above all, women's bodies are taken back by the women themselves; their breasts are screaming their message to the world. She believes that the extreme negative reactions that people have to her small naked body expose their fears and repressions. Like Amina, her body bears the burden of their honour somehow, or the honour of the nation, and in that process of objectification, her human rights are made invisible. She comments that "when we put a naked woman in the situation, the location, the place where no one expects, it's something that is kind of working like a bomb".⁷⁰ Rather than using actual violence, Shevchenko's breasts are her ideological bombs; her approach is the nonviolent use of taboo.

Maryam Namazie expresses this sentiment succinctly:

> Commodification relies on an objectified image that is separate from the reality of women's bodies, minds and lives. This image is used to regulate, control and suppress. And this is what religion and pornography share, albeit in different forms. The actuality and frankness of women's bodies as a form of protest challenges and upsets both. Nudity is deeply humanising and revolutionary because it challenges the religious/pornographic view of women's bodies and reclaims a tool used for women's suppression. Nudity outrages and offends because of this very challenge. And it is taboo-breaking in the most progressive sense of the word since progress often comes as a result of offending deeply held and misogynist views and sensibilities. (Namazie 2013)

The positioning of women in public spaces draws attention to the masculinization of public space. This effect is exaggerated by the exposed breasts of Femen activists contrasted against the Christian men in anti-gay rallies, predominantly male neo-Nazi crowds, men at conservative political rallies, and the male police officers who handcuff Femen and drag them away.

Oksana Shachko being detained by police in February 2013.

According to Mariam Betlemidze:
> Historically, public space has been a domain for masculine actions, while feminine actions were mainly restricted to domestic arenas (Lefebvre, 1991; Wigley,1992; Sennett, 1994). […] By attacking the public spaces of Paris, Kiev, Tripoli, Rome, and other places landmarked by iconic symbols, FEMEN is "sub-verting uses of urban space" (Sennett, 1994, p. 24) and becomes a "force of disunity" in these settings (p. 66).
> (Betlemidze 2015: 376).

In November 2012, Catholics organized a massive, 100 000-strong demonstration against gay marriage in Paris. Nine women of Femen France attended dressed as nuns, carrying white fire extinguishers labeled "Holy Sperm". In the midst of the protest Femen stripped off their robes to expose their breasts emblazoned with the words "In Gay We Trust", and "Fuck Church". They proceeded to spray baby powder over the crowd of people who in turn began beating them, kicking them, knocking out their teeth and breaking one woman's nose. LGBT (lesbian, gay, bisexual and trans) people rushed in to shield Femen with their backs and take them to safety.[71]

Femen continued their battle with the Catholic Church. In February 2013, a day after Pope Benedict XVI's resignation, eight Femen activists entered Notre Dame in trench coats, surrounding the Cathedral's new bells. They whipped off their coats exposing breasts painted with the words "Pope No More", "No More Homophobe", "Saved by the Bell", and "Bye Bye Benedict", referencing Joseph Ratzinger's statement about homosexuality as a "strong tendency ordered toward an intrinsic moral evil; and thus the inclination itself must be seen as an objective disorder".[72] They rang the bells for several minutes before being hustled out by security. This message was splashed across their Facebook page the day of the action:
> FEMEN is congratulating the whole progressive world with the resignation of fascist Benedict XVI from the place of the head of the Catholic mafia. It's symbolic that today is the day of voting on law of same-sex marriage in France. The ex-Pope was a fierce opponent of gay marriages. FEMEN applaud the complete capitulation of medieval homophobia! Pope go to the devil! Viva common sense! Viva freedom!
> (Femen International 2013)

For this action they faced charges for degrading a place of worship, going through two years in courts of appeal before the charges were dropped. The 'Holy Sperm' counter-protest was widely applauded as a clever and brave stunt, however, the 'Pope no More' act earned Femen widespread disapproval. People felt that it was disrespectful and insensitive to the Pope, and neo-Nazis saw it as an insult to the national icon Notre Dame.[73] Where Inna Shevchenko was once a local celebrity and a prized political refugee, she was now told to watch out and lay low or go back to Ukraine. She did an interview with *The Atlantic*:

"Our protest did one thing: it stripped the French of their masks and showed what their so-called progressivism really is. Their reaction was purely *Catholic*. Their liberalism is just a cover-up, there's nothing behind it. It's all fake." This is strong, uncompromising anti-Gallic verbiage from one who is petitioning the French government for political asylum. Was she worried that such words, to say nothing of a criminal conviction, might adversely affect her chances?

"I'm not a slave to papers. I came here to carry on my work, not for the sake of a residency permit... I won't give up demonstrating."
(Tayler 2013)

More anti-gay demonstrations took place in Paris. The disturbing popularity of the anti-gay movement in France was emblematic of a growing hostility toward marginal people all over Europe. Anti-Semitism, Islamophobia, and neo-Nazism were also on the rise, as a subculture of hate brewed in the background of the world news declaring economic hardship and the displacement of many people by war.

Just after the Second World War, Hannah Arendt, a witness to the catastrophic events of the climax of the twentieth century mass hatred of Jews, wrote:

Nothing perhaps illustrates the general disintegration of political life better than this vague, pervasive hatred of everybody and everything, without a focus for its passionate attention, with nobody to make responsible for the state of affairs—neither the government nor the bourgeoisie nor an outside power. It consequently turned in all directions, haphazardly and unpredictably, incapable of assuming an air of healthy indifference toward anything under the sun.
(Arendt 1948: 335)

Example of graffiti I saw scrawled on buildings in Brussels in 2014.

In May 2014, I was in Sweden for a conference, where I was surprised to see anti-Jewish graffiti scrawled on buildings in Uppsala. I showed a Swedish colleague, who explained that the 'cultural Christian' terrorist Anders Breivik was from one such network of ethno-nationalists increasing in popularity in Scandinavia. Breivik's manifesto says that "if you have a personal relationship with Jesus Christ and God then you are a religious Christian. Myself and many more like me do not necessarily have a personal relationship with Jesus Christ and God. We do however believe in Christianity as a cultural, social identity and moral platform. This makes us Christian".[74] He writes that he prefers Christianity to neo-paganism as a personal banner because it has pan-European 'mass appeal'; he wants his movement to be equally attractive to Italians, Greeks, and other Europeans who are inclined to support 'cultural conservatives'. Christianity thus functions as a universalizing ethno-ideology against Muslims, who he sees as irrational barbarians, and Jews, who he sees as conniving atheist Marxists. Breivik is orthodox in his scapegoats. Women, and feminists in particular, as well as gays, are responsible for both the decreased birth rate of white people (leading to a takeover by Muslims)[75] and the "rise of matriarchal systems which are now dominating Western European countries".[76] He is far from alone in this thinking; Breivik's manifesto describes meetings across Europe with wealthy and powerful supporters of this movement.[77] In 2011, Breivik planned a bombing of government buildings in Oslo, an attack for which he knew that Muslims would be targeted, to distract police while he killed 69 people execution-style at a camp for youth run by the Labour Party. He selected the camp, full of young feminists and anti-racists, to deliver a decisive blow to the next generation of socialists.

After the conference in Sweden (2014), I further noticed anti-Jewish messages at train stations in Antwerp, Belgium, and swastikas on buildings in Brussels. Several days later, an attack at the Jewish Museum in Brussels killed three and left one wounded. The next day, I watched on television with my friends in Brussels as two seats in the European Parliament were won by neo-Nazi parties, and many other seats went to far-right parties in nations across Europe.

Femen predicted the dangers of this hate mobilization long before the European Parliament elections. In May 2013, Inna Shevchenko lead an action intended to make a farce of a neo-Nazi rally in Paris. Every year, the group Nationalist Front gathers at the statue of Jeanne d'Arc to commemorate the ousting of the British from France. Nationalist Front claims to be a right-wing group supporting family values and love of France. In 2013, Shevchenko and her topless cohorts climbed onto the roof of a hotel facing the Jeanne d'Arc statue, dramatically unrolling a massive banner that read "Sextermination for Nazism", playing on their notion of 'sextremism' protest tactics. Immediately National Front members made the Nazi salute and shouted Nazi slogans, "instantly show[ing] what they're really about".[78] The National Front members hurled invectives like 'sluts, go kill yourselves'. Femen's Anna Hutsol later cheekily remarked "[w]hy is this sex object protesting? I'm used to seeing her in porno films, in magazines, in my bed, or in the kitchen. I'm not used to seeing this object protesting".[79]

Shevchenko sees her activism as a call to action for people in the left-wing whom she sees as 'regressive' and passive. She calls on the people of France to use their freedom of speech to stand up against the National Front and the rising fascist movement. She believes that young people will see Femen's action online, and be emboldened to oppose hateful ideology in their own way the next time an opportunity arises.[80] In Alain Margot's 2014 documentary *Je Suis Femen*, on a train winding sluggishly past the suburbs, Oksana Shachko says as she points out the window: "I want to give people a wake-up call. I want to wake up all these people sleeping in these houses, happy with their little piece of land and any old job. I want to give them a wake-up call, to make them rise up, and help us change the world order".[81]

THE UKRAINIAN REVOLUTION OF DIGNITY: MAIDAN

Independence Square in Kiev: 2009 and 2014.

    The revival of fascist ideological movements helps to explain where a radical response movement like Femen comes from. Far-right extremism precipitates the radical left corollary. The history of Ukraine demonstrates that where freedoms of human dignity, like freedom of speech or freedom of assembly are repressed, the upshot is rebellion bursting from the seams.

    The Ukrainian Revolution of Dignity, or the revolution of the Maidan, was one such burst of rebellion. Viktor Yanukovych, the pro-Russian oligarch who tried to circumvent democracy in 2004 and was defeated in the Orange Revolution, was elected in 2010 to the dismay of Femen. He overturned the 2004 transparent government reforms fought for in the Orange Revolution, and pushed to stop pursuing NATO membership. Yanukovych won the election again in 2012, despite concerns raised by international observers over the legitimacy of the elections. During his campaign he promised to deepen ties with the European Union,[82] but in 2013, the Ukrainian government backed out of a plan to sign an association agreement with the European Union in exchange for a $15 billion payoff by Russia. This dismayed Ukrainians yearning for a European standard of living and European human rights laws.

This time, the generation of Ukrainians who had lived their whole lives in a post-independence democracy, and who had watched the success of the Orange Revolution on television, were now voting-age adults. More than that, they had access to Western media all of their adult lives and were mobilized on social media networks. When the Yanukovych government made the announcement that Ukraine would pursue ties with Russia and distance from Europe, the reactions were swift and decisive.

"I opened my computer to social media," said Maksim Panov, a young law student featured in the documentary *Winter On Fire: Ukraine's Fight For Freedom,* "and I saw a post from Mustafa Nayyem. It said 'Let's meet at 10:30 pm by the Independence monument. Dress warm; bring umbrellas, tea, coffee, a good attitude, and friends. Re-post highly appreciated!'. I closed my laptop, and the next time I opened it was a month and a half later".[83] A young translator named Ekaterina Averchenko described how on the day of the announcement, November 21, 2013, her Facebook page was covered with messages and posts telling people to 'come to the Maidan' that evening.[84]

Through social media, students knew when to show up, what to wear, and who would be there. Images, videos, stories and music popped up in their social media newsfeeds and they knew exactly what was happening in Maidan Square in Kyiv from 10:30 pm onward. Protesters poured into the square from every corner of the city, dancing, sharing food, singing Ukrainian cultural music and peacefully showing their solidarity with the sentiment that Ukraine would be part of Europe now. Ukraine would be a democracy, and the time of dictators and human rights violations was over. These children were born in the 1990s; they were raised in an independent Ukraine by parents suffused with the enthusiasm of living through the struggle to independence. "I came here because our government crossed out the future of Ukraine, and the aspirations of Ukrainian youth," said a boy full of passion and hope who looked no more than seventeen years old.[85] "I came here to defend my future and the future of my children".[86] Half of the people in the crowd were women. "We are standing here to prove that Ukraine is a European country," said a smiling teenage girl wearing bows the colour of Ukraine's flag. "We dream of a better future".[87] The crowd chanted "Ukraine is part of Europe", "together until the end" and "Sign! Yanukovych sign the agreement" believing that it would happen.

On November 30, 2013, thousands of Berkut—meaning 'golden eagle', a special paramilitary police force—circled the Maidan. They bludgeoned the protesters with truncheons; students ran screaming, and those who fell to the ground were beaten over and over. One witness, a surgeon named Valerii Zalevskiy, recalled: "The troops beat everyone with iron batons instead of plastic ones. It seemed that even they were surprised at the injuries they made using them".[88] While many were rushed to the hospital, minor injuries were treated at the Mykhaylivs'kyi Zolotoverkhyi Monastyr (St. Michael of the Gold Dome Monastery) a few blocks from the Maidan where they were sheltered from the police.[89] In the early morning hours, pools of blood and crumpled Ukrainian flags dotted the square. The police tried to convince the protesters to leave the monastery, but the dissidents locked the gates; the state was afraid to violate the church.

Happy and hopeful the day before, today they were outraged at the government's brutal reaction. This was the first time that Soviet measures were taken against peaceful protests in the history of independent Ukraine. By 11 am, the monastery and courtyard were filled with protesters. Major Archbishop of Kyiv-Halych, Sviatoslav Shevchuk, said "everyone realized that if today students are beaten, tomorrow anyone can be beaten as well. From that came the March of Millions".[90]

The protesters resolved to continue occupying the square. They were joined by millions of people of all ages, setting up food lines, tents and shelters, and even a 'tech tent' where people could stay in touch with family members and broadcast their stories.[91] People from out of town held up signs for the press calling on their neighbours to come to Kyiv and join the movement. Other signs read "They give us corruption, we give them revolution", "We are against the police state", and "only a coward can hurt a child". Toothless grandmothers held up icons of the Virgin Mary. Ukrainian musicians played live performances to keep up the spirits of the protesters. There was a sound stage, and religious leaders held prayers. Protester Marieluise Beck recalled that an Open University was organized; every morning at 10 am there was a stage for academics to give lectures.[92] People made rousing speeches—one man, Ukrainian singer Svyatoslav Vakarchuk, said "there are two European values: freedom and human dignity. We will not let them take these away from us" with emotion in his voice.[93] The youth were learning through experience how to organize. Ukrainian orphans moved into the encampments, where they were fed and housed, and they volunteered all over the Maidan. The encampment offered family and a reprieve from poverty. It was a (religio) nationalist, revolutionary coming-of-age for them. Polish-Ukrainian Slawomir Sierakowski described the sense of community in the Maidan encampment:

> People are never as well organized as they are during a revolution – anyone who saw the kitchens at Euromaidan knows what this means. We do not know whether the invisible hand of revolution would overpower the invisible hand of the market. […] At the realized utopia of the Maidan, the private became public. Provisioning, sleep, healthcare, security. You walked through the Maidan and you are presented with food, clothing, a place to sleep, and medical care. Even the services of a massage therapist or a psychologist. At the Euromaidan, everything was shared. Even if the taste of coffee or "everything soup" had their own revolutionary character, they tasted exceptional, as exceptional as the event itself was.
>
> (Snyder and Zhurzhenko 2014)

Femen activists participated in the Maidan activities; after all, before they were an international movement, they volunteered with children in orphanages.[94] Group members still in Ukraine prepared food and liaised with journalists, while the Paris headquarters staged an action. On December 1, 2013, Shevchenko and four others undressed in front of the Ukrainian embassy in Paris. They then peed and "defecate[d] on an image of Ukrainian President Viktor Yanukovych, shouting slogans such as 'Yanukovych piss off' and 'Ukraine to the EU'".[95] Shevchenko made this statement:

> Dictatorship in its pure form is already in Ukraine. That's why we are coming today here to pee on this face and the face who is bringing dictatorship, pure dictatorship, to Ukraine and protection and influence of Russia, of Putin. And we are giving an alarm to Europe that we need help.
>
> (Now World News 2013)

Long before Maidan, Femen was protesting the corrupt politics of Yanukovych. Fearing another fraudulent election, Shevchenko and a group of other girls stripped at a polling station in Kiev in February 2010 bearing signs which read "The War Begins Here" and "Stop Raping the Country".[96] After another protest in 2010, and after Ukrainian secret servicemen entered Shevchenko's apartment and threatened to break her legs if she did not stop interfering with Yanukovych's campaign,[97] she passionately cried "[j]ust look at our cabinet; it says it all. There isn't a single woman in the Ukrainian cabinet. It's a man's country, run by men. So we've decided to take matters into our own hands and fight for our rights".[98]

While the core Ukrainian civilians in Maidan constructed shelters for a long occupation, the Berkut set up outside the square. Priests of every denomination, muftis, and old Ukrainian grandmothers holding rosary beads and praying stood in a line between the police and the protesters. Several masked young men tried to incite the crowd to storm the presidential headquarters; when questioned under duress these provocateurs admitted to being paid $25 to 'cause trouble', but it was unclear who had paid them.[99] American journalist Marci Shore wrote that "[p]rotestors were disappearing, their bodies sometimes found frozen in the forest, signs of torture on the corpses".[100]

In the darkness of night on December 11, 2013, the Berkut gathered in formation, armed in riot gear, along with the Ukrainian military, and struck the Maidan. The peaceful protesters stood shoulder to shoulder in lines, holding hands. The police pressed forward as screams filled the air and people were bludgeoned. Their hands began to weaken. Suddenly, a different sound rose. It was the voices of thousands of people singing the Ukrainian national anthem, a song which overwhelmed the sounds of screams.[101] From several blocks away, Ivan Sydor, the young bell-ringer at St. Michael's monastery, pulled the bells like never before, signalling the beginning of an eight-hour assault by the state on Maidan.[102] "The last time Mykhaylivs'kyi Monastery rang all the bells like that was in 1240 when the Mongols invaded Kyiv," he said.[103] The number of protesters swelled as people heard the bells and poured into Kyiv to support the demonstration. Taxis gave free rides to the city centre. The protest was intimidating but not violent. Ukrainian citizen Ivan Suharenko describes that night the next morning in Russian:

> The Maidan crowd [was] ready for bloodless resistance. I would not call it peaceful resistance, but rather bloodless resistance. Those who were longing for blood were quickly excluded. Those people who had the idea to disarm the Berkut policemen and take their shields and helmets were quickly calmed by others – and the police were given back their things. No one was allowed to take clubs away from the policemen.
> (Snyder and Zhurzhenko 2014)

The 4000 police and military troops were unable to disperse the fifteen thousand protesters.[104] The resolve of the Maidanistas was stronger than ever.

On January 16, 2014 Yanukovych passed a series of laws, colloquially termed the 'Dictatorship laws'. These laws included preventing people from wearing helmets, driving in groups of more than five cars, and covering their faces. They also restricted access to foreign websites, threatened imprisonment for journalists investigating police officers, and "judges [were] allowed to conduct trials and sentence defendants in absentia", permitting immediate incarceration of protesters.[105] People all over Ukraine were outraged. They wore bicycle and ski helmets, colanders, pots, pans and costume masks to work in protest and in solidarity with the Maidanistas.[106] Tensions were high and there were several skirmishes with police, including injuries caused to police by a cobblestone catapult constructed by protesters on January 20.[107] Military reinforcements were called in from Dnipropetrovsk by train and a group of nonviolent activists lay across the railroad ties; the driver refused to crush them.[108]

Barriers were constructed out of furniture, tires, wood, and blocks of ice. Priests in full regalia constructed barricades. "From the very beginning, the representatives of all religions were on Maidan, as the 'Men of Prayer'", said Major Archbishop of Kyiv-Halych, Sviatoslav Shevchuk.[109] "Different religions came together without conflict, in order to achieve one mutual and important goal," said Said Ismagilov, Mufti of Administrations of Muslims of Ukraine.[110] "When people were singing the national anthem every three hours, I had this feeling that it became a prayer," said Bogdan Dubas.[111]

Retired military members and reservists came to Maidan to train the students how to resist the riot police. "I was worried about them, and live not too far from here" said retired soldier Sergei Kibnovsky, a rarity considering that the average Ukrainian man lives to be 62 years old.[112] Maidanistas organized into defense units with shields. Protests erupted across Ukraine in major cities and small towns. In Lviv classes were canceled on rally days and twenty thousand and thirty thousand students attended. People from all over sent medical supplies, fuel, and food to the Maidan. Observer Yaroslav Hrytsak noted that the collective building of barricades, preparation of food and organization of patrols was essential to keeping the restless, frozen, anxious protesters busy and engaged amidst increasing frustration with the government.[113]

On January 22, 2014, the Berkut assembled. Teenagers called their mothers to tell them they loved them.

Protester Nataliya Stelmakh wrote that "[t]hey were shaving and putting on clean clothes in case they should die that night".[114] The police burned the Maidan encampment to the ground, gunning down men, women and children from the rooftops with rubber bullets and live rounds. The scene was grave; twelve-year-old Ukrainian orphan Roman Savelyev shot at police with stones in his slingshot.[115] Reflecting on this day, surgeon Valerii Zalevskiy recalled bleakly, "[C]an you imagine? Infuriating people to such despair that a banker and one of the most influential attorneys from Lviv came to Hrushevskogo Street to throw stones at the police".[116] Priests stood in the billowing smoke praying aloud, their hands shaking as they held Bibles and shots rang out and protesters fell around them. The monastery set up an emergency hospital, but many people were horribly burned, and some lost their eyes, and others their lives.

On February 18, 2014, a peaceful, unarmed group of protesters walked to Parliament. Again, they were brutally beaten by police. There were multiple casualties, especially the elderly who were unable to run away or withstand the head trauma of the beatings. A group of 40 police officers from neighbouring city Lviv traveled to Kiev, reportedly defecting from the government, vowing to protect the demonstrators.[117] Video footage of February 18 showed Kiev police descending upon old people, raining down blows on them, screaming "come on, finish them!".[118] German-Ukrainian protester Marieluise Beck recalled how "[p]riests, crying, blessed the dead".[119]

That night, the Maidanistas declared that if Yanukovych did not resign by 10 am, they would storm the capital with live weapons. Yanukovych fled into hiding in Russia and the Ukrainian parliament made Oleksandr Turchynov interim president. Yanukovych's palace was peacefully—or more accurately, bloodlessly—overtaken; the impoverished "people gaped at the wealth".[120] Several members of Yanukovych's party issued statements denouncing the use of violent measures against peaceful protesters. On February 24, 2016, after 93 days of protest, the Ukrainian government classified former president Viktor Yanukovych "a fugitive on charges of mass murder".[121] The pro-democracy reforms reducing the direct powers of the President's office which Yanukovych had overturned were re-instated.

The contemporary story of Maidan echoes one from the not-so-distant past. The passage below is a worker's account of a 1918 strike in St. Petersburg right before the fall of the Imperial Russian dynasty:

> Many thousands of workers had then clashed with the police—at times fighting them with clubs, or hailing them with rocks from behind improvised barricades. Women and children had joined in building these barricades—out of telephone and telegraph poles, overturned wagons, boxes, and armoires. No sooner was a demonstration dispersed, or a barricade destroyed, than the workers, after evacuating their wounded, would regroup, and clashes would start all over again. Whole districts were without light, their gas and kerosene lamps having been destroyed.
>
> (Hasegawa 1981: 10)

History repeats itself. "I can't accept that after all the wars we've had in this world, we are still resolving our problems by killing one another," said Ekaterina Averchenko, a mobilizer at Maidan.[122] The peasants who resisted and died for a regime change in 1918 were nameless, uncelebrated victims. The resisters of the Maidan were splashed across social media, their deaths captured on video clips to be replayed over and over again by people sitting at home perusing YouTube.com. Such a user, living anywhere in the world, could then search on Facebook and spend an hour looking at photos, messages and posts by the deceased protesters while they were still alive. When people die, their digital lives remain online, frozen in time, like a personally curated shrine. The digital world has changed the stakes of revolutions and protest internationally. From the day Oksana Shachko attended Ukraine's Independence Day celebration topless, Femen understood this and operationalized the internet as a portal to social change.

While Maidan was a testament to the power of collective action against corruption, the losses should not be underestimated. An old man cried quietly, recalling the people he lived alongside during the occupation of Kiev's square. "We lost here the best people in our nation," he said.[123] Thanks to the digital age, there is a record of their contributions.

Femen activist Anna Hutsol was interviewed by Euroradio about her hopes for improvement and reform by opposition leaders after the flight of Yanukovych. She liked none of them, remarking that they were all oligarchs and cowards, but she added that "[t]his revolution may produce new leaders and they may come from the barricades, from Maidan".[124] She may be right. Maidan brought hardened former Soviet prisoners together with educated and energetic young people. Some of these young people have since been employed by opposition leaders and positioned within the Ukrainian National Guard.

Femen, being fiercely pro-democracy, are resisting the prospect of dictatorship any way they can. Inna Shevchenko says in an interview with *Dazed*:
> Feminism is at that point again where you have to make people interested. People think a lot of things are done already, that there's no need any more. We realised you can attract people by breaking rules and creating new ones. So we started taking off our tops, not for promoting beer or a sex club but to promote our political idea, and moving our body not in a sexy way but an aggressive way, running and screaming. Ukraine at that time was going from this Orange illusion of democracy back to dictatorship, to a Russian way of organising the political situation. For us, the younger generation, we were just terrified. So we did a radical thing.
> (Gray 2014)

It is within the context of the slippage back to dictatorship and the Russian state collusion with the Russian Orthodox Church and what it means for women's rights that Femen position themselves.

There is a lack of consensus in the international community as to whether or not Ukraine has a right to self-determination and autonomy as a sovereign state. Peter Pomerantsev examines the reporting of Maidan in the international press, writing that the story of the revolution has been "spun in a hundred ways".[125]

> "It's a fascist / CIA / Masonic / Zionist / anti-Semitic coup," the Russian press declared. "It's all the fault of the EU's empire-building ambitions," insisted the anti-EU crowd in Western Europe. "Russia has a right to rule over Ukraine," reasoned the big power realists. And the Ukrainians who actually made, or were caught up in, the revolution had their own ways of telling the story [… as] Putin has sponsored, armed and helped man a war against Kiev.
> (Pomerantsev 2015)

Russian president Vladimir Putin took the turmoil surrounding the ousting of Yanukovych as an opportunity to seize Crimea, a region in southern Ukraine. The territory was formally absorbed on March 18, but Putin later commented that implementation of the plan began February 22, the night of Yanukovych's defeat.[126] Crimeans were traditionally conservative and largely sympathetic to Russian influence on Ukraine, so their secession allowed for more liberal politics in the rest of the country.

However, the taking of Crimea was proof for Putin that the international community would do nothing to stop the annexation of Ukraine, and the Kremlin continued to push westward, taking Donetsk and Luhansk. The rise and fall of nation-states in Europe and elsewhere is a constant flux, and the confederation of sovereign Ukraine is currently at a particularly high risk of jeopardy.

East-west allegiance is a difficult question for Ukrainians. The Soviet regime exterminated millions of Ukrainians, and 'The West', meaning Nazi Germany in the twentieth century, slaughtered millions as well. The youth of Maidan, and Femen activists as well, are currently favouring the West in hopes of building a corruption-free democratic government modelled on European Union conventions. While the young are throwing in with Europe, a not insignificant portion of the population sees control by the increasingly autocratic and colonial Russia as inevitable, and are daunted by the often bloody and dismal task of building a democracy.

2014 protest. Photo courtesy of Anna Hutsol.

CHAPTER TWO

BEYONCÉ FEMINISM, FEMEN, AND SEXTREMISM

CHAPTER TWO
BEYONCÉ FEMINISM. FEMEN. AND SEXTREMISM

CRITICS OF FEMEN

Now consider this. If you had a pack of wild, "stray" dogs in a pen, would you let them out to run all over the neighborhood? No, of course you wouldn't. Why? Because dogs, being what dogs are, will wreak havoc and spread mayhem throughout that neighborhood, and they'll cause a great deal of long-term trouble. That being the case, you keep them in a pen, or on a leash. And yes, you already guessed that this same principle applies to women. Why? Because women, being what women are, are more akin to animal than human ... being human in appearance only, yet having little to no logic to use, or loyalty to have, and going chiefly off instinct, emotions and primitive drives. In fact, being completely ruled by them. Think of them as being more-or-less the "midway point" between man and animal. - Now, ask yourself this question; would you give a group of chimpanzees (or children), being very logically and cognitively immature, a bunch of knives or nukes to play with? Of course you wouldn't. But unfortunately we did. So in summary (this can turn into a VERY long topic), when men allowed feminists to create feminism ... and allowed women to have whatever they want, no questions asked .... they effectively "opened the door" on the dog pen. And that's why you see what we're seeing today; women completely out of control. - As women will immaturely and inherently use, abuse and corrupt everything given them eventually, it was our place (the place of men) to keep them in check from the beginning.
—YouTube user Bob Frye, commenting on a video of Inna Shevchenko (Frye 2015)

The passage above may be a wildly irrational statement on social media, but it conveys a distillation of the fears of women and feminism that Femen draws out. The irrationality of women, as noted in highly regarded data collection organizations like Gallup, is the basis for denying women access to power and rights all over the world.

Screen captures from a viral Vocativ video of a Ukrainian pensioner reacting to a Femen protest.

When Femen emerged in Ukraine as a protest group, they received a great deal of support from locals who admired their bravery and enthusiasm, particularly pensioner women. In recent years, the Ukrainian government has cut funding to pensions to meet the conditions to receive a $17.5 billion International Monetary Fund (IMF) bailout package. Pensions are largely collected by women. The average life expectancy of a Ukrainian man is 62 years old, so the 'elderly' category is comprised mostly of women who are often impoverished. There were also many locals who dismissed the protests outright as foolish, and others who shouted their disapproval.

In the early years of Femen, before their strategy had been worked out, Ukrainians, and men especially, were often confused as to what Femen activists were even protesting about. News reports described them as prostitutes seeking sex work legal reform, and the early charges against them were for mental illness.[127] The youths themselves did not have an elaborate, articulated message.

> **Sex tourism is a major problem in Ukraine, and every woman is victimised as a result, says Alexandra. "You'd walk down the street and foreigners, men, would come up to you, ask how much, touch you." […] In those early days they were just developing their views. Feminism was unpopular in Ukraine; saying you were a feminist was "something similar to saying you're an idiot, you're crazy," says Inna. Alexandra says she used to believe the "image created by patriarchy, where feminists are ugly women with moustaches who want to cut off men's penises". (They've played with this imagery themselves. Until recently, their website featured a picture of a woman holding an enormous scythe in one hand, a bloody scrotum in the other.)**
> **They embarked on long, lively discussions about women's rights. "We're not based on 700 pages of doctrine," says Inna, "instead we would come in and saying 'can you believe that fucker? He just touched my arse and said he wants to fuck me, and he will pay me with a cocktail.' The discussion was very primitive, and we became angry, and wanted to express it, so we started doing street performances."**
> (Cochrane 2013)

Femen activists were cheered, protected, scorned and jeered at in Ukraine. They quickly noticed that the press cropped their signs out of the published photos, so they wrote the messages directly on their breasts.[128]

What began as a Eurasian flavoured protest group tackling local issues was not perceived as threatening until they started criticizing government policies and specific Russian-linked conservative politicians. This earned them police beatdowns and local news reports, but it was not until Amina Sboui posted her solidarity photo online in Tunisia and disappeared shortly after that the movement exploded into global recognition. With global recognition came a flurry of excitement and support, as well as waves of condemnation.

Femen activists are most often criticized for protesting topless. Naysayers argue that Femen's nominal modus operandi, gender equality, is lost in the distraction of boobs. Countless articles ranging from calling them sluts and heretics to thoroughly argued treatises on performing for the male gaze abound. Canadian editor of the blog *Feminist Current* Meghan Murphy is a vocal opponent of Femen, writing that "[t]he only message is: 'look at me'".[129] Reddit user 'stephen89' calls Femen "a radical group who cares less about feminism and more about putting down men. They don't really help the cause of feminism at all and are only doing more damage than helping".[130] Likewise, Murphy says that "there is a wrong way to do feminism. And Femen is doing it wrong".[131] There is a tension between Shevchenko's on-the-ground approach to activism and the more academic approach highly concerned with etiquette and scholarly grace. Here is Shevchenko's position: "I would never criticize someone else's activist tactic".[132]

Murphy and stephen89's responses are emblematic of the neoliberal capitalist approach to feminism which reads Femen as white girls undervaluing their white bodies for the benefit of men. Shevchenko undercuts the normative use of female nudity to sell a product by using it instead "to protest and fight".[133] The Murphy/stephen89 perspective is tied to the twentieth century concept of 'performing for the male gaze'.

The idea of 'gaze', and particularly 'the male gaze' was first explored by Laura Mulvey in her 1975 essay "Visual Pleasure and Narrative Cinema", and developed further in later writings. Mulvey expands the Freudian notion of scopophilia, the pleasure of subjecting persons as objects to "a controlling and curious gaze".[134] According to Mulvey, Freud posits that scopophilia, which encompasses both the pleasure of seeing and being seen in particular coded ways, is "one of the component instincts of sexuality which exist as drives quite independently of the erotogenic zones".[135] Freud must have imagined the scopophilic gaze of a doctor examining his patients. Mulvey focuses on the power dynamics between gazers and the gazed-at. She notes that systemic hierarchies are reinforced through the gaze as a mechanism. She writes that "[m]ainstream film coded the erotic into the language of the dominant patriarchal order".[136] According to Mulvey, the glossy pages of advertisements using the female body as scopophilic, phallic-reinforcing object and the representations of women in 1930s Hollywood films exaggerate and bolster the 'controlling gaze' of the male as subject. In her work, Mulvey uses psychoanalytic theory "as a political weapon, demonstrating the way the unconscious of patriarchal society has structured film form".[137] Femen uses and queers the taboo of bare breasts to scandalize and make front page headlines in the media.

In 2011, before Femen entered the international spotlight, a New Zealand radio station hosted a competition called "Win a Ukrainian Wife". The prize of the competition for winner 'Greg' was a two week vacation to Ukraine with a new wife every day. An image appeared on Femen's website with Inna Shevchenko holding a sickle in one hand and a bloody scrotum in the other; the caption read "Greg! We are Waiting! Try to Win a Wife Again!" This image has been shared and cited over and over again in antifeminist circles online as evidence of an international feminist conspiracy to slaughter men.

Perhaps the most well-known criticism of Femen comes from a controversy spawning from the 2013 documentary, *Ukraine is Not a Brothel*. In 2011, Femen was joined by Kitty Green, an Australian-Ukrainian filmmaker. She lived with 5-10 women in their crumbling two-bedroom Soviet-era apartment for fourteen months and traveled with them to protests, shooting their footage, and doing interviews. She edited the film on her laptop computer, and released it under the title *Ukraine is Not a Brothel* in 2013. The film exposes the increasingly controlling role of Viktor Sviatsky, a Ukrainian dissident and former Soviet prisoner, in the organization of Femen actions. Footage appears in the film of Sviatsky screaming at the girls and insulting them. Green said in an interview with *Vice* that if they had not joined Femen, "they would all be working as strippers or topless models or just be married with children by now".[138] Websites across Europe and North American alleged that this man in the documentary was the patriarchal mastermind behind Femen, that the whole thing was thought up and organized by men. These allegations ultimately led to his exile from the group. The activists felt betrayed by Green, but also felt that leaving Sviatsky behind was a necessary development. In news articles reporting on Femen actions, commenters still regularly allege that Femen is actually an organization run by men. Equally common is the assertion that Femen is funded and managed by the Israeli government.

Condemnation of Femen by blogs like *Feminist Current* demonstrate a desire to fight for equality for women in a way that preserves upper-class 'good manners' and 'civility' rather than the 'lower-class debauchery and crudeness' of street theatre styled activism. This is why Femen makes "all feminists look barking mad"—in this case, "all feminists" is coded for upper-class.[139] 'Feminist' is a universalizing identity category, and 'sextremism' occupies an ideological space within the 'feminist' category that highlights class differences between members. The idea that Femen "are causing more division than unity among the feminist world", as stated by Laura Santos-Bishop, reveals a tension between the 'moderate', 'modest', 'civil' approach of women who have access to privileged spaces of 'respectability', and women who do not, but who still want to claim a space in the 'feminist' identity category.[140] In an article in *Head Space* called "Why as a Feminist I Will Never Identify With Femen" by Toula Drimonis, commenter Arturo Rivera writes:

> I was a little startled by how FEMEN debases itself as a spectacle, while unwittingly tarnishing what feminism actually stands for. None of them are looking at the bigger picture. There was this protest in front of a church, I don't remember the name or place, but FEMEN held a protest there that ended up offending and traumatizing the patrons attending. It was so ridiculous. Just plain ridiculous. That is radical and extreme behavior at its finest, and it definitely doesn't do anything other than make a mockery of the very cause that they claim to be fighting for.

(Drimonis 2015)

Femen's crudeness is not compatible with upper-class sensibilities and 'manners politics'. These 'manners politics' preserve respect and deference for churches. The mainstream discourse draws a line at challenging the politics of religion.

The perspective that Femen's topless protest tactic is a sexual performance for the benefit of men is constructed on the premise that women's breasts are inherently sexual objects for the pleasure of men, and thus uncovering them is giving men pleasure. Within the boundaries of this premise, women can choose to reveal their breasts to please men, or cover their breasts to withhold pleasure from men.

There is no scenario which does not revolve around men's pleasure, and there is no space to consider women's pleasure, except within the limited role of being the scopophilic object.

It is clear from the thousands of comments by appalled men who are disgusted by Femen protesters that the premise of women's breasts equalling male pleasure is flawed.

As Inna Shevchenko points out, moving naked breasts from the privacy of a brothel room, or a housewife's bed, into the public realm of men functions like a taboo-exploding 'bomb'. Breasts are coded as pleasurable only within particular spaces. The image of women's breasts in front of Parliament or on the steps of Notre Dame Cathedral takes control and directs the male gaze, drawing attention to the constraints of women's bodily agency to submissive, powerless poses. Mulvey writes that "destruction of pleasure is a radical weapon", shattering the voyeuristic ph/fantasy of the male gaze.[141]

Watson button by *Jordystories* via Redbubble. (https://wanelo.co/search?query=jordystories)

"Feminism makes women automatically ugly, Emma Watson went from a 10 to a 6 once I heard she was a man eating Feminazi."[142] When actress Emma Watson became a vocal advocate of feminism, tweets like this one revealed that submissive postures and ideology play a far greater role in public performance than the two-dimensional critiques of Femen by many bloggers.

If this is the case, then on what grounds does a feminist critique of 'sextremism' stand? After all, a basic definition of feminism is bringing to light unexamined systems of power.[143] After a lecture I gave about Femen to an undergraduate class on gender and religion, a student raised her hand and said that these particular activists are bad girls who make all feminists look bad. She was worried that these kinds of radicals make men dislike feminists. This insightful comment echoes a stream within the wider realm of feminist thought that desires to maintain middle-class sensibilities of moderation.

Image posted by Janet Mock on Twitter in 2014.

Ever since Beyoncé walked out onto a stage emblazoned with the word FEMINIST in silver lights three meters high at the Video Music Awards (VMAs) in 2014,[144f] girls around the world have taken on the feminist label. It was a turning point in the history of the feminist movement. What was once a taboo political word for bad girls has now permeated the mainstream as an acceptable identity. This pop-culturation (ie. gentrification) of feminism is a depoliticizing mechanism; feminism has been reverse-queered to accept the conservative capitalist elements of mainstream society, subject to commodification and monetization. The Guardian contributor and commenter 'Bulletpoint' calls this generation of young bloggers "feminist

---

[f] Beyoncé's statement became "the subject of two-thirds of all tweets [in the history of Twitter] about feminism in the 24 hours after her appearance," according to a Twitter data analysis by Jessica Bennett. (Bennett 2014)

lightweights".¹⁴⁵ She argues that the faction of feminists who are uncomfortable with Femen oppose the group because of neoliberal sympathies. Bulletpoint writes that:

> **The prudish protestants in Britain are quite happy to let modern capitalism have anything as its commodity - they see no alternative to neo-liberalsm [sic] and as they have no meta-narrative they simply accept its constructs as facts on the ground. What they find offensive is the female body itself exposed -and the fact that the Ukrainians are devaluing the female body as a commodity. [...] What we are talking about is the fight of so called feminists who regard the female body as a valuable commodity not to be wasted with needless exhibition and the Ukrainians who are old school and are saying F*** your commodification of the female body.**
> **(Bulletpoint 2013)**

Bulletpoint's comment points to the preservation of conservative ethics in expanding the feminist movement to include 'lightweights'. Commenter 'Loumo' asks Bulletpoint to explain the meaning of 'meta-narrative'. Bulletpoint responds:

> Ideological constructs are not natural phenomena. When you lack the tools or the desire to question ideological constructs then you accept them as truths that correspond to nature and human nature.
>
> Yet, neo-liberal and capitalist economics are failed ideological constructs. They are ruinous. People who live in the ruins of this ideology, but who have no way to put it in perspective and critique it, live as if ideological fiction were fact. This leads you into a sorry cul-de-sac. [...]
>
> There is no critique of capitalism if you think capitalism is the end of history. So in this way we don't criticise capitalism but racism, not capitalism but sexism, not capitalism but religious intolerance, not capitalism but poverty.
>
> And so on and so on. The result is ridiculous. Imagine a critique of poverty without a corresponding critique of capitalism. If that's your party trick then you are lost up sh** creek, because poverty is a consequence of exploitation, of capitalism.
>
> (Bulletpoint 2013)

This conversation points to the wide-ranging debates between anarchists, socialists and the New Left, and conservative neoliberals within the expanding feminist movement.

Another source of intense criticism of Femen comes from their "Topless Jihad" project. When Amina Sboui posted her topless solidarity photo ("My body belongs to me and is not the source of any man's honor") and was expeditiously punished for it, Femen began a media campaign to exert international pressure on Tunisian officials to keep Sboui out of harm's way. Femen activists protested outside of mosques all over Europe as well as at Tunisian embassies. This elision of Muslims generally, rather than Tunisian officials specifically, characterizes a majority of racism directed against Muslims and drew heavy criticism from anti-Islamophobia groups. It should be noted that it was not the Tunisian state that abducted Sboui, but her family and 'religious' clerics, so a protest of the 'religious' system was appropriate; however, Femen's intention was to pressure the Tunisian state to step in, so the message was muddled. A core principle of Femen is excoriating critique of all religions as tools of patriarchy, seeing Christians and 'secular' right-wing fascists opposing gay marriage, for example, as equally dangerous forces working together to fuel hatred. The 'Topless Jihad' action entangled gender, race, sex, religion and politics.

Despite the controversy, Femen's goal to create a viral buzz online throughout the world to draw international attention to Tunisia so that Amina would not be tortured or imprisoned was successful. Sboui was released; however, a good many feathers were ruffled along the way. With slogans such as "Nudity is Freedom", "Free Amina!", "Muslim Women, Let's Get Naked" and images of topless women with beards and turbans down on their knees praying, the criticism is not surprising. Ilana Alazzah called it "blackface", and "CNN, the New York Times, Al Jazeera English, and the *Huffington Post* (and elsewhere) [called] the group racist, classist, imperialist, colonialist, Eurocentric, Islamophobic, orientalist, neo-orientalist, cowardly, or, at best, naïve, and foolish".[146] Most of these international commentators coded Femen activists as wealthy white American or western European women rather than women who grew up in poverty from a country in ruins and at war. While Femen branches in developing countries were more focused on fair elections and human rights abuses, the American Femen branch became entwined with the Free the Nipple movement, and this was the kind of lens a casual observer in USA or Canada saw the protests through. As explained by Agata Pyzik in *Poor But Sexy: Culture Clashes in Europe East and West,* the existence of this group of women, documented in images splashed across the features of websites all over the world, challenges the contemporary assumptions of rich whiteness in complicated ways.

Feminism as a vast international movement struggles with both its universalizing function as a category and the desire to be intersectional, or reflect many dimensions of perspective. This gets complicated in the post-globalization age. If an activist like Ilana Alazzah, born in San Francisco and attending Smith College in Massachusetts where tuition is almost $70 000 USD per year,[147] is allowed to identify with someone calling themselves a Muslim in Tunisia, then ostensibly a Ukrainian woman is allowed to identify with someone who calls herself a woman in Tunisia, and indeed, the latter probably have more in common.[148] However, the (male-centred) category of religion often trumps the category of woman for solidarity, and access to rights.

A very important issue that often gets sidelined in the conversation about 'Topless Jihad' is the protection of 'religion' from critique. On this subject, Jeffrey Tayler of *The Atlantic* writes:

> The media has long fostered the view that religion should be de facto exempt from the logical scrutiny applied to other subjects. I am not disputing the right to practice the religion of one's choice, but rather the prevailing cultural rectitude that puts faith beyond the pale of commonsense review, and (in Amina's case), characterizes as "Islamophobic" criticism of the criminal mistreatment of a young woman for daring to buck her society's norms…

(Tayler 2013)

The identity category of 'religion' retains a privileged status amongst identity categories. Intersectionality has made needed spaces for diverse perspectives within the feminist movement, particularly in regard to race, but somehow patriarchal ideology in 'religion' gets preserved in the application of intersectionality, threatening the foundation of feminism itself.

Where 1970s feminism gave rise to slogans such as Mary Daly's "if God is male, then the male is God", contemporary mainstream feminism is deeply divided on the patriarchal category of religion.[149] In "Why as a Feminist I Will Never Identify With Femen", Toula Drimonis writes that "[p]robably the aspect that most troubles me about FEMEN is their blatant disdain of religion and the people who practice it… It's a daily battle not to be perceived as nagging, whining, overindulgent, man-hating bra-burners without having a bunch of women flashing their boobs in protest to undo all that work and make all feminists look barking mad".[150] Women demanding the right to vote is no longer perceived as 'barking mad' in mainstream discourse, but exposing breasts against God's will still is. Likewise University of Exeter professor Francesca Stansfield writes that "Femen have a ridiculous white saviour complex, they should respect the religious sensitivities of Bethlehem and stop giving feminism a bad name".[151]

As in the past, many young women today are striving to be 'good girls', and indeed there continues to be a market for literature and products for women to consume and buy in this genre. In the 1950s, it was little etiquette books of how to behave, what you should and shouldn't do, what is appropriate and inappropriate. Today, there are websites like *Everyday Feminism* pumping out articles about all the bad things bad girls are doing wrong. These well-mannered ladies have all the zeal of yesterday's evangelicals and high school cheerleaders for telling you how to behave, but none of the rule-defying trailblazing attitude of the loud and proud suffragettes. A lot of the pop-culture 'lightweight' feminism you see on blogs on the internet is paralyzed with concern for using the appropriate euphemisms, and avoids taboo topics like religion. The internet is flooded with this kind of concern-troll version of feminism, but there is still a vibrant contemporary contingent of critics of religion in the on-the-ground feminist movement like Women Against Fundamentalism, Pussy Riot, the Southall Black Sisters, and renowned feminists like Taslima Nasrin, Maryam Namazie, Susan Jacoby, Katha Pollitt, Annie Laurie Gaylor, and Sikivu Hutchinson. The tradition of feminist critiques of religion has a long and rich history; as Katha Pollitt remarked at a Women in Secularism conference in 2013, it was Job's wife who exclaimed "curse your god and forget him!" when Yahweh killed all their children and blighted their crops in the Old Testament. Mary Wollstonecraft (author of *A Vindication of the Rights of Woman: With Strictures on Political and Moral Subjects* 1792), Matilda Joselyn Gage (author of *Women, Church and State* 1883), Emina Slenker, Annie Besant, Lucy Parsons, Marian Sherman, Queen Silver, Margaret Sanger, and many more understood the role of the church in the social structures oppressing women. First-wave feminist icon Elizabeth Cady Stanton famously wrote the 19th amendment of the American constitution, giving women the right to vote, but she also wrote *The Woman's Bible* (1899), expanding her 1896 essay, "The Degraded Status of Woman in the Bible". Women's rights movements and critiques of religion have long been complementary endeavours.

Ernestine Rose, for example, lectured extensively on atheism; her "Defense of Atheism" lecture delivered in Boston in 1861, praised by George Bernard Shaw, included the theory that it is "demonstrable fact, that all children are atheists, and were religion not inculcated into their minds they would remain so. Even as it is, they are great skeptics, until made sensible of the potent weapon by which religion has ever been propagated, namely, fear" (Huberman, 2008, p. 258). A Massachusetts newspaper responded that "We know of no object more deserving of contempt, loathing, and abhorrence than a female atheist. We hold the vilest strumpet from the stews to be by comparison respectable" (Jacoby, 2012). Perhaps these kinds of characterizations help to explain why women today are moving toward the 'holistic milieu' and 'spiritual-but-not-religious'
identity rather than calling themselves out-and-out atheists.
(Montgomery 2012: 12)

It is unsurprising that Femen's attack on religion is 'too much' for North American popular culture, where patriarchal Christian influence is deeply rooted. When asked by Jennifer Aniston "[w]hat do you think the biggest problem with feminism today is?" at the *Makers: Women Who Make America* conference, Gloria Steinem "named religion as one of three 'biggest problems' after anti-feminism and income disparity".[152] She said that "religion is just politics in the sky. I think we really have to talk about it".[153]

I have noticed in the classroom that many of today's young feminists are avoiding the difficult and taboo critique of religion, and often are unaware of the classic feminist texts which offer a treasure of analysis. When the young Ukrainian teenagers who became Femen started meeting to discuss their ideas and plan actions, they had never heard of 'feminism'. They had never been introduced to feminism in schools, at home, or amongst their peers, and they had certainly never heard about it in church. They simply saw that the conditions of life for women around them were deteriorating, and their own options as young women were narrowing as the country became more conservative. They developed a strategy through trial-and-error to address it. They were not in touch with an international or even national discourse on feminist philosophy, and so when they were labelled 'bad feminists' in the international press, it was a meaningless insult. Their activism emerged as a response to personal experience, unlike many contemporary middle or upper class feminists whose consciousness-raising is based in theory, or through blogs. Inna Shevchenko epitomizes Rudnytsky's (1987) analysis of working-class Ukrainian dissidents who are first generation intellectuals. For example, she contributed an opinion column to the *Huffington Post* which was theoretically rudimentary, but contained a kind of activism realness that is often absent from contemporary mainstream feminist discussions. Her column, titled "Sextremism: The New Way For Feminism To Be!", argued:

> The body of the woman is always too much. Or not enough. And this idea has infected up to women themselves. The biggest concern of modern feminism is how to take back the female body from the cultural and financial machine of the patriarchal system, and return it to its rightful owners - using this body, instead, to protect the interests of women across the world.
> (Shevchenko 2013)

Writers at *Everyday Feminism, Feminist Times, Jezebel,* or *Bitch Magazine* might look at this comment as a prosaic reinvention of the wheel, but Shevchenko's impoverished upbringing in a dictatorship means that translated copies of classical feminist texts were not available in her school library. As Pyzik points out in *Poor But Sexy: Culture Clashes in Europe East and West,* Femen:

> [W]ere dismissed by Western feminists for crypto or even open racism and nudity-obsession, regardless of the context. In this case, both sides misunderstood the delicate circumstances. Intersectional, progressive Western feminists, concerned with the risks of racism and (post) colonialism, speak of Femen's unhealthy obsession with nudity with suspicious disdain, not seeing that behind the admittedly "primitive" methods and controversial approach there's a very specific reality that Femen are fighting.
> (Pyzik 2014: 41)

Anna Hutsol, a member of Femen since the beginning, explains how Femen has always been excluded from bourgeois feminism. In Femen, there is no "set of strict rules you have to adhere to or you're out. We distinguish ourselves very clearly from feminist organisations with high intellectual standards. For example, if a woman hasn't read a particular book, she can never be part of that organisation. These types of organisations ignore ordinary women. They are excluded for various reasons. We value all women. Each woman counts for us and can become a fighter and change her life".¹⁵⁴ It is clear that the focus for Femen leaders is on direct action; their feminism is defined in terms of actions rather than verbally supporting or disagreeing with particular arguments. After Amina Sboui posted her solidarity photo, a Facebook group was started called *Feminists against Femen*, filled predominantly with 'men's rights activists'. Group member Xuan Matta commented on a photo in the group, "I can't really tell so I have to ask, is this page feminist or anti-feminist?".¹⁵⁵ He was not the only one who was confused. In a time of significant social transformation, the line between what is and what is not feminist is blurred.

Feminist Times author Charlotte Raven reported that "Femen are one of many depressing features of the internet age – an international brand with as much name recognition as Hermes that captures attention and doesn't convert it into anything".¹⁵⁶ Meanwhile, Femen women have done the footwork, putting their own bodies and safety on the front lines, inspiring the Maidan Revolution, and even the Occupy Movement, thanklessly it seems. In February 2016, Shevchenko was giving a talk about freedom of speech and women's rights in Copenhagen, and she was fired at with a Kalashnikov over 200 times. While several people were killed or injured, miraculously, Shevchenko escaped. After receiving death threats on a regular basis, she dropped to the floor as soon as she heard shots ring out. The shooter, 22-year-old Omar al-Hussein, was shot dead by police.

What Charlotte Raven is referring to in her disparagement of the internet age is a common criticism of contemporary social media users, sometimes called 'armchair activists'. Users will share content on their Facebook and Twitter accounts, and write strongly worded comments on articles and blogs about issues they presumably care about, but for some reason their activism does not progress to mobilization. The screen stultifies, and desires for change are soothed by clicking 'like' and 'share'. Mustafa Nayyem, the Afghan-Ukrainian journalist who catalyzed the initial Maidan protest, posted an update on his Facebook page calling out this trend. He wrote: "Come on, let's get serious. Who is ready to go out to the Maidan […] by midnight tonight? 'Likes' don't count".¹⁵⁷ Facebook users in particular will share post after post about injustices internationally, but never get involved in projects improving those situations.

I sometimes refer to this kind of material as '**sadporn**'—users will watch horrifying videos of slaughtered children, police shootings, and Trump rallies, experience an intense moment of sadness, and then go on with their day.

What Charlotte Raven does not seem to realize is that Femen's actions and their impacts are real, reminiscent of the theatrical and influential street protests of the 1960s and 1970s, which were often criticized for being fruitless at the time. Further, these street movements, whether at Ukrainian Maidan fighting for a democratic revolution, Femen demanding equality for women, Idle No More challenging colonial sovereignty over First Nations in Canada, the Black Lives Matter actions protesting police brutality and systemic racism, or the Fight for 15 strikes against wage slavery in the fast food industry in the United States, represent a powerful return to direct action people's politics. Youth are tuned in online, as well as 'unplugged' in the street irl, and the media revolution is an integral part of this shift. As Shevchenko says, there is "no feminism in the street anymore. We are trying to push it".[158]

In the *Feminist Times* article, Raven also criticizes Femen for performing for the male gaze. One of the important prospects of post-Beyoncé feminism is that members of Femen are not necessarily performing for the male gaze at all. In Noah Berlatsky's article for the Pacific Standard, he argues that Beyoncé's fanbase is overwhelmingly comprised of women and gay men. He asks "if Beyoncé's fans are mostly women and gay men, why the stripteases, the thrusting, the shaking, and the sexualized performances in general? If she's not on display for the male gaze, who exactly is she on display for?".[159] Women and gay men are deriving scopophilic pleasure from Beyoncé's thrusting and shaking, not straight men, who "have no interest in Beyoncé whatever, and even seem to be averse to her".[160]

An important aspect of Mulvey's analysis of the male gaze was the 1930's Hollywood representations of women in positions of submission and sexual vulnerability. Beyoncé's sexualized performances are powerful, and probably terrifying[g] to the kind of straight men looking to consume a submissive image. The director positioning Greta Garbo on set to look meek and soft was not impressing the male gaze with sexuality, but with

---

[g] I acknowledge that this is a speculative comment. I was walking in a mall past a Victoria's Secret underwear store in 2015, and noticed the massive floor-to-ceiling billboards featuring statuesque, bronzed, chiseled women wearing lingerie and standing in power postures. The man beside me gestured to the images, commenting that they were "intimidating and terrifying." This comment made me question my assumptions about the different purposes, audiences, and intentions of the uses of female bodies for advertising.

passivity and timidity. Beyoncé may be a heterosexual woman, but the sexuality represented in her performances on stage is not aimed to please heterosexual men in general. Likewise, Femen members are not screaming with their breasts exposed to get boyfriends or to make men happy, and neither are they trying to please feminist bloggers. Femen aim to inspire women with their brazen and radical actions to step outside the boundaries of what they are 'allowed' to do, no matter what other men or women think is appropriate. In that sense Femen are performing radical rebellion for the female gaze. Femen do not care about looking like 'bad girls' to politicians, the church, or moralizing women. Their message is speaking to women ready to tear down social constraints, and men who are prepared to be allies of women's freedom of speech. Building on Mulvey's analysis, Femen's public displays 'destroy the pleasure' of the image of the naked female body as compliant, vulnerable and private. Further, women, gay or straight, can derive scopophilic pleasure from the sight of Femen's empowered self-representation, like the women and gay men who love Beyoncé, and who derive non-sexual scopophilic pleasure from her performances.

Azarov pursued by Bloody Tits Krovosisi.

Victoria Sendón, a Spanish feminist philosopher and professor who is a member of Femen Spain. Whose gaze is Sendón performing for here?

Femen activists stage an action during the anti-abortion rally in Madrid in 2014. On their chests are written 'your morals are killing me', 'abortion is sacred', and the rhyme 'pro-vida genocida', which translates to 'pro-life genocide'.

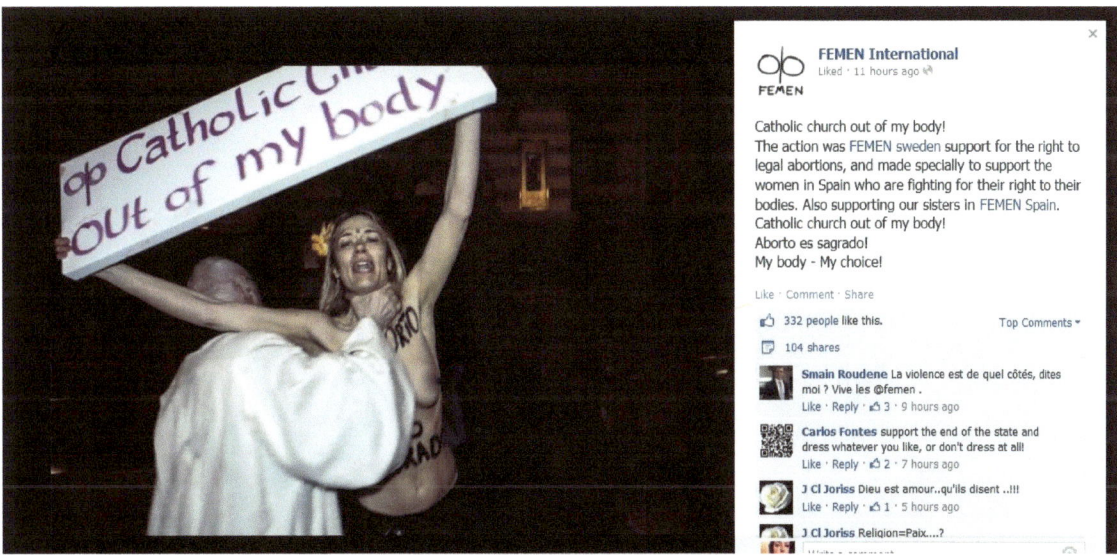

This image shows a solidarity action in Sweden in support of Femen Spain's pro-choice action pictured above. The caption reads:

> *Catholic church out of my body! The action was Femen Sweden support for the right to legal abortions, and made specially to support the women in Spain who are fighting for their right to their bodies. Also supporting our sisters in Spain. Catholic church out of my body!*

Aborto es sagrado! [abortion is sacred]
My body – my choice!
(www.Facebook.com/femenmovement 2014)

French Arab women protesting for laïcité in Paris in 2012. Eco-feminist and anti-racist activist Safia Lebdi invited Femen Ukraine to participate. In the picture below, Oksana Shachko wears her cultural regalia in solidarity with the French Arab women's protest, along with the 1970s Muslim star and crescent painted on her arms.

FEMEN IN CANADA

Femen Canada in 2013. www.facebook.com/FEMENCanada

Femen Canada in 2014. www.facebook.com/FEMENCanada

Neda Topaloski of Femen Canada.

Femen's international movement has gained much traction and popular support in social justice movements under repressive regimes, like Tunisia, Ukraine, Belarus, Egypt and Erdogan's Turkey, but continues to face intense criticism from North American audiences.

In May 2014, Neda Topaloski and Delphine Bergeron of Femen Canada protested the Ottawa March For Life rally. The focus of the 2014 rally was to prevent Canadian women from taking pills (called RU-486) which trigger menstruation up to seven weeks after pregnancy.

> **Neda Topaloski:** We were protesting for every Canadian woman to have free access to abortion, in a medical and safe way. We were also protesting against the powerful lobbyists that work all year long to try to make abortion illegal. We want them to stop organizing these events and doing such massive propaganda against women. In a democracy like Canada, people should be stopped and denounced when they make anti-human lobbies. We want to drag the attention to the alliance of church and state on this abortion debate. It is extremely dangerous.
>
> **Interviewer: So you believe that church and state are working together here?**
> Yes, exactly. On Thursday the Archbishop of Quebec was on stage. He was speaking when we intervened. There were a couple members of parliament from Stephen Harper's Conservative party, as well as senators, all together on one side. Church and state are supposed to be separate. When you have political and religious leaders organizing these types of things, with history and money and power backing them, it worries FEMEN. Religion is way too close with the government. Together they are trying to achieve legislation against women's rights in general.
> (Hennessey 2014)

The interview with Vice was posted online, and the comments posted below it are not favourable. Reader Dan Andrew "Canadian Teacher" writes: "Well, as a man who supports feminism this is a total failure. Too bad most women think these two are idiots who went about this entirely the wrong way. Radicalism is for the Taliban not for privileged white women. If you want real change organise respectfully. The whole idea of Femin is to have "more women rebel" thats pretty pathetic [sic]. Way to make women's rights activists look like immature, angry teenagers with an attitude problem".[161] Reactions to Femen in Canada have been lukewarm on the average.

Femen-style activism is more warmly embraced in countries that more closely resemble Ukraine economically and politically. The group inspires resistance in countries where dictatorships rule. In November 2015, journalist Can Dündar was imprisoned for publishing footage of the Erdogan regime in Turkey providing weapons to the Islamic State in Syria (ISIS, or ISIL in popular media coverage). In December, Inna Shevchenko and Femen France staged an action in support of the imprisoned journalists of Hurriyet, decrying the increasingly authoritarian government of Turkey under Erdogan. The Canadian branch of Femen also participated in this action. Can Dündar wrote to Femen from prison, to say that the journalists were proud "to see our names written on the most effective rebellion boards of the recent years, on your breasts, just above your hearts. From Silivri with love and thanks, I salute your movement which is always on the side of those who are oppressed. Viva FEMEN! Yours, Can Dündar".[162]

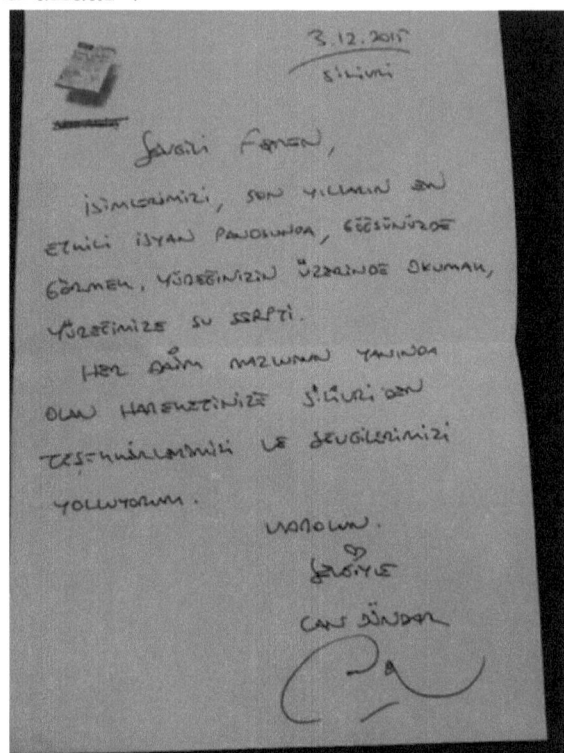

Letter of thanks to Femen from imprisoned journalist Can Dündar.

Femen responded that "FEMEN are proud to read those words, FEMEN are proud for the strong spirit and convictions of jailed journalists of Cumhuriyet. Our resistance goes on! FREEDOM TO CAN DÜNDAR AND ERDEM GÜL!" (femen.org).

Turkish woman demanding the release of Turkish journalists.

Canadian women in solidarity with imprisoned Turkish journalists.

Campaign of support for imprisoned Turkish journalists.

Femen also organized a campaign of support for Raif Badawi, the Saudi Arabian blogger who was publicly flogged for publishing a website debate forum about the influence of religion on law. In 2012, he was arrested for "insulting Islam through electronic channels" and cited for apostasy, "a conviction which carries an automatic death sentence".[163] He was officially charged with "setting up a website that undermines general security", "ridiculing Islamic religious figures", and "going beyond the realm of obedience".[164] In 2013 Badawi was sentenced to seven years in prison and 600 lashes, because his website "violates Islamic values and propagates liberal thought".[165] In May 2014, his sentence was amended to ten years in prison and 1000 lashes, and he was fined 1 million riyal. In January 2015, he was "flogged 50 times before hundreds of spectators in front of a Jeddah mosque, the first in a series of 1,000 lashes to be carried out in over twenty weeks".[166] This event was so widely publicized and criticized internationally that Badawi's next scheduled flogging was postponed, and he has since been hospitalized. Badawi's wife and children are living as asylum-seekers in Quebec, Canada. Many people have made statements of support for Raif Badawi, including Salman Rushdie, Ayaan Hirsi Ali, Noam Chomsky, Sam Harris, and even Bono. Here is Femen's statement of support:

> **If one considers that there are heroes in our time, Raif Badawi is definitely one of them. His simple sense of freedom is a threat to the entire dictatorial state of Saudi Arabia, his ideas and words are a revolution for us all. Whereas Saudi Arabia's bloody regime is torturing Raif's body and limiting his freedom through imprisonment, they cannot prevent making his ideas stronger and bigger... Badawi's ideas are everywhere now, in many people, and they are in me as well.**
>
> **Criticising religion is our duty today as Badawi's case proves it. It is what we are supposed to call 'freedom'. My only request will not be to the Saudi Arabian state to release Raif (it wouldn't be successful anyways) but instead to Raif and everyone including you, to keep these ideas, to spread them more, to be proud of them, so that soon, everyone will be able to enjoy fully his freedom, including the heroic Raif Badawi.**
>
> **We will win this fight!**
> **Femen**

FEMEN IN IRAN

Iranian artist Moujan Taher: "I'd rather be a rebel not a slave."

In March 2016, 36 year-old Iranian artist Moujan Mohammad Taher staged a topless action in Tehran with the words "I'd rather be a rebel not a slave" painted on her breasts. She was speaking out against the Islamic Republic's new anti-woman laws and the increasing influence of religious clerics on governance in Iran. As an artist, she was frustrated that she could not make the kinds of films or art that she dreamed of. She issued this statement to her friend Hessam Yousefi in Germany to share with 'western' media:

> My message to women is that they can be active inside Iran and demand their rights loudly… This kind of protest can give Iranian women more courage to engage in struggle against current conditions […] I did this as a representative of all women who are not heard. I did it under very difficult and hard conditions, under the shadow of a government that arrests women who demonstrate, and throws them into prison. Women must have their own organizations and fight against unjust laws. They must support each other and go forward hand in hand. Without power and without knowledge and unity you cannot get anywhere. (Iranwire 2016)

Mohammed was inspired by Femen protests, particularly that of Alia Al Mahdi, the young Egyptian Femen activist fighting against the Islamicization of the Egyptian constitution. One day, after Al Mahdi's action, Mohammed saw that her friend and former classmate Solmaz Vakilpour had participated in a protest in Germany. She writes: "It gave me a very good feeling and I thought that I too could do a protest in a fundamental and radical way. We agreed that if the conditions were right both of us would participate in an act of protest. Almost a year after we talked, preparations were underway in Germany to stage a nude protest on March 8, International Women's Day. I decided to do the same thing in Iran on the same day".[167]

Close friends who knew what Taher was planning tried to talk her out of it for her own safety, but her biggest critic was herself; she said in an interview with Iranwire that "it was very hard for me to break this taboo in my own head. I had to damage my reputation among close family members. Showing the body of a woman in Iran is breaking a taboo in itself. I very consciously wrote what I wanted to say on my body and got naked, even though I was afraid".[168] Taher and her friend went to a park together, where Taher, both nervous and excited, took off her clothes while her friend quickly snapped the photograph. The entire action took just a few minutes. What seemed to be a tiny act of rebellion made a huge impact on social media. Taher's image was shared and viewed by millions of people around the world. This is her perspective on the responses to her photograph:

Some think we should move forward slowly — or as they say, engage in reforms. But I hope the protest will ripple like throwing a stone into stagnant water. I am actually happy about the objections, because they show that my protest has been noticed. I hope that in the same way that Femen's actions gave me the courage to do such a thing, my act will give others courage.
(Iranwire 2016)

When the Femen movement began in Ukraine, the girls had only their own communities to fear. The relocation to France, and the subsequent chapters opening all over the world makes the movement truly international. Shevchenko writes flatly: "I get death threats from Islamists daily, they have murdered my friend and tried to kill me. The only thing I have done is to show breasts and say what I think. I intend to continue".[169] Despite the scathing critics, the challenges of becoming a global feminist movement, and the threats of violence and death from fundamentalists, the Femen movement continues to spread to different cities around the world and to non-violently combat corruption, tyranny, and injustice the best that they can.

Bare Breasts, a Femen Hymn by Paris-based band Western Fiasco

Our cause is human
Our god is woman
Our mission is protest
Our weapons are bare breasts
Our bosom, for freedom
Vagina, our kingdom
Our mind, our battle, a fight

You're the slut, you're the whore
Merciless and hardcore
Male domination in our head?
Why don't you stick it in your ass instead?

Our cause is human
Our god is woman
Our mission is protest
Our weapons are bare breasts
Our bosom, for freedom
Vagina, our kingdom
Our mind, our battle, a fight
(Western Fiasco, 2013)

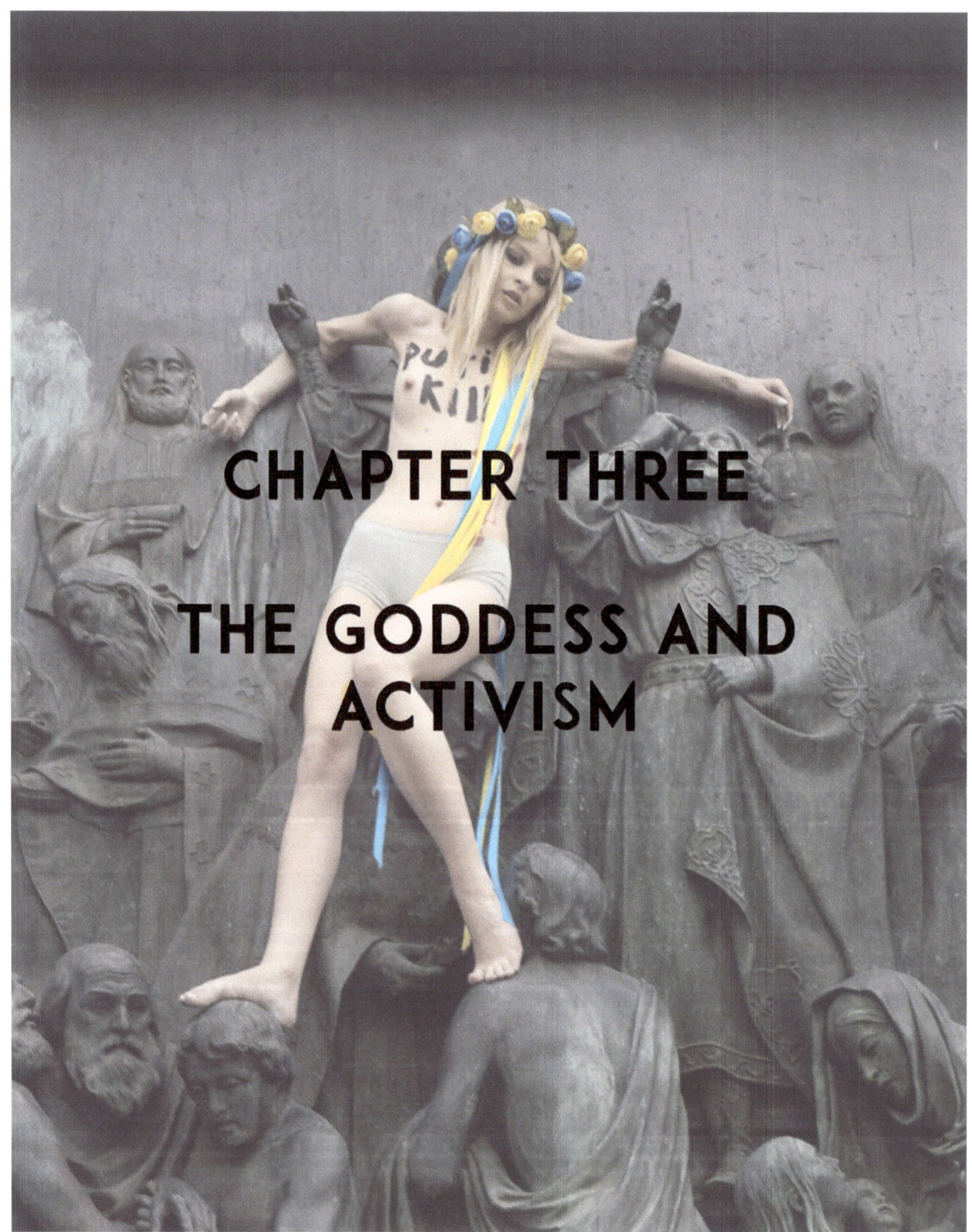

CHAPTER THREE

THE GODDESS AND ACTIVISM

CHAPTER THREE

THE GODDESS AND ACTIVISM

When I was a student at Cambridge, I remember a professor holding up a picture of a bone with 28 incisions carved in it. 'This is often considered to be man's first attempt at a calendar,' she explained. 'My question to you is this – what man needs to mark 28 days? I would suggest to you that this is woman's first attempt at a calendar.' It was a moment that changed my life. In that second I stopped to question almost everything I had been taught about the past.
—Sandi Toksvig
("Sandi Toksvig's Top 10 Unsung Heroines", 2009)

GOD THE FATHER

Don't play stupid, don't play dumb
Vagina's where you're really from
—Pussy Riot
(*Straight Outta Vagina*, 2016)

In 2012 I worked at a program at Queen's University in Kingston, Ontario called *Future Quest*. It was intended to promote the Religious Studies program of Queen's University to interested teens. The program was described in a brochure as a non-denominational "summer experience for youth" which was "exploring community, theology and leadership".[170] Participants visited a variety of 'religious centres' to participate in or observe ritual practices of different groups in the Kingston area. For most of them, it was their first time in a mosque, Cathedral, temple, or non-Protestant community centre.

"I prayed in a mosque," said one participant to her father when he came to pick her up from camp. "I got down on my knees and prayed to Allah. They pray to God just like us, dad; we're all one people."

He turned angrily to me as a facilitator and said: "My daughter ain't no Islam!"

The program coordinator explained to me that 'non-denominational' for many meant "both Protestant *and* Catholic."

The group attended a small Catholic service. The priest began by saying that he knew we were a non-denominational group, and that he was open to all the names of god because Catholicism is an inclusive tradition. This made me feel welcome despite not being a Catholic, and during a group prayer that involved reading from a screen, I participated and exchanged 'Goddess' for the word 'God'. The priest was so angry with me that I thought he was going to hit me. I remember how confused I felt. Why was he so angry? I could not understand his reaction. If Catholicism is an inclusive tradition, and if Catholics believe that 'God' is just a name for what is a universal deity, then why did feminine pronouns disturb the priest so deeply that I felt like he was going to strike me? Why did the goddess scare him so much?

Since then, I encountered Hanisch's (1970) feminist slogan, "the personal is political", and Goldenberg's (2015) twist, "the religious is political", and it became clear. There is no such thing as personal religious belief for women. Everything women do with their bodies is a political statement and a public affair that is subject to policing. Calling on the Goddess, whether I chose it to be so or not, was an inherently political act. Invoking the goddess is activism.

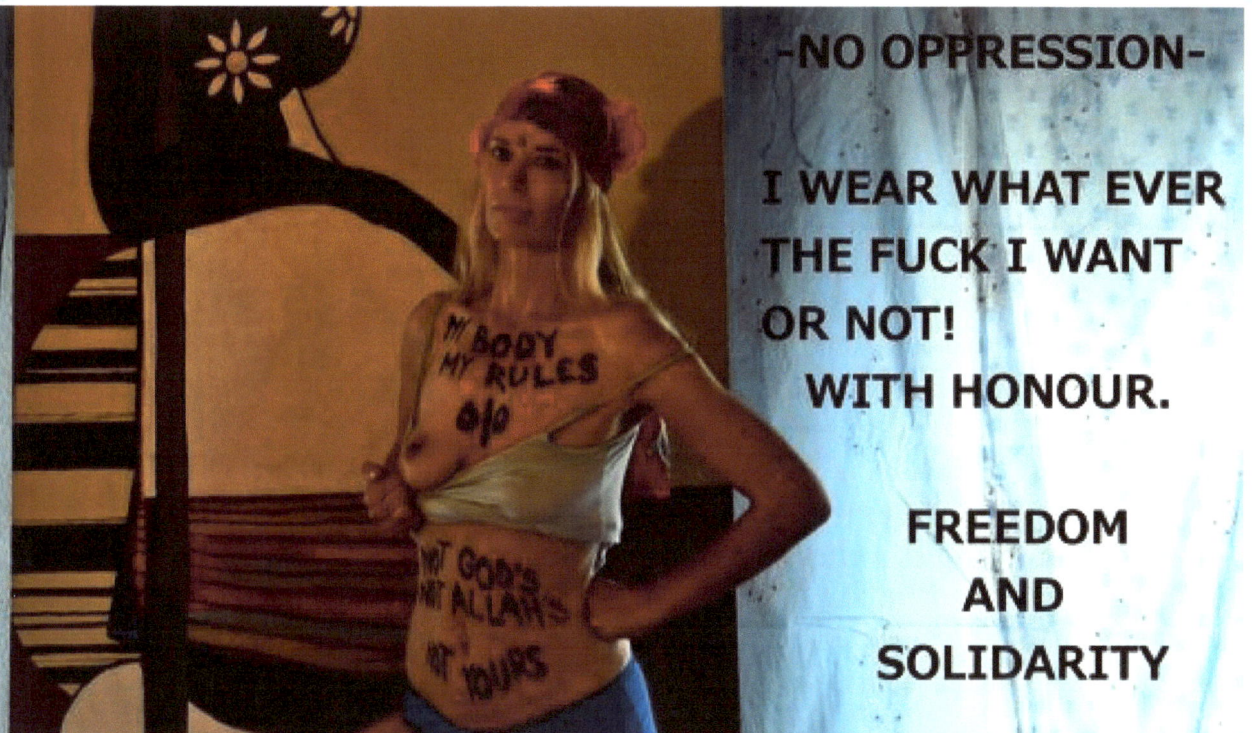

In August 2013, a pregnant Swedish Muslim woman was grabbed from behind, her headscarf torn off and her head slammed into a car until she passed out. Foujan Rouzbeh and Nabila Abdul Fattah started the Twitter hashtag #hijabuppropet, calling on Swedish women to wear headscarves in solidarity with Muslim women. Many high profile Swedish politicians answered the call and posted their photos online. Jenny Wenhammar of Sweden, a self-described "sextremist, atheist, feminist" created this solidarity image with the Femen symbol painted between her breasts widely shared on social media (Femen Sweden 2013). She wrote:

I dress in solidarity with your message - how I dress or do not dress myself does not give anyone the right to hurt me. We wear what we want and cover what we want. Anyone who decides over me and my body is not God, Allah or any other. My body, my rules.

Jenny

(Femen Sweden 2013)

Self-described feminist freethinker[h] novelist Katha Pollitt gave a talk at *Women in Secularism II*, a Washington D.C. conference in 2013 entitled "Sexism and Religion: Can the Knot be Untied?" After the talk, a member of the audience asked her what the world would look like if the 'end goals[i] of the feminist and atheist movements' were achieved. She responded that for feminist and freethinking objectives to be realized in society it would mean opening a history book and finding that they had always been popular. Pollitt is describing the feminist (and Critical History) understanding that historical narratives are embedded within a discourse of patriarchal hegemony. In the words of Gloria Steinem's famous rally refrain, 'women have always been an equal part of the past, we just haven't been a part of history'. (Or, more ironically, "the history of the world is but the biography of great men," to quote Thomas Carlyle in *Heroes and Hero-Worship, The Hero as Divinity,* 1840). For example, the first named author in known history is the Akkadian/Sumerian poet Enheduanna (living in approximately 4300 before present), but her name is little-known, even to historians. Pollitt calls the process of bringing women's histories into the cultural imaginaire 'seeking the usable past'.[171]

Roland Barthes writes that mythology is depoliticized speech; the depoliticization inherent to the category of 'history' is the underlying power relations driving the narrative. When history is called 'the account of what happened', the reader has forgotten that, to quote Virginia Woolf, "nothing has really happened until it has been described".[172] History is a mythology of ourselves—with 'ourselves' as the privileged authors and authorities of history-writing. Mythology narrates the plot of the present. According to Pollitt, the scholarship of drawing out the historical significance of women in mythology and history is a necessary precondition for civic rights for women in contemporary times.

For example, in ancient Sparta, women were granted full citizenship at the age of 18, including the right to own and inherit property. Since women lived longer than men and so many men died in war, a significant portion of the land in Sparta belonged

---

[h] 'Freethinker' is an alternative term for a secularist or atheist. 'Freethinker' is different than 'secularist' because the latter term preserves a religion/secular binary, which in turn re-inscribes the problematic category of religion. It is different than 'atheist' because the movement is not focused on disproving a Christian or Muslim deity, as 'atheist' implies, but on turning to science and reason for public decision-making, as well as justice-grounded social theory. For more information about the Freethinking movement, see Annie Gaylor's work.
Gaylor, Annie Laurie. *Women Without Superstition: 'No Gods, No Masters'*. (Madison, Wisconsin: Freedom from Religion Foundation, 1997)
[i] Merely as an aside, I want to iterate that while feminist actions or feminist movements may have end goals, such as repealing a particular law, gaining particular human rights like voting, or getting public funding for necessary services, 'feminism' as a theoretical discourse does not have 'end goals'. Theory is fluid, and feminist theory is dependent on context. Feminism shifts as the notion of 'feminine' shifts. The goal posts are always moving with the discourse.

to and was managed by women.¹⁷³ The Spartan political system was split between the assembly of soldiers, presided over by men aged sixty or more (the *gerousia*), and the two royal houses, where daughters and queens were vocal representatives. In the 2006 Hollywood film *300* chronicling Spartan heroism in the battle of Thermopylae, Queen Gorgo addresses the *gerousia*, and she is chastised for entering a male space. The script reads: "my little whore queen… Remove her from this chamber before she infects us further with her inglorious and shabby self".¹⁷⁴ In a previous scene, she was raped by the man who chastises her in the council chamber. ("This will not be over quickly; you will not enjoy this…") The pop-culture glorification of rape culture combined with the erasure of women as state figures in ancient Sparta in the 'retelling' of *300* patterns contemporary misogyny anachronistically onto an ancient context. Proleptically disempowering Spartan women justifies a contemporary environment in which women are disenfranchised from state leadership. Pollitt's argument is to tell the stories of feminism and atheism in history. These stories form the basis of a new mythology to inspire the present. Andrew Robinson writes that "they must return to the level of constituent power or the creative social imaginary to generate the new set of myths, and to pit these myths against the fixity, the apparent obviousness and eternity, of the existing social order."¹⁷⁵ Changing the mythology changes reality. Although the angry priest told me to use whatever inclusive language I wished to use, when I invoked the Goddess he must have felt at some level that 'religion' is not some ubiquitous, universal category making reference to an eternal, unchanging deity; the god-image is the god.

What Pollitt and others' work recognizes is that the mythology of a supreme universal male God is analogous to a social conditioning of male supremacy. Carol Christ argues that "[r]eligions centred on the worship of a male God create 'moods' and 'motivations' that keep women in a state of psychological dependence on men and male authority, while at the same time legitimating the *political* and *social* authority of fathers and sons in the institutions of society".¹⁷⁶ Mary Daly argues in *Beyond God the Father* that the term 'mankind' is neither a mistake nor a universal; books and articles which use 'mankind' are referring only to men and must be read as such to be understood.[j][177]

Naomi Goldenberg takes this critique one step further, arguing that not only does God the Father reify male dominance, but that "the category of religion is always a support for male hegemony".¹⁷⁸ According to Janet Jakobsen and Ann Pellegrini, discourses on religion take place in constant reference to a hegemonic Cultural

---

[j] See Mary Daly's *Beyond God the Father* for a more detailed explanation of the unreadability of the 'sisterhood of man'.
Daly, Mary. *Beyond God the Father: Toward a Philosophy of Women's Liberation.* (Boston: Beacon Press, 1973)

Christianity, namely Christian notions of governance, sexuality and gender duality policing, patriarchy, personal exclusive relationship to a modern Christian God-image, and particularly Christian notions of secularism.[179] The category of religion, perpetually privileging a Christian framework, inherits and re-inscribes the patriarchal social arrangements advocated by Christian traditions. Pollitt argues that "religious texts are the rulebooks of misogyny", and Brent Nongbri explains how the category of religion itself protects (and even invents) these texts.[k][180] The World Religions Paradigm, reducing complex cultural formations to a Christian definition, promotes the most conservative interpretations of these groups as the 'true' or 'authentic' versions. The further a group moves away from the Christian norm, the less they are validated by the state definition of religion.[l] Groups with female deities or no deities at all, non-Christian family social arrangements, or non-preoccupation with death are tenuously marginalized to the fringes of the category as 'spirituality' or 'alternative movements'.

Muslim and ex-Muslim feminist public intellectuals like Maryam Namazie or Ayaan Hirsi Ali who challenge misogyny in Islam are ignored or attacked as 'not really Muslim' by male 'religious' leaders, men preserving male power in the state, and even some intersectional feminists who hesitate to support critiques of Islam for fear that they might be racist. Muslim feminists are at times left with little support from some other feminist communities, whose critiques stop at the ideological wall built around the category of religion. This can sometimes be a problem within liberal communities generally; Muslim activist Maajid Nawaz calls this "Islamsplaining"[m].

---

[k] In *Before Religion,* Nongbri gives the example of the first written mention of "the religion of India" by Henry Lord, an agent of the East India Trading Company and chaplain, who in 1630 wrote about "a booke of theirs called the SHASTER, which is to them as their Bible, containing the grounds of their Religion in written word" (Lord 110-111 in Nongbri 2012: 208). Nongbri writes that "'Shaster' in all likelihood refers to the Sanskrit term śāstra, which is a general term for a rulebook rather than the name of a specific text" (2012: 208). This is an example of the way that the category of religion invents examples of 'religion' around a Christian framework, including the textual literalism produced by the Protestant Reformation.
Nongbri, Brent. *Before Religion: A History of a Modern Concept.* (New Haven: Yale, 2012)

[l] The Canadian government's definition of religion is built on a case-by-case basis via precedent. For example, federal Crown attorneys Nicholas Devlin and Donna Polga denied the claims of the Church of the Universe case on the basis that the movement "offers no insight or answers into the existential questions (of) 'ultimate concern' which are the chief domain of religion; offers no comprehensive system of belief by which to live and offers no moral or ethical code".
Saint-Cyr, Yosie. "Defining Religion Under the Charter—Church of the Universe Case." *Slaw: Canada's Online Legal Magazine.* (April 15 2010. Accessed February 15 2016. Retrieve at http://www.slaw.ca/2010/04/15/defining-religion-under-the-charter%E2%80%95church-of-the-universe-case/)

[m] "Islamsplaining" remixes the feminist term 'mansplaining', which refers to when a man will patronizingly explain something to a woman that she has well qualified knowledge of.

Through the counter-extremism organisation Quilliam that I founded, I have spent eight years defending my Muslim communities in Europe, Pakistan and beyond from the diktats of Islamist theocrats. I have also argued for the liberal reform of Islam today, from within. But, in a naively dangerous form of neo-Orientalism, the SPLC [Southern Poverty Law Center] just arrogated to itself the decision over which debates we Muslims may have about reforming our own religion, and which are to be deemed beyond the pale. Let us call it "Islamsplaining." In a monumental failure of comprehension, the SPLC have conflated my challenge to Islamist theocracy among my fellow Muslims with somehow being "anti-Muslim." The regressive left is now in the business of issuing fatwas against Muslim reformers.
(Nawaz 2016)

In public discourse, the category of religion is reserved for what is conservative and regressive, so attempts by Nawaz and others toward reform are fiercely criticized for resembling the 'occidental secular' category. Nawaz explains that the SPLC's characterization of him as "anti-Muslim" is in the best interests of theocrats, "who argue that any internal criticism is but heresy", as well as the best interests of xenophobes, who argue that "every Muslim is a jihadist in waiting".[181] The SPLC seeks to reduce Islamophobia, but by defining Islam in particularly conservative ways, they are reinforcing the construction of a 'straw Muslim' who is regressive and conservative. Scholars of Religious Studies who struggle to pin down a universal, timeless definition of a thing called 'religion', without recognizing the contingency of the term, are condemning all groups to be stuck within the narrow limitations of the category.

Muslim feminists like Riffat Hassan (1979), Fazlur Rahman (1984, 2002), Amina Wadud (1992), Sa'diyya Shaikh (1997), Asma Barlas (2002), Azizah Al-Hibri (2003), and Aysha Hidayatullah (2014) are reclaiming Islam by subverting the patriarchal domination of *tafsir*—exegetical interpretation of Islamic texts—as well as taking aim at the Christianization and patriarchalization of Islam. Hidayatullah's book *Feminist Edges of the Qur'an* examines the "use of dynamic epistemological tools to challenge the abuse of male power in the interpretation of the Qur'an".[182] The notion of 'God the Father' is contrary to the many citations within Muslim texts and traditions expressing the female aspects of Allah.[n] Hassan investigates the Garden of Eden story in the Qur'an, noting that although it does not include verses about women being made from men's ribs like the Christian version, some Muslims have been conditioned to believe that it does.[183] Hidayatullah places particular emphasis on contextualizing the suras, noting

---
[n] Al Lat

that "reading the Qur'an historically does not limit its meaning to the context of revelation; rather, reading the Qur'an historically allows the Qur'an to be read in light of changing historical circumstances, thus making it relevant and applicable universally. In other words, to read the Qur'an in historical context is to uphold the Qur'an's universality".[184] She also uses the verses about idolatry to discuss equality, arguing that "sexism is a form of idolatry since it attributes a God-like role for men over women.[185] Hassan, Wadud, and Al-Hibri draw inspiration from the figure of Hajar (Hagar in the Christian tradition) as a foremother of Islam and feminist theology icon. Wadud explores the trials of Hajar as a single mother abandoned by Abraham, making her own way and founding a nation. The field of feminist Quranic tafsir defies Orientalist characterizations of Islam by offering a uniquely Muslim methodology for renewing the movement to fit non-Arab contexts.

FEMINIST THEOLOGY

Rita Gross' *Feminism and Religion* argues that "when contemporary academic scholars study the history of a religious tradition, they usually focus on what the tradition itself has emphasized—the records of its male heroes".[186] The recourse to patriarchal ways of approaching traditions leaves dismal options for women, and necessitates both critique of these modes of knowledge production and the excavation of women's stories from the accounts.

In his book *God as Woman, Woman as God*, J. Edgar Bruns excavates a usable past for women by chronicling the story of Pope Joan, a woman who allegedly ascended to the papacy. He wrote that a young woman from England fell in love with a wandering scholar, who took her to Rome disguised as a man named 'John'. John was exceedingly intelligent and attracted a great deal of attention, including a following of brilliant disciples. S/he became Pope from 855-858, but was discovered when she gave birth. Bruns records that the story was widely known "from the thirteenth century to the time of the Reformation. No one seems to have thought it an unlikely story, and at least three popes could not have found it embarrassing since they made no effort to remove the portrait of Pope John (Joanna) which had been placed in the Cathedral of Siena, where each of them had sat as archbishop before assuming the papal tiara".[187] He writes that Olivetanus (Marius Equicola d'Alveto) argued in the early sixteenth century that the election of Pope Joan was proof that God "wished to make clear that women are not inferior to men".[188] The example of Pope Joan demonstrates the importance of the recovery of usable history; although the contemporary Catholic Church argues that Pope Joan was never real, her story inspired Olivetanus to argue for the personhood of women in the 1500s.

Elizabeth Schüssler Fiorenza's text *In Memory of Her* demonstrates the importance of feminist exegesis. She writes:

> In Mark's passion narrative, there are three major characters, two well-known men, Judas and Peter, and the nameless, who anoints Jesus. Of her, Jesus says: "And truly I say to you, wherever the Gospel is preached in the whole world, what she has done will be retold in memory of her" (Mark 14:9).
>
> The inconsistencies in our New Testament sources indicate that the early Christian traditioning and redactional processes followed certain androcentric interests and perspectives. Therefore the androcentric selection and transmission of early Christian traditions have manufactured the historical marginality of women, but they are not a reflection of the historical reality of women's participation in the early Christian movement. (Schüssler Fiorenza 1995: 52)

This passage of *In Memory of Her* examines the discrepancy between the content of the Biblical quote within the text, Christ commanding that she be remembered, and the erasure of the woman's name in the transmission of the quote. Schüssler Fiorenza argues that assumptions about the patriarchal organization of early Christian movements are inaccurate and require deeper investigation.

Schüssler Fiorenza draws attention to the nameless women erased from the textual record. Other exegetes make contributions to feminist work through the resurrection of stories of women from Biblical texts, like Karen King's (2003) important translations of Gnostic texts and research on the historical role of Mary Magdalene in her book *The Gospel of Mary of Magdala: Jesus and the First Woman Apostle*. This book and its implications have profoundly affected studies of Early Christianity. King's work is a reminder that advances in theological scholarship for the voices of women are recent, with much potential for elaboration.

No discussion of feminist theology would be complete without exploring Mary Daly. Daly began her feminist exegetical work by writing a careful and well-evidenced critique of the church in 1968, *The Church and the Second Sex*. By 1973, she decided that the only way for the church to change was for women to leave it in a mass exodus. In *Beyond God the Father,* Daly (1973) used more poetic and mythical language to discuss and develop the ideas laid out in *The Church and the Second Sex*. The chapter "Exorcising Evil from Eve: The Fall into Freedom" critiqued the notion of Eve the sinner and women as sinners. Other themes explored in *Beyond God the Father* include the concept of Christolatry, phallic morality, and the Death of God the Father, as well as the development of 'Sisterhood' as an escape from patriarchal religion. Daly described Sisterhood as a "Cosmic Covenant" that is enacted when women declare themselves witches.[189]

In 1972 Rosemary Ruether named the shift away from doctrinal Christianity in women's spirituality the "awakening of a critical consciousness" in her book *Liberation Theology: Human Hope Confronts Christian History and American Power*.[190] Ruether developed the theory of woman-church, paralleling the Christian notion of the Church as the bride of Christ. Daly and Ruether's 1970s writings were representative of the growing collective agitation of women unrepresented in the icons and ideologies of their church traditions. Rita Gross drew attention to the continued lack of representation of women in institutional worship settings, particularly in Buddhism, her area of focus. She notes:

> The female life cycle, including menarche, menstruation, menopause, and even childbirth, is completely uncelebrated and unmarked in most traditional liturgies. Divorce, abortion, lesbian sexual orientation, the trauma of sexual violence—these common experiences of women do not even exist in the vocabulary of most conventional liturgy.
> (Gross 1996: 205)

What many women felt they were missing in churches they found or built in the Goddess movement. Lithuanian archaeologist and philologist Marija Gimbutas's (1989) work was central to the Goddess movement. Based on her archaeological findings, she developed the Kurgan Thesis, or the theory that Old European societies were goddess-worshipping, peaceful societies which were structured around economic equality, and that these cultures were invaded by Indo-European andocrats in the Bronze Age. Gimbutas photographed and documented over 12 000 female figurines. Proponents of the Goddess movement are motivated by the idea of a 'usable history' for women to cite a mythological narrative of equality that pre-dates the Christian patriarchy narrative. Elinor Gadon writes "[I]n reclaiming the Goddess, in recovering our full human history as men and women, we can learn other patterns of behavior. We can redress the imbalance between the human species and our natural environment, between men and women, exploring the possibility of living in harmony and justice with all things".[191]

Now, as much as ever, the field of Religious Studies benefits from the research being carried out in feminist theology. As Leslie McCall argues, feminist theory is uniquely positioned to both acknowledge difference and to transgress the limitations of hegemonies.º

Mary Daly wrote that the stories of women have historically been treated as "nondata".[192] Through exegesis and tafsir, these stories are heard and understood, making space for mythologies of liberation.

WHY WOMEN NEED THE GODDESS

> A woman who echoes Ntosake Shange's dramatic statement, "I found God in myself and I loved her fiercely," is saying "Female power is strong and creative." She is saying that the divine principle, the saving and sustaining power, is in herself, that she will no longer look to men or male figures as saviors. The strength and independence of female power can be intuited by contemplating ancient and modern images of the Goddess.
> —Carol P. Christ, "Why Women Need the Goddess"
> (Christ 1979: 367)

"Why Women Need the Goddess: Phenomenological, Psychological, and Political Reflections" is a chapter by Carol Christ in *Womanspirit Rising: A Feminist Reader in Religion*. Christ addresses the question: "does the emergence of the symbol of Goddess among women have significant political and psychological ramifications

---

º "[F]eminist researchers [are] acutely aware of the limitations of gender as a single analytical category. In fact, feminists are perhaps alone in the academy in the extent to which they have embraced intersectionality—the relationships among multiple dimensions and modalities of social relations and subject formations—as itself a central category of analysis."
McCall, Leslie. "The Complexity of Intersectionality." *Signs: Journal of Women in Culture and Society*. (vol. 30, no. 3. Chicago: The University of Chicago, 2005) p. 308.

for the feminist movement?".[193] In *The Church and the Second Sex,* Mary Daly uses Simone de Beauvoir's theory from *The Second Sex* that "one is not born, but, rather, becomes a woman" to explore the role of the Catholic Church in 'making' women.[194] Daly was influenced by the growing Goddess movement, and criticized the Catholic Church for its focus on death. She compared the Tree of Life in the Goddess movement to "the Christian cross, the dead wood rack to which a dying body is fastened with nails".[195] Despite her excoriating critiques of the church, Daly considered herself a Catholic feminist theologian, leading the revolution from within the church. It seems that the Goddess was not a theological object to Daly, but an analytical tool of symbolic significance. The question of whether or not group members 'believe in' the Goddess or 'merely' appreciate her as a cultural symbol is frequently asked and considered within the groups I worked with in this ethnographic research. In "Why Women Need the Goddess", Christ discusses whether the Goddess is "out there", or is a symbol which represents female power.[196] Following Pollitt's argument and Barthes' theory, this distinction—between "out there" and symbolic—is unnecessary because both the literal divine and the Goddess as discourse of power are co-constitutive.[p] Christ remarks that discourse "transforms mythos into ethos, symbol system into social and political reality. Symbols have both psychological and political effects, because they create the inner conditions (deep-seated attitudes and feelings) that lead people to feel comfortable with or to accept social and political arrangements that correspond to the symbol system".[197] She argues that "women's unique position as menstruants, birthgivers, and those who have traditionally cared for the young and the dying" would add a dimension to the social and political world ignored by worshippers of God the Father.[198]

I challenge you to imagine not only what God the Mother looks like, but what a society worshipping God the Mother would look like.

"Feminist priestess" Starhawk invoked the Goddess as a feminist statement, practicing "**feminist witchcraft**".[199] She broke down the religion/secular binary by refusing to acknowledge the ideological separation between the Goddess as 'religion' and the Goddess as a political symbol. In "The Three Faces of Goddess Spirituality", Merlin Stone explains the movement from the perspective of the group *The Great Goddess Collective*. She writes:

---

[p] The distinction—between "out there" Goddess and symbolic Goddess—is unnecessary because both the literal divine and the Goddess as discourse of power are co-constitutive, like male authority in the Church as well as in the state.

The first aspect of Goddess spirituality is the emerging interest in the history and prehistory of ancient cultures that worshipped a female deity and in the laws and customs of those societies. Through research in archaeology, history, anthropology—and using this information to analyze ancient literature and mythology—we have begun to discover that far from the generally accepted idea that the Judeo-Christian religions rescued women from supposedly more barbarian and anti-woman societies, women have actually lost a great deal of status and physical and material autonomy since the inception of these and other male-worshipping religions. […] The second aspect is that of a growing concern with a feminist perception of spirituality and theology. […] The third aspect of Goddess spirituality is concerned with the more circumspect observation of the organized male-worshipping, male-clergied religions of today—an examination of the specific ways in which these religions have instituted and maintained a secondary status for women.
(Stone 1978: 1-2)

Whether intentional or not, invoking the Motherhood of God is a political statement.

In a paper[q] delivered at a conference in Bethlehem, Pennsylvania, Naomi Goldenberg said "I would like to see a Goddess Movement that is not a religion".[200] This is how I see Femen—as a collective of women who believe in their power and who are not vestigial. Feminist theology and the Goddess Movement of the 1960s and 1970s manoeuvred at the edges of the religion/secular binary. The contemporary Goddess Movement and feminist theology, as evidenced through groups like Femen, Pussy Riot[r], and the Native Faith movement, are moving into a space beyond the binary, and beyond both secular and religious systems built around patriarchal social arrangements.

---

[q] The paper was called "What is this Slouching Toward Bethlehem?: Is it a New Feminist Defense of Religion?" Goldenberg, Naomi. "What is this Slouching Toward Bethlehem?: Is it a New Feminist Defense of Religion?" Presented at *Feminisms Beyond the Secular: Epistemologies and Politics for the 21st Century*. (Lehigh University, Bethlehem Pennsylvania. March 22 2016)

[r] Pussy Riot is a feminist Russian punk band started in 2011. Performers wear colourful balaclavas on their heads and protest the collusion of the church and state, supported by an anarchist collective that helps with the logistics of the performances. They only perform in illegal locations. Their 2012 'flashmob' performance of the song "Punk Prayer: Mother of God, Drive Putin Away" at Cathedral of Christ the Saviour in Moscow resulted in two members being sentenced to several years in a Russian penal colony. "We were deeply saddened that you allowed the Church to become a weapon in a dirty election campaign," they wrote on their blog, referring to Patriarch Kirill's public endorsement of Vladimir Putin's electoral campaign.
Russia. "Pussy Riot Hit Back at Church Criticism." *Sputnik News*. (March 27 2012. Accessed March 30 2012. Retrieve at https://sputniknews.com/russia/20120327172417090/)

Imagine the ancient Ukrainian goddess Mokosh rising up from the fields, shaking off the dirt and slapping the cold of a long hibernation out of her hands, her feet firmly rooted in the earth. Unafraid and unashamed, she wears nothing but a crown of flowers in her hair. She grows larger and stronger to non-violently oppose the destruction of the earth. In the contemporary moment, she looks like Femen. The protest group's larger-than-life, outrageous, and fearless demonstrations are an ode to a contemporary embodiment of the goddess, free of distinctions of secular or religious.

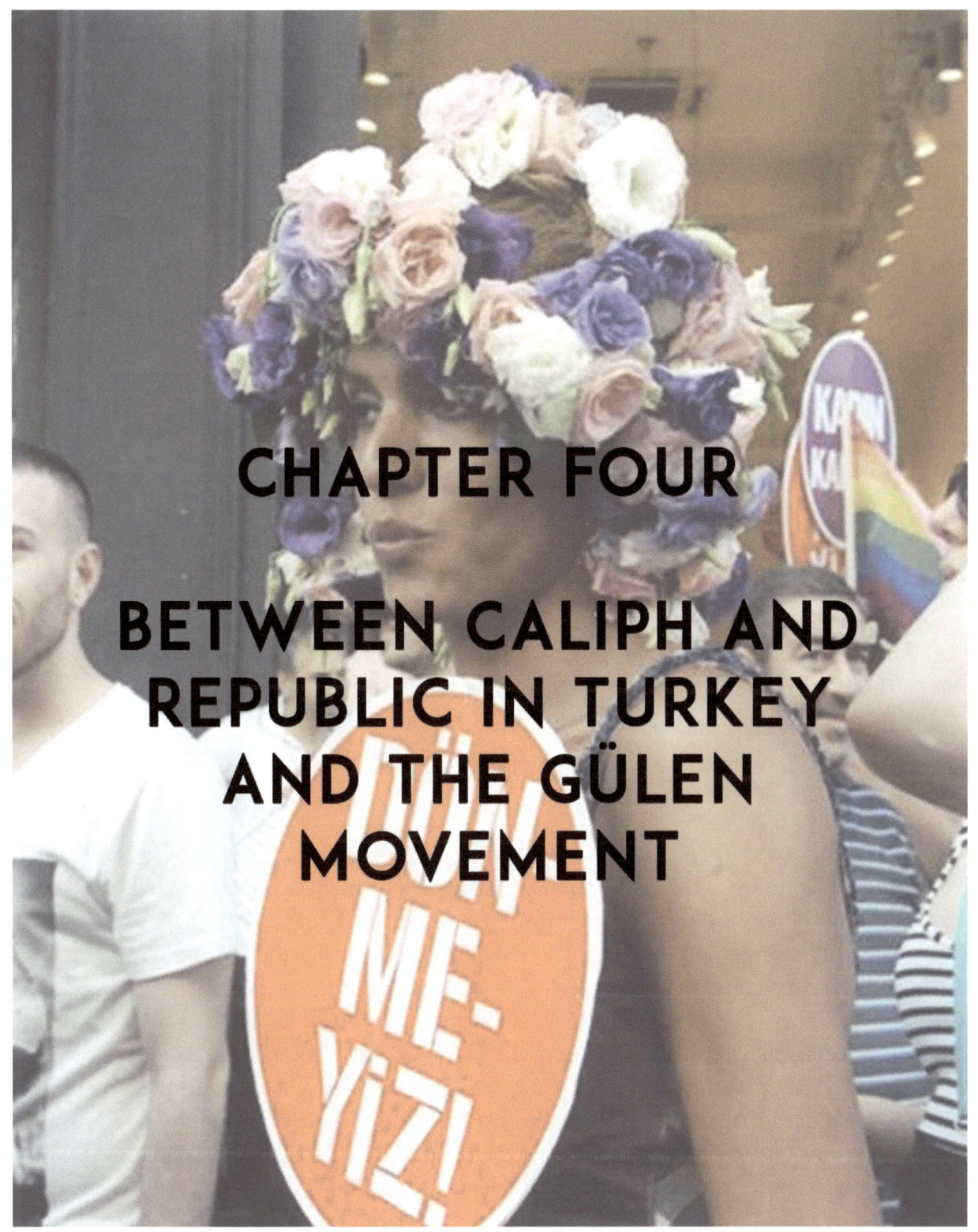

CHAPTER FOUR

BETWEEN CALIPH AND REPUBLIC IN TURKEY AND THE GÜLEN MOVEMENT

CHAPTER FOUR

BETWEEN CALIPH AND REPUBLIC IN TURKEY AND THE GÜLEN MOVEMENT

GEZI PARK

> Don't it always seem to go? You don't know what you got til it's gone; they paved paradise, and put up a parking lot.
> —Joni Mitchell
> (*Big Yellow Taxi*, 1970)

In the early morning hours of May 27, 2013, a group of approximately fifty Turkish environmentalists headed to Gezi Park, one of the last large green spaces in the crowded city of Istanbul. The government had decided to raze the park adjacent to fashionable Taksim Square and build "luxury residences and a shopping mall".[201] The intrepid protesters marched nervously to the park, and sat down in front of the bulldozers. Except for the shouting of a few frustrated workers who just wanted to get on with the demolition, the sit-in was quiet and peaceful. The protesters did not leave. On May 30, 2013, police entered the park with tear gas and water cannons, and applied forceful measures to oust the demonstrators, resulting in several injuries. The use of severe measures against the peaceful protesters sparked outrage in Turkey. Thousands of people joined the protest, building an encampment in Gezi Park, and thousands of protesters were fed each day with donations solicited via the social network Twitter.

Some statistics suggest that up to 3.5 million Turks participated in protests and general strikes, not only in Gezi Park, but in major cities across the country in May and June of 2013.[202] In particular, a photograph of a woman in a red dress being blasted with tear gas at close range by an officer became a symbol for the movement. 'The Woman in Red' was shared by millions on social media, and her image was used in posters, on stickers and in advertisements for the movement. Erdoğan called the protesters 'radical terrorists'; the woman, later identified as Turkish academic Ceyda Sungur, appears to be just an average citizen walking through the park in her simple red dress, a white bag over her shoulder. The contrasting iconography of Sungur against the police office in riot gear spraying her from a metre away is striking. Her silhouette inspired hundreds of artistic derivatives.

The original Lady in Red photo.

Top: Stencil by Ari Alpert of the Lady in Red. (Alpert, *Lady in Red,* 2013)

Bottom: Anonymous Lady in Red stencil.

Top: Occupied Gezi Park in Istanbul, Turkey.

Bottom: Ballet show at Gezi Park protest in Taksim Square. From *Twitter* user EsraFurtana.

Top: *Work by Day, Protest by Night*, by Tumblr user ilariagenovesio.

Bottom: This woman's eyes were burned by tear gas. By Emine Gozde Sevim, from the series *Homeland Delirium*, 2013, on Ilariagenovesio.

Pelin Turgut interviewed a protester at the park, Ali Riza Gurs:
"It's grown like an avalanche," Gurs said, beaming. "I haven't really slept. I haven't gone to work. This sense of solidarity is a super feeling." He is one of thousands who have turned what began as an environmental protest into an experiment in social change.
(Turgut 2013)

The threat to destroy Gezi Park was only the beginning; Turkish people came out into the streets to protest police brutality and Turkish Prime Minister Recep Tayyip Erdoğan's increasingly authoritarian and increasingly Islamist regime. Like the protests following the Chernobyl disaster in Ukraine in the 1980s, environmental degradation was the conduit through which many more politically volatile frustrations were expressed. Liberal and moderate citizens were getting nervous about Erdoğan's turn to right-wing extremism after Turkey's historic struggles toward secularism. What made this protest different than the well-organized anti- Erdoğan protests by upper-class secularists during the election was that it managed to involve the middle class. Turgut describes the atmosphere in the neighbourhood adjacent to Gezi Park:

My apartment in central Istanbul is now part of the 'Occupied Zone'. No cars rumble by, just a sea of very cheery people, witty hand-drawn posters, graffiti, tents and makeshift barricades. My friends have become expert demonstrators. They carry goggles and masks in their bags and mix bottles of detergent water against the sting of tear gas. My sister takes her toddler to sit in the park. At 9pm, everyone in the neighborhood comes outside and bangs loudly on saucepans in protest. The middle class has turned militant and their mood is catching.
(Turgut 2013)

The modern state of Turkey, bordering the south of the Black Sea with Ukraine bordering the north, has a long and interesting historical relationship to Islam, a community that was founded in the Arabian Peninsula in the seventh century. Muḥammad ibn ʿAbdullāh ibn Abdul-Muttalib ibn Hashim, colloquially referred to as Prophet Mohammed, united Arabia into one large polity, creating an urban legal framework and colonizing diverse indigenous regional systems. He enlisted the support of younger sons of prosperous merchants, and men who had failed to earn higher status within their tribes.²⁰³ When he died without a male heir, his friend and associate Abu Bakr was elected as the first Caliph, or leader of the community. The position then became monarchical, and the Umayyads, and then the Abbasids ruled. In 1517, Selim I, then Sultan of the Ottoman Empire, conquered the Egyptian Sultanate, annexing the entire caliphate, including the special cities of Mecca and Medina in the Arabian Peninsula. He forced the Abbasids to surrender the title of Caliph, along with the symbolic Mantle of Muhammed and his sword.²⁰⁴ These items have been kept ever since in Topkapi Palace in Istanbul. According to Paul Pitman, the Sultan of the Ottoman Empire was called *padishah* ('highest king') by the Persians, the 'Emperor' by the Christians after the capture of Constantinople, and "[a]mong the Turks he was, as his nomadic warrior forebears had been, the khan, a master of the tribal ruling class".²⁰⁵ After Selim I, the Sultan was also called Caliph by the Arabs, signifying that he was the "chief executor" of Islamic sharia law and master of the Ummah, or the Muslim diaspora.²⁰⁶ Pitman writes that within the cosmopolitan Ottoman Empire "[a]ll offices were filled by his authority, and all legislation was issued by him in the form of a *firman* (decree). He was supreme military commander, and he had basic title to all land".²⁰⁷ The Ottoman system structurally informed later ways of thinking about the role of the caliph.

The region enjoyed several generations of prosperity and expansion, and although the elite class was comprised mostly of wealthy, educated Muslims, the empire supported pluralism. At one time, Christians comprised up to 80% of the population of the Ottoman imperial territory.²⁰⁸ As the empire began to decline, Christian countries to the west began poaching territories of the Ottoman Empire occupied by Christians. At the turn of the twentieth century, nationalist movements, mentioned earlier in relation to Eastern Europe, agitated within imperial borders all over Europe and Asia, and countries like Bulgaria emerged from the Ottoman Empire as independent states with a distinct culture and language. Ottoman Sultan Abdülhamid II consolidated the remaining Muslim-majority territory in 1900—he could be called the first Islamist, in the sense of galvanizing a protectionist ideology of Muslim nationalism and expelling non-Muslims from the empire.²⁰⁹ Under the direction of Sultan Abdülhamid II, the Ottoman caliphate committed a mass genocide of the Armenian population within Ottoman borders, as well as the ethnic cleansing of Assyrians and Pontic Greeks. This earned him the title of "Bloody Sultan", and was the beginning of the end of the empire. In July 1908, the Young Turk Revolution broke out, where a group of young educated ethnic Turks frustrated by censorship and repression revolted against the conservative, old-fashioned caliphate institution, which "stood for ignorance, backwardness, corruption and decline".[210] Abdülhamid II capitulated immediately to their liberal reforms, including the restoration of the suspended constitution and lifting restrictions from education. During World War I, Abdülhamid II joined the Central Powers, the alliance of Germany, Austria-Hungary, and Bulgaria. The Central Powers were ultimately defeated by the Triple Entente, and the Ottoman Empire dissolved into several new states.

Mustafa Kemal, an Ottoman military commander who had been fighting the Russians on the Eastern front when the Russian Revolution broke out, had travelled to the German front and realized that the Central Powers would lose the war.[211] He resigned his position in the Ottoman army and made plans to create a state of ethnic Turks which he would arm and defend while the Entente forces conquered other Ottoman territories, like Syria, Israel, Iraq, Jordan, Egypt, Saudi Arabia, Kuwait and others. Kemal founded the Turkish National Movement, and led and won the War of Independence. Mustafa Kemal was given the honorary name Atatürk, meaning "Father of the Turks".[212] He founded the modern state of Turkey.

This state was no caliphate. Atatürk was committed to building a modern secular democracy free of dogma; he felt that dogma had led to the decline and fall of the Ottoman Empire. He moved to ideologically separate the caliphate from the Sultanate. The caliphate was the judiciary foundation of the Islamic state, and Atatürk did not believe it was an adequate system of governance for the modern state, which required a mechanism of legislative reform to adapt to a rapidly changing world. By separating the Sultanate and caliphate, he was able to overthrow the monarchical political system and its powerful royalty without interfering with the lower-order Muslim administrators who provided social services to the public. He institutionalized the roles of clerics and imams as public servants, and abolished the royal family. Islamic courts were replaced by a legal system based on the Swiss legal code. Atatürk built thousands of new schools, and had a new alphabet created with Latin-derived letters for the Turkish language. Al Rasheed, Kersten, and Shterin emphasize that the new written Turkish language to be taught in the new public education system would provide a mechanism of Turkification of the new citizenry, so that being Muslim was not the primary identity factor tying them together.[213] Primary education was made compulsory for girls and boys, and all women were granted equal civic rights to men.[214] All clerics had to pray and perform the call to prayer in the Turkish language—Atatürk remains the only leader in the world to have instituted this change. He was concerned that Islamism would subsume the Turkish identity within a universalizing ideology. If he rid the state of Islamist politics then he could build a state for the Turkish people, who he saw as culturally unique and pre-Islamic. Moreover, he wanted to secure Turkey a position in the emerging world order of post-war nation states.

Atatürk was charismatic and won widespread support from the Turks, both civilian and military. He was embraced as a powerful conqueror and was offered the position of Caliph, in the same way that Selim I had taken it in the sixteenth century. He refused the title. Atatürk was staunchly opposed to dynastic rule, believing that monarchical systems were corrupt; he intentionally produced no biological offspring, instead adopting many daughters as well as a son and providing them with excellent education. Atatürk was a scientist and felt that 'sacred texts' had served their purpose and were now eclipsed by more relevant contemporary philosophies, and he was a socialist who supported building a strong middle class by shifting the burden of taxation off peasants and distributing it more democratically.[215]

The caliphate continued and Abdülmecid II was elected in 1922. Atatürk immediately became concerned that there would be conflict between the new republican government and the caliphate system when Abdülmecid II attended public ceremonies and engaged in international relations as though he were a head of state. Not only that, but opposition forces were plotting to use the Caliph's authority to overthrow Atatürk.[216]

In 1924 Atatürk abolished the caliphate in Turkey as well, and transferred the personal military and personal treasury of the Caliph's office to the state. The caliphate was made vestigial, and became a private organization separate from the modern state. In May 1926, A Caliphate Conference was hosted in Cairo to discuss the future of pan-Islamism. A resolution was passed that the caliphate was necessary to the future of Muslims, and several candidates came forward from Egypt and Tunis, but no leader or family was selected to take the title.[217]

Further conferences were held in Mecca and Jerusalem, but again no decisions were made.

Although Atatürk nominally founded a democracy, he ruled autocratically as the head of a one-party system until his death in 1938. Atatürk never endorsed Communism, but his one-party government, with widespread socialist and liberal reforms, and state management of religious institutions, in many ways mirrored Vladimir Lenin's government in Imperial Russia taking power at exactly the same time. After Lenin died suddenly and Stalin took over the Soviet Union, he jealously guarded the vast imperial borders, divesting a crippling amount of funds and resources into preventing member states from seceding. Atatürk, on the other hand, could see that the Ottoman Empire was over. Al-Rasheed, Kersten, and Shterin write:

> The realities of the post-First World War world, where the Turkish heartland was surrounded by the Soviet Union, traditionally hostile Balkan states, and British and French colonial forces in Iraq and Syria, made the pursuit of pan-Islamic and pan-Turkic policies virtually impossible. What remained were Turkish nationalism and the safeguarding of new borders.
> (Al-Rasheed, Kersten, and Shterin 2012: 46)

The Ottoman Empire throughout the 1800's was indebted to financiers in England and France, slowly bleeding its economy to death.[s] Atatürk's policy of secularism and his clear stance against pan-Islamist foreign policy was a survival tactic. He mapped the boundaries of the Republic of Turkey around borders he could defend, and territory the republic could afford to sustain without colonial patronage, paving the way for a century of security and economic stability. If Stalin had abandoned the imperial borders, like Atatürk, and focused on the Russian federation rather than the empire, modern history may have turned out significantly differently.

The Republic of Turkey flourished modestly, opposing and warding off colonial intervention in Turkey, unlike Sudan, Tunisia, Algeria, Morocco, Libya, and Saudi Arabia and the other Arabian states, who were plagued by colonial forces more intensely after the discovery of massive oil reserves in the area during the Second World War.

---

[s] "The establishment, in 1863, by British and French capital of the Imperial Ottoman Bank, which would act as a quasi-central bank for the Empire in addition to its commercial operations, further consolidated the position of European capital in the Ottoman financial markets."
Pamuk, Şevket. *A Monetary History of the Ottoman Empire*. (Cambridge: Cambridge University Press, 2000) 204.

In 1950, the United States Sixth Fleet was designated to be stationed in the area to protect imperial interests. In 1969, the fleet was slated to drop anchor just offshore of Istanbul in the Bosporus Sea. Over thirty thousand left-wing activists, consisting mainly of students, marched on Taksim Square, adjacent to Gezi Park, to peacefully protest the 'friendly' American ships in Turkish waters, which they perceived as colonial trespassers. A police faction and a massive mob of conservative Islamists armed with clubs, Molotov cocktails and other improvised weapons attacked the demonstrators. Several of the leftists were killed and many were injured. Called Bloody Sunday, this was the beginning of right-wing violence in Turkey; it was the prelude to attacks in 1971, the 1977 Taksim Square Massacre, and the context underlying the contemporary Gezi Park protests.

1983 marked a conservative turn in Turkey. Turgut Özal was elected, leading the right-wing Motherland Party, combining Islamist revivalists and fiscal conservatives. According to Nas Tevfik, Özal had worked for the World Bank in the United States and promptly initiated widespread privatization in Turkey, which temporarily supercharged the Turkish economy with foreign interest but led to economic crashes in 1994, 1999, and 2001.[218] Andrew Mango writes that a "nineteenth-century Ottoman reformer wrote that Istanbul might well become orderly and prosperous like Paris or London, but 'we would not be the ones who would profit from or taste these delights... Rather, we would turn up from time to time as sellers of firewood and charcoal and gaze at it sadly'".[219] It appears that the colonial financiers that Atatürk had worked to safeguard the Republic of Turkey against had finally found a way in.

In 2001 conservative parties in Turkey amalgamated to form the Justice and Development Party, also called AKP, led by Recep Tayyip Erdoğan, a man who had recently been sentenced to 10 months in prison for inciting religious hatred. The party, known for being socially conservative, capitalist and Islamist, has steadily gained power since 2001. With the help of Fethullah Gülen, a powerful Muslim cleric, he was able to increase the executive powers of the presidency, "slowly but surely travelling the dark path toward a presidential dictatorship".[220] Erdoğan and the AKP are engaged in a politics of pan-Islamist neo-Ottoman ideology. They are steadily increasing their presence in former territories of the Ottoman Empire, like Russian President Vladimir Putin in 2012 before the 2014 annexation of Crimea, and the ongoing annexation of eastern Ukraine.

Two topless women with the words "Ban Erdogan" written on their chests protested fraudulent elections at a polling station in eastern Turkey.

THE GÜLEN MOVEMENT

Like Erdoğan, Fethullah Gülen is critical of Atatürk's suppression of Muslim practice. Gülen is the leader of a Turkish pan-Islamic organization, called the Hizmet Movement. In 2014, I travelled around Turkey with organizers of this movement, learning about their beliefs and organizational structure. They often cited Atatürk's Hat Law as an example of his going too far in separating Islam from the Turkish Republic. In 1925, Atatürk passed a law requiring citizens to wear western-style hats.[221] Women could not wear headscarves to work in the public service; Atatürk said: "let them show their faces to the world, and see it with their eyes... Don't be afraid. Change is essential".[222] Men were banned from wearing the hats of their many cultural traditions, including turbans, the fez, and any other headgear that marked cultural difference in the new republic. Atatürk was not taking aim specifically at Islam, he was trying to build an assimilationist monocultural Turkish identity, where the Republic of Turkey would become a European country and participate in European international conferences. He believed that the only way to protect territorial sovereignty from colonial control was to engage in cultural colonialism. Hizmet is a Wahhabi movement, part of the wave of reactionary 1970s Islamist movements which adopted the practice of hijab wearing for women.[223] However, unlike Erdoğan, Gülen is a socialist and staunchly nonviolent. While Erdoğan's fiscally conservative government has opened formerly public social services to private divestment, private enterprises like the Hizmet Movement have filled in the gaps.

Gülen's Hizmet Movement operates public schools for the poorest children in Turkey, and provides disaster relief in times of environmental crisis. The movement is affiliated with over 300 schools around the world, and these schools cater to predominantly lower class students.[224] The movement also runs orphanages, and manages aid operations in the poorest African contexts through their NGO Kimse Yok Mu, an affiliate of the United Nations Department of Economic and Social Affairs. They provide food and medical care to inmates in Somalian prisons.[225] Although there are many organizations associated with the movement, there is no central administration. 'Hizmet' means service. The Hizmet Movement is one of the world's largest civil society organizations, and it is widely considered a world leader in moderate, liberal Islam. It is no surprise that Erdoğan feels threatened by this powerful and wealthy network. Within the Republic of

Turkey, Gülenists hold a great deal of democratic power.

Gülen is socially conservative in his support for the modesty of women, and he is an advocate of solidifying the Muslim identity of Turkey, but he supports the pluralist republican state. In an interview with the press responding to criticism of his schools, he said: "[i]f, in these schools, you can show me one word that is against democracy, the Republic or Kemalism and its principles, I shall kiss your hands and feet and I'll say 'close these evil nests'".[226]

The 'religious' Gülen was an outspoken supporter of the 'religious' Erdoğan, who ran on a platform of moderation and positive relations with the west from an Islamic perspective. Gülen provided opportunities for Erdoğan to speak at major intercultural dialogue events around the world to build his international reputation. Gülen money funded Erdoğan's campaign, and in exchange Erdoğan and Gülen worked together to imprison the top secularists of the Turkish elite, making way for religious organizations to take over state services.[227]

According to Barış Karaağaç, Fethullah Gülen then became too powerful. Tensions between the two "started to increase two years ago [2012], when the Gülen community tried to take control of the national intelligence agency and they failed".[228] Erdoğan arrested members of the Gülen community.

When Erdoğan ordered the police to so violently suppress the Gezi Park protests, Gülen commented: "Is the shopping center that was to be built there worth a single drop of blood?" signaling the public end of their allegiance.[229] Gülen backed the anti-government Gezi protesters by appealing to left-wing sentiment, stating:

> Everyone must respect diversity. Freedom of speech and expression cannot be restricted. While the views of the majority certainly deserve respect, the views of minority groups should be treated with the same level of respect as well. If you suppress the masses, this will cause friction along social fault lines.

(*Hürriyet Daily News* 2014)

Since the massacre of a generation of left-wing youth in the 1970s, there is a visible lack of a left opposition in Turkish politics today. The 2012 protesters represent the coming-the-age of a new generation of liberal youth. Erdoğan and Gülen represent two brands of conservatives. Gülen is pro-west and supports allying with European and American forces and markets as a Muslim capitalist country, and Erdoğan is leaning toward eastern alliances as a Muslim capitalist country.

December 17, 2013, information was leaked to media about far-reaching corruption in the Erdoğan government. The Gülen community was blamed, and according to Karaağaç, a Canadian specialist on Turkish affairs, was indeed responsible for the leak. Top officials and allies of Erdoğan were charged and imprisoned. The Gülen Movement publically criticized Erdoğan's hard line against Israel. In response, Erdoğan passed a law forcing the closure of the Hizmet Movement's schools. Both the public and politicians reacted against this measure, because it "would exclude the most disadvantaged students from the most sought-after universities and increase the impact of socio-economic differences on entrance exam results".[230] The court reversed the law, finding it unconstitutional. Kar-aağaç describes the relationship between Erdoğan and Gülen as "a struggle, a fight over more political power in the country, a struggle, a fight over who controls a larger part of the Turkish state".[231]

This framing of the relationship between Gülen and the republic is very much focused on the top of the movement's hierarchy. On the ground, the people driving the Hizmet Movement—the thousands of volunteers who care for orphans, who devote their lives to providing poor children with access to better education, the doctors and the nurses who provide necessary life-saving services—see and express their participation in this organization as their 'religion'. In the case of Turkey, the secular/religious binary framework of Religious Studies does not clarify analysis of an organization like the Hizmet Movement, so clearly discursively religious, and so clearly discursively political. On July 25, 2016 I was interviewed by SiriusXM about my work with the Hizmet Movement in Turkey. This work was difficult to describe in terms of my field, Religious Studies, because the terminology associated with a movement that otherwise fits so well within the 'religious' category does not adequately convey the movement's political relationship to the state. Fethullah Gülen is described in the Western media as a 'cleric', but this title does not effectively communicate who he is. The Hizmet Movement is sometimes described as a 'civil society organization'. This term does not adequately encapsulate the bureaucratic level of involvement the group has in the workings of the Turkish government, or the charismatic worship aspect of the group. As longtime supporters of Erdoğan's Justice and Development Party (AKP), the movement followers are not an official political party either. The Gülenists are socially conservative like Erdoğan, but the recent split makes them disenfranchised outliers.

After the split, Erdoğan's paranoia has only increased. He imprisons those who criticize him, like the Hurriyet journalists Can Dundar and Erdem Gül. International tensions rise as he is criticized for violating human rights, but no measures are taken to do anything about it.

July 19, 2016 newspapers around the world announced that a faction of the Turkish military had staged a coup against the Erdoğan government. The president announced the following day that the coup had been carried out by the military, but was orchestrated by Fethullah Gülen. This could easily be true, but equally plausible is the prospect that the traditionally secularist military establishment acted out against Erdoğan's abandonment of democratic processes and disturbing support for ISIS. The possibility also exists that Erdoğan himself staged the coup to gather and arrest his enemies and free his allies from prison. Although only several hundred people were said to be involved in the coup, upwards of 60 000 people have been arrested, including members of the judiciary who convicted his party members of corruption and teachers at Hizmet schools, and to date (August 2016) the number of targets rises. According to Tim Arango and Ceylan Yeginsu, Erdoğan is emptying the country's prisons to make room for all of the arrests.[232] Over 38 000 prisoners have been released.

It is a difficult time in Turkey. The coup represents an attempt to fight back against a regime violating human rights, but it also undermines Turkish democracy. The other powerful player in Turkey, Gülen, is socially conservative. The prospects are grim for a liberal political alternative in Turkey.

I met a Turkish graduate student named Poyraz Kolluoglu at a conference at Queen's University in 2013 who presented a moving talk on his participation in the Gezi Park protests. He described how Muslim practices were observed during the protests, which overlapped with Ramadan. Calls to prayer were performed, and the protesters organized a mass Iftar dinner open to all. The simplistic characterization of the protesters as 'secularists' versus 'religious Muslims' by the western media was inaccurate.

Kolluoglu's talk prompted me to enroll in a program, coincidentally planned and run by the Gülen Movement, to travel to Turkey and learn more about the context of the Gezi events. When I arrived in Istanbul in 2014, I headed straight to Taksim Square, to stay in a hostel at the edge of Gezi Park where these events had taken place. I spent my days chatting with artists, socialists, stateless refugees and shop owners about the situation in Turkey.

 alizex786   5m

I bought a newspaper from the feminist society of Istanbul, who had set up a table for the parade. Photo courtesy of Alyshea Cummins.

alizex786 @dreamshare supporting the feminist society of Turkey 💗

Screen capture of an Instagram video of the parade.

    I watched the Gay Pride Parade of Turkey from the second floor of a Taksim coffee shop. I leaned over the balcony to watch thousands of smiling people waving rainbow flags; half the crowd would shout and the other half would respond, back and forth. I asked the man beside me what they were saying, and he translated for me.

"WHERE IS MY LOVER?"
"HERE I AM!!"
"WHERE IS MY LOVER?"
"HERE I AM!!"

    The atmosphere was joyful and optimistic. When I wandered down amongst the people in the crowd after the parade was over, I heard young people talking about Gezi Park. I bought a newspaper from the feminist society of Istanbul, who had set up a table for the parade. This was a celebration of the young liberals of Turkey. Most of them were Muslims, all of them supported a liberal and democratic Turkey. The event was "the most important LGBT gathering in a Muslim country", because Turkey has traditionally been a safe haven for gay Muslims in a region of nations where their existence is illegal.[233]

    In 2015, the parade was banned, for "safeguarding security and public order".[234] The police descended on the celebration, firing tear gas and rubber bullets at attendees. This year (2016) was met with similar violence.[235]

The protest crowd represents a collection of disenfranchised youth from diverse backgrounds, who agree that they want change in their country. Jay Cassano critiques the simplified 'religion' versus 'secularism' narrative that is so often used in the western media to describe contemporary politics in Turkey:

> 'Saying the protest is about secularism or religion misses the point completely,' says Zeyno Üstün, a demonstrator who participated in the occupation of Gezi Park on the very first night, May 27. Üstün was one of only fifty activists who occupied Gezi Park on the 27th. Now the movement she helped launch has been taken up by hundreds of thousands.
>
> She continued, 'Sure, there are hardcore secularists in the crowds. But there are also feminists, LGBT activists, anarchists, socialists of various stripes, Kurdish movements' leaders, unionized workers, architects and urban planners, soccer hooligans, environmentalists, and people who are protesting for the first time! Someone wearing an Atatürk [the founder of the Turkish Republic as a secular, ethnically Turkish nation-state] T-shirt walks alongside another waving a flag of [imprisoned Kurdish leader] Abdullah Öcalan.'
>
> (Cassano 2013)

This description of events mirrors Pomerantsev's observations of the Maidan. A diversity of interest groups were united through a collective critique of the state of affairs.

In a follow-up talk at Queen's University in 2016, Kolluoglu discussed a concept of 'postmodern sacred'; he asked: "Why are protesters trying to maintain and form solidarities in these communal sites despite their sociocultural and political differences? I would argue that the protest repertoires of the 21st century are mostly shaped by the affective ruptures emerging in daily politics and affective ties created by the participants themselves; and urban spaces such as Gezi Park in the Turkish case arise as affective hubs[…] Are these encounters harbingers of post-Islamic values and affective ties in a belated modern milieu?". His arguments point to major contemporary paradigm shifts in identity and knowledge mobilization.

Varol, Ferrara, Ogan et al.'s study of social networks and systems mapped a transformation from "a broadcasting model (one-to-many, like radio and TV) to a peer-to-peer (many-to-many) distribution system".[236] The mass diffusion of communications and information has played a significant role in social uprisings around the world in the 21st century. Government restrictions on journalism and access to information are undermined by peer-to-peer social media networks. Varol, Ferrara, Ogan et al. note that "the use of social media in the Egyptian protests allowed people to make informed decisions about participation in the movement, provided new sources of information outside of the regime's control, and increased the odds that people participated in the protests on the first day".[237] Technology changes too rapidly for the highly regulated organizational structures of nation states to adapt in time to control peer-to-peer digital 'sharing'.[†] Grassroots action is sometimes better suited to the networks of 'religious' organizations than state ones. Indeed, peer-to-peer knowledge mobilization is the communication mechanism of 'elective affinities', the network of identity formation in the 21st century.

[†] The increasingly rapid advancement of technological innovation is colloquially referred to as Moore's Law. Specifically, it refers to the rise of silicon semi-conductor electronics and the miniaturization movement. In 1965, Gordon Moore predicted that the number of transistors installed into an integrated circuit would double every one-two years. Increased 'memory', or data storage on digital devices and higher pixel count on digital cameras are tangible examples of this principle, but the near future of Moore's Law holds self driving cars and sex robots, as well as speculative research in nanotechnology and AI (Artificial Intelligence).
Brock, David C. *Understanding Moore's Law: Four Decades of Innovation.* (Philadelphia: Chemical Heritage Press, 2006)

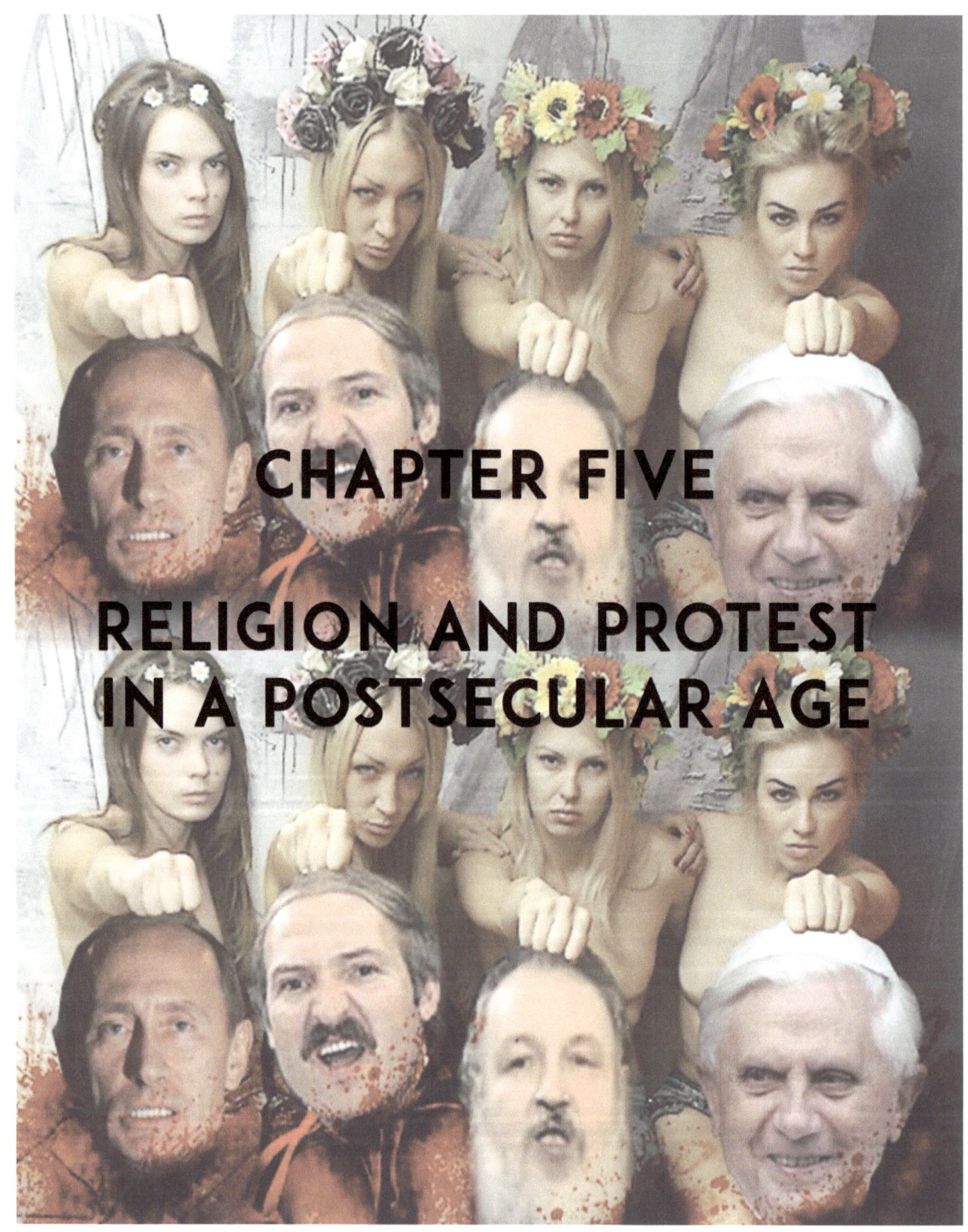

CHAPTER FIVE

RELIGION AND PROTEST IN A POSTSECULAR AGE

CHAPTER FIVE

RELIGION AND PROTEST IN A POSTSECULAR AGE

The chief reason warfare is still with us is neither a secret death-wish of the human species, nor an irrepressible instinct of aggression, nor, finally and more plausibly, the serious economic and social dangers inherent in disarmament, but the simple fact that no substitute for this final arbiter in international affairs has yet appeared on the political scene.
—Hannah Arendt, *On Violence*
(Arendt 1970: 46)

THE RELIGION/SECULAR BINARY

Who controls the past controls the future, who controls the present controls the past.
—George Orwell, *Nineteen Eighty-Four*
(Orwell 1949)

Femen is an Eastern European protest group hailing the spirit of early women's street theatre styled protests and literature, and using contemporary tactics and tools. They are combatting the rise of right-wing extremism with outrageous antics and relying heavily on the internet and social media to draw attention to their actions. At various points in history, the church has been an institution that led revolutions, and supported progressives. There are pockets of progressive movement in church communities, but overwhelmingly, we are living in a time when 'religion' is synonymous with backward, anti-intellectual, and tacitly supportive of state violence. The church as a historical and powerful institution is uniquely positioned to criticize the nation state, but instead works with conservatives to take away the rights of women around the world. Femen activists are taking aim at this unholy alliance that is detrimental to women.

Patriarch Kirill I of the Russian Orthodox Church and Russian President Vladimir Putin. Nadezhda Tolokonnikova and Maria Alyokhina spent two years in a Russian penal colony for performing the hit song *Holy Shit* with the feminist punk band Pussy Riot at Moscow's central Russian Orthodox Saviour Cathedral. They performed the song to protest against Patriarch Kirill's official endorsement of Vladimir Putin's campaign.

Sister Marie Veronique, a Dominican nun says "I think they're absolutely right to do this... It's a good way to shock people and call attention to this [gang rape of two 16-year-old girls in Paris]".

In 1912, influenced by theories of evolution, Emile Durkheim mused that over time, the ideologies of Testamenters would transform into social constructs like nationalism, the way that he thought animistic traditions were primitive precursors to polytheism and then monotheism. He argued that their *sui generis* cosmological formulations represented a simplistic, imprecise version of science or moral philosophy which would eventually fade into history.[238] This sounds as though Durkheim was an atheist, but he also wrote about the categories of sacred and profane as universal categories. In *The Elementary Forms of Religious Life*, he wrote of the sacred and the profane that:

> In the history of human thought, there is no example of two categories of things as profoundly differentiated or as radically opposed to one another. The traditional opposition of good and evil is nothing beside this one: Good and evil are two opposed species of the same genus, namely morals, just as health and illness are nothing more than two different aspects of the same order of facts, life; by contrast, the sacred and the profane are always and

everywhere conceived by the human intellect as separate genera, as two worlds with nothing in common... The fact is universal.
(Durkheim 1912: 36)

Emerging theory in the field of Critical Religion argues for a theoretical framework which sees the secular/religious binary as 'opposed species of the same genus', culturally and contextually relevant, and not universal. Durkheim struggled to come to terms with the Christian tradition of cosmology he was raised in on one hand, and new information about indigenous traditions on the other. His hierarchy of traditions which theorized that the practices of Western Europeans were superior and the practices of people of colour were "primitive" was tainted by racism and social Darwinism. On some level however, he was beginning to understand that what gets called religion referred to a form of governance displaced and replaced by a new order. He could not abandon his notion of the sacred/profane absolutism; he seemed to be something of a deist, criticizing the medieval Christian social order in Europe, while holding onto the idea of a universal 'sacred' concept (and its 'profane' mirror). In the following passage, Durkheim attempts to 'secularize'—or explain with social science—the Church as a social institution which interprets a universal 'sacred'. Thus 'religion' the category was theorized as a study of interpretations of a universal concept called 'sacred'.

Religious beliefs proper are always shared by a definite group that professes them and that practices the corresponding rites. Not only are they individually accepted by members of that group, but they also belong to the group and unify it. The individuals who comprise the group feel joined to one another by the fact of common faith. A society whose members are united because they imagine the sacred world and its relations with the profane world in the same way, and because they translate this common representation into identical practices, is what is called a Church. In history we do not find religion without Church. Sometimes the Church is narrowly national; sometimes it extends beyond frontiers; sometimes it encompasses an entire people (Rome, Athens, the Hebrews)...
(Durkheim 1912: 41)

Durkheim ultimately theorized a universal religion/secular binary to overcome the logical fallacies which arise when competing cosmologies interact. As Tomoko Masuzawa explains in *The Invention of World Religions: Or, How European Universalism Was Preserved in the Language of Pluralism*, this system of comparative religion privileged Christianity at the expense of non-Christian systems. Any cosmology without a sacred/profane binary was rendered invisible by the field of Religious Studies, because the binary was supposed to be 'universal'.

In A Secular Age, Charles Taylor argued that while the church was not the center of twentieth century communities in the same ways it had been in previous centuries in Europe and North America, the identity category of religion firmly and undeniably remained a factor in people's self-descriptions, political platforms, and social organizing. Taylor's argument showed that the systemic aspects of what gets called 'religion' are more deeply embedded in the workings and constitution of what gets called 'secular' than on a simply ideological level. Foucault writes that:

> [T]he real political task in a society such as ours is to criticize the working of institutions which appear to be both neutral and independent; to criticize them in such a manner that the political violence which has always exercised itself obscurely through them will be unmasked, so that one can fight them.

(Foucault 1984: 6)

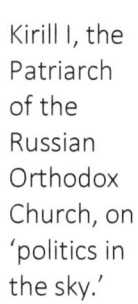

Kirill I, the Patriarch of the Russian Orthodox Church, on 'politics in the sky.'

The political violences operating through the category of religion are obvious to rights activists. The violences operating through the category of secularism are less obvious. What Charles Taylor seems to be concerned about in his articulation of 'secularism' is that tearing down the idols of the old gods merely makes room for the idols of the new ones. Specifically, he deplores the gods of "efficiency or cost benefit" of market capitalism.[239] Taylor's antidote for these heartless gods is a kind of social communitas sharing structural aspects with Christianity but based on collectively reached contemporary values; *The Ethics of Authenticity* argues for reaching beyond selfish individualism toward "horizons of significance", or shared moral commitments to each other and the environment.[u] For Taylor's vision to be realized, the category of religion itself (and the shadow it casts called secularism) must be deconstructed and overcome, ie. understood as 'opposed species of the same genus'. Only then can the new idols be critiqued and a contemporary vision actioned.

The category of religion is constructed so that organizations classified within it operate beyond critique. It is necessary to break down the category by putting the history of its development into context to 'unmask' the political violence exercised within it. In his book *1984*, George Orwell (1949) theorizes a language called *duckspeak*. This language is the reductionist result of a regime that continuously forbids politically-charged words from being spoken to prevent social uprising. In the book, the activists are unable to vocalize their dissent; they look at each other and feel the unease and injustice, incapable of putting it into words. The histories of many 'religious' regimes are marked by periods of silencing dissent, and this silencing is intrinsic to the modern formulation of the category of 'religion' itself. The "ineffability of religion" is the inability to deconstruct the category of religion.[v] Efforts to deconstruct it

---

[u] Taylor's perspective stands in contrast to Habermas, who argues for public recognition of 'religions'. Habermas, Jürgen. *Between Naturalism and Religion*. (Cambridge: Polity Press, 2008)
See Maria Birnbaum's critique of "the kind of religion Habermas envisions entering the public sphere and […] the way in which his postsecular arguments constitute a legitimate speaker under the banner of 'religion'."

[v] "The ineffability of religion" refers to an academic argument which posits that there is an essential object called religion that either *is not* explainable in words or *should not* be explained in words (Scharfstein 1993; Jacobs 2015; Jonas 2016). I am implying here that the history of the 'ineffability' runs parallel to the modern development and attempts at definition of the category of religion.

should be welcomed by scholars of Religious Studies, both sociologists and theologians, for a clearer understanding of the many composite elements the category strives to encapsulate.

How are we to study movements like Femen, or the protests in Gezi Park? 'Religion' as a discourse is deeply embedded in the language of these events and 'affective hubs', as Kolluoglu calls them. What is lost when protest is studied as strictly a 'political' matter? And yet, to study protest in the depoliticized discursive realm of 'religion' would be utter nonsense. Study of these groups is not served by a top-down application of the religious/secular binary which mischaracterizes what McGuire and others call 'Lived Religion', or what is lost in the higher-order, abstract definitions of institutional elites.[240] These movements of dissent move dangerously and freely in the borderlands of the jurisdictions of church and state institutions in defiance of lines of demarcation. The classical Durkheimian definition of religion as binary opposite of secular in the field of Religious Studies does not offer an analytical apparatus which is able to make sense of contemporary post-9/11 globalized identity categories and subject positions. [w] Contemporary theories emerging from the impact of postcolonial studies, queer theory, and feminist theory and methodologies in the field of Critical Religion offer new ways of thinking about and understanding religion.

Jacobs, Jonathan D. "The Ineffable, Inconceivable, and Incomprehensible God Fundamentality and Apophatic Theology." *Oxford Studies in Philosophy of Religion*. (Oxford: Oxford University Press, 2015)
Jonas, Silvia. *Ineffability and its Metaphysics: The Unspeakable in Art, Religion, and Philosophy*. (London: Palgrave Macmillan, 2016)
Scharfstein, Ben-Ami. *Ineffability: The Failure of Words in Philosophy and Religion*. (Albany New York: State University of New York Press, 1993)
[w] The ideological religious/secular divide is a mainstream Religious Studies framework. I could point it out in just about any theoretical lineage in the field, but for the sake of specificity, I point to Maria Birnbaum's critique of the work of Jürgen Habermas as "one of the most prominent contemporary liberal theorists" (p. 182). Birnbaum argues "that there is a distinctive productive power in Habermas' argument for the recognition of religion and that he 'makes' religion through arguing for its recognition. [...] Habermas' vision of religion is conservative, that is, reproducing the social and political structures within which this recognition takes place" (p. 183). Her chapter offers resources for further critiques of specific authors reifying a religion/secular binary, including Dressler and Mandair 2011; Joas 2008a; 2008b; Chatterjee 2006; Kehrer 1998.
Birnbaum, Maria. "Exclusive Pluralism: The Problems of Habermas' Postsecular Argument and the Making of Religion." In *Religion as a Category of Governance and Sovereignty*. (Trevor Stack, Naomi Goldenberg, Timothy Fitzgerald, eds. Leiden, Netherlands: Brill Publishing, 2015) p. 182-196.

NAOMI GOLDENBERG: THEORY OF VESTIGIAL STATES

In *Religion as a Category of Governance and Sovereignty*, Naomi Goldenberg operationalizes the deconstruction of the category of religion within the field of Critical Religion to propose a theory of vestigial states.[241] This theoretical lens sees religions as the vestiges of former sovereignties of regions now controlled by nation states. The modern word 'religion' then refers to the hierarchy of this pre-nation system existing as an ideological apparatus within the new state system. Goldenberg gives the example of Judaism; she writes that Jewish people were the people of Judea, indigenous to a particular region with its particular community conventions. When Judea was conquered by the Romans, the continuation of indigenous regulations and practices, such as matrilineal descent, and a shared ethnic identity formed around the continuation of these practices are what constituted 'Judaism'. This was not a belief-based conversion group, but a community who shared a language and ancestral stories. In her article "There is No Religion in the Bible", Goldenberg writes that "[i]n the ancient, social worlds spoken of in the Bible, religion has not yet been invented. Instead of narratives about groups and individuals interacting in arenas of life that we now differentiate as religious or secular, governmental or ecclesial, political or clerical, we are presented with stories and reports in which these distinctions have no meaning".[242] Thus the terms 'secular' and 'religious' are anachronistic when applied to the Biblical context. Goldenberg continues that "[c]ontemporary dualistic formulae of religious/secular or religious/political had no meaning in the societies that produced the Bible. When these terms are applied to biblical history and literature, they distort our understanding of ancient peoples by presenting their ways of organizing and describing authority as too similar to our own".[243]

Vestigial state theory makes sense of modern systems which get called 'religions' as the vestiges of former sovereignties within a new government. A vestigial state encompasses more than what is categorized as 'religion', rather than being a substitute for the term. This means that ethnicities, neo-imperial politics, nationalist movements, religions, and other ideological movements emerging from former sovereignties can be understood within the theory of vestigial states. Goldenberg writes:

> **By designating religions as vestigial states, I am identifying them as the structures of former sovereignties that continue to operate with differing degrees of autonomy within present-day governmental domains. Vestigial states called religions are composed of discursive and institutional practices similar to those of fully functioning states. However, the particular non-vestigial states that contain their predecessors determine**

the parameters of the vestigial varieties: religions are accorded limited powers and special privileges by the states in which they operate. (Goldenberg 2015: 8)

As evidenced in the contemporary case study of the Druid Network outlined by Suzanne Owen and Teemu Tara, vestigial states are only 'accorded the powers and privileges' of being classified as a religion by the nation state in relation to their emulation of a dominant Christian model.[x] Owen and Tara demonstrate in their work on the Druid Network that the contemporary category of religion is predominantly defined by the state. In parliamentary democracies, and other contemporary government systems, groups designated 'religions' receive exemption from particular taxation. They also receive allowances, like rights to collect money, provide social services and have charitable status. According to Owen and Tara, druids were the members of Celtic society who were teachers, managed medical treatments, and made laws. After the Romans invaded the British Isles, the new administration took over those functions. The symbols and stylings of druids became symbolic of the old order, rather than socially functional. When the Roman Empire receded from bureaucratic control of the Isles, the Christians established their own administration of teaching, medicine and law. When English law developed, Christian symbols and stylings became ritualistic rather than functional the way the Druid social arrangements had become vestigial under Roman rule. Contemporary British people practice Druidry, as well as Christianity, ritualistically rather than functionally within the jurisdiction of England. Owen and Tara write that Christian groups are afforded the tax exemptions and other benefits of the status of 'religion' by the Charity Commission in Britain, and the Druids sought the same status and benefits. Owen and Tara explain that establishing Druidry as a religion in Britain required arguing that Nature could be God: "the rhetorical excess of religious-sounding key words in the application, such as spirit, deity, divine and sacred… helped TDN's argument that nature can be regarded as a supreme being".[244] This metric based on the Christian framework requires vestigial states seeking 'religion' status to emulate Christianity. England's policy on categorizing religion, then, is an evangelical policy, requiring all groups seeking status to become systemically Christian.

Timothy Fitzgerald writes that "we are rendered impotent by our ignorance of the semantic and ideological bias of our tools of analysis… we do not notice that the very elusiveness of the definitional problem in religion is a sign of its disguised ideological function".[245] This disguised ideological function is particularly troubling for

---

[x] Owen, Suzanne, and Teemu Tara. "The Category of 'Religion' in Public Classification: Charity Registration of The Druid Network in England and Wales." 2015

women, considering that the administrations of organizations called religions are the most patriarchal in the world, following the model of the Vatican's anti-woman policies.

GOLDENBERG EXPLAINS THAT "[B]Y MOVING THE CATEGORY OF RELIGION INTO THE SPHERE OF STATECRAFT. BY UNDERSTANDING THAT GENDER ARRANGEMENTS DERIVE FROM THE HISTORIES OF EARLIER FORMS OF GOVERNMENT RATHER THAN FROM INSCRUTABLE STRUCTURES OF MYSTERY. PIETY MIGHT BE PARALLELED MORE CLOSELY WITH POLITICS AND THE INFERIOR POSITION OF WOMEN WITHIN THE ONCE AND FUTURE STATES NAMED RELIGIONS MIGHT BE SUPPORTED WITH LESS CONVICTION".[246]

    The universalizing function of the category of religion is evident when looking at 'interfaith dialogue' events. After a talk in April 2016 about colonial formulations of 'world religions' in a Christian-dominant society, an Afghani Muslim visiting graduate student pointed out that random Canadian imams are invited to speak at interfaith events and act as representatives of Canadian Islam, but within her community, these imams were merely responsible for organizing group prayers, not for acting as leaders or ambassadors of the community at large. Muslim imams in Canada are constructed by the hegemonic knowledge producers of the category of 'religion' in Canada. They are modelled after priests, and thus compelled to emulate the patriarchal hierarchy of the College of Cardinals of the Catholic Church, and all within a supposedly 'secular' state. Sheila Jeffreys argues that homophobia is re-inscribed by this ecumenical Interfaithism as well.[247] In the case of Tunisian activist Amina Sboui who posted the topless photo of herself on social media, several imams called for her to be lashed and stoned.[248] These men were not representatives or ambassadors of specific Muslim communities the way that a priest is considered the spokesperson of 'his flock'; they were individual conservatives voicing their own opinions outside of an institutional authority. The fatwas of these fringe radicals are given more weight in the international news media than by Tunisians themselves, as frustrated Muslim feminists repeatedly explain.[249] The category of religion carries the structural baggage of Christianity.

    An important aspect of Goldenberg's theory of vestigial states in the notion of 'once-and-future states'. By this she means that just behind the organization's non-state status is the aspiration or potential for future sovereignty. This can be seen in the contexts of both the collapsing Soviet Union and the collapsing Ottoman Empire. Andrew Mango writes:

> There was this difference between Christian and Muslim communities: among the former... clerics often encouraged or even took part in violent action; among the Muslims, nationalism developed in opposition to religion. The Muslim religious establishment stood for the whole Muslim community (ummet), and not for the nations that were arising in its midst. On the other hand, the Greek, Serbian, and Bulgarian Eastern Orthodox Churches, and the Armenian Gregorian Church, had become by the end of nineteenth century bearers of their respective nationalist ideologies.

(Mango 2011: 10)

The term 'religious' in the passage above obscures the author's meaning, but reimagining the passage outside of the religious/secular binary opens up productive possibilities. Applying the theory of vestigial states, it is possible to see that the Armenian Gregorian Church, for example, formed the proto-government structure of the later attempts to build an Armenian state. In that case, there is no need to call the movement 'religious' or 'secular'—the binary becomes irrelevant to understanding the history.

The Gülen Movement is a fitting contemporary example of how a so-called religious group operates closely parallel to the nation state. After the falling out of Turkey's great political allies, Fethullah Gülen and Recep Tayyip Erdoğan, the Justice and Development Party of the Turkish government classified the Gülen Movement, and all affiliated networks, as the Gülenist Terror Organisation (Fetullahçı Terör Örgütü, FETÖ) or Parallel State Organisation (Paralel Devlet Yapılanması, PDY). Erdoğan accurately evaluated the Gülen Movement as a challenge to the existing nation state with their state-like social services and influence in all levels of jurisdiction, whether intentional or not on the part of Gülen.

Perhaps this kind of insight on the part of the republic of Turkey derives from their history of separation of Sultanate and caliphate. However, Christendom is seemingly forgetful of the similar history of the Catholic Church. The Papal States, a small empire which survived almost a thousand years (754 CE – 1870 CE) encompassing parts of what is now modern Italy and France, was a sovereign nation which was conquered by the Kingdom of Italy in the nineteenth century, transforming it into a vestigial state, or once-and-future-state. Subsequent popes, who still wielded a significant amount of popular control despite being overthrown as a nation, refused to cooperate with the Italian state. The State of Vatican City was made a micro nation in the Lateran Treaty by Benito Mussolini in 1929.

A precondition of the negotiations was destruction of the parliamentary Catholic Italian Popular Party. Pius XI disliked political Catholicism because he could not control it. Like his predecessors, he believed that Catholic party politics brought democracy into the church by the back door. The demise of the Popular Party caused a wholesale shift of Catholics into the Fascist Party and the collapse of democracy in Italy.[250]

In a speech following the finalization of the treaty, Mussolini stated that "[i]nside the State the Church is neither sovereign nor free… We have not resurrected the temporal power of the popes: we have buried it".[251] In *God in the Tumult of the Global Square: Religion in Global Civil Society* by Mark Juergensmeyer, Dinah Griego, and John Soboslai, the authors write that in "the political instability that rose at the end of the twentieth century, with the dawn of the global era, secular leaders have recruited religious ideologies and leaders to their side, hoping that the legitimacy of religion would shore up their flagging power".[252] This description of trends could easily describe the Lateran Treaty between Mussolini and Pius XI. However, the use of the terms 'religious' ideologies and 'secular leaders' actually obscures the context of events. The analysis of Juergensmeyer, Griego and Soboslai would be more precise if they explained exactly what they mean when they use the term 'religious ideologies'. Discussing these movements more precisely within their historical contexts reveals a great deal about their significance to today's global milieu.

The Islamic State (often called ISIS in the media) is similarly a contemporary attempt in a longtime project to resurrect the Muslim caliphate's sovereign domain. Al-Rasheed, Kersten and Shterin describe how the caliphate became vestigial:

> Ultimately, once the sultanate was abolished and the republic was declared, the caliphate became an anomaly. The Caliph's position in, and relation to, the emerging national state was never clearly defined.[…] With its inherent extraterritorial dimensions, the institution of the caliphate was in total contradiction to the conception of the state that was being implemented in the Turkish Republic. From the point of view of its creators the modern Turkish state could no longer shoulder the responsibilities that the caliphate implied. (Al-Rasheed, Kersten, and Shterin 2012: 47)

The possibilities are vast in the potential application of vestigial state theory in the context of the former Ottoman Caliphate states. Andrew Mango explains that the term *millet* in Turkish was the word used to describe Christians, Jews, Armenians, and other non-Turk minority groups within the Ottoman Empire.[253] Brent Nongbri's work explores indigenous terms which are later translated as 'religion', but in this case, the word *millet* is later translated as nation:

> The Ottoman state was Muslim, dynastic, and medieval in its organizing principles. Its government was based on Muslim religious law (*sharia*, in Turkish spelling *şeriat*), which was supplemented by royal ordinances (*kanun*) and customary law (*örf*), and stretched, sometimes beyond reason, to cover day-to-day requirements. In accordance with that law, non-Muslim monotheists who submitted to Muslim rule were given protected status and allowed to run their communal affairs. The three main non-Muslim confessional communities-- Greek or Eastern Orthodox Christians, Armenian Gregorian (Monophysite) Christians and Jews-- were known as *millet*, a term which later acquired the secular meaning of *nation*.
> (Mango 2011: 4)

Mango's use of the word 'secular' in the passage quoted above is unnecessary as it is anachronistic. The millet was a group or tribe of people identifiable as part of that particular group—millet was a "cultic distinction", to use James Diamond's term.[254] The modern nation state with its unmoving territorial borders did not apply to the pre-republic context. Atatürk used the term millet to describe the Turkish nation. For example, he said that "unless a nation's life faces a peril, the war is murder", translated from "millet hayatı tchlikeye maruz kalmayınca, savaş cinayettir".[255] It is difficult to say whether or not he meant the Turkish people or the Turkish sovereign territory, but Atatürk himself marked the shift in the meaning of millet.

Goldenberg explains how the word 'religion' is applied strategically when referring to post-caliphate Muslim community contexts. She writes:

> Innovative vocabulary pertaining to Islam has blossomed in recent years. Terms such as political Islam and Islamism are invented to cordon off appropriate forms of Islam from those that are considered dangerous to public order as defined by ruling governments. I suggest that Islam is in the process of being turned into a religion – i.e. of being made vestigial – within some contemporary states at the same time that it functions non-vestigially in other parts of the world. Debates about Islam illustrate how religion as a discursive category operates as a regulatory description in Western democracies.
> (Goldenberg 2015: 5-6)

Ukraine has struggled in and out of once-and-future statehood since the eighth century. Ukraine was declared a sovereign nation in 1991, but the current (as of 2016) war with Russia demonstrates that Ukraine may become vestigial once more. It is no coincidence that in 1990, on the brink of Ukraine's 'secular' declaration of independence, Stepan Ivanovych Skrypnyk returned from exile in Canada and the United States after 46 years—as 'Patriarch Mstyslav I of Kiev and all Ukraine'—to declare independence from the Russian Orthodox Church and the Moscow Patriarchate and lead nationalist rallies as the head of the Ukrainian Autocephalous Orthodox Church (UAOC). If the modern state of Russia reconquers all of Ukrainian territory, perhaps the vestigial state of the UAOC will be all that remains of the Ukrainian state. More likely, the UAOC will be banished, their leaders rounded up and executed, as was the case 46 years before Skrypnyk's return, because once-and-future states, whether labelled 'religious' or 'secular', are 'states-in-waiting'.

Today, Russian President Vladmir Putin is strengthening ties with the Moscow Patriarchate, contributing to theories of the postsecular about people becoming 'more religious'. These contemporary developments make more sense when analyzing the historical context through the lens of the governmentality of religion. Why did Vladimir Putin forge an alliance with Kirill I, the Patriarch of the Russian Orthodox Church? Putin declared that he had been secretly baptized as a child and he then paid to resurrect 23 000 churches, in Russia and the West (which here means Ukraine).[256] A decade later, Putin invaded Ukraine with soldiers and guns. Vladimir Putin knows that Ukrainian nationalism, or an identity of Ukraine as separate from Russia, is professed in the pews of the Ukrainian Orthodox Church. I am not arguing that Putin's turn to religiosity was insincere, and I am not arguing that Patriarch Kirill I was meddling in politics. I am arguing that those verbal distinctions here, religious and secular, actively mischaracterize the patriarchal governmentality of these organizations. The distinction of religious and secular is irrelevant to the women whose homes have been burnt down in the War in Donbass, to the women who go to a church to get emergency care while Ukrainian state social services are withdrawn from the seceded territories, and when Putin's 'secular' democratic government made it a crime for people who are gay to show it in public in 2013 to the applause of the Russian Orthodox Church, the religious/secular categorization did not matter either.[257]

In December 2015, Ukrainians yearning to shore up their relationship with the European Union protested against Russian military attacks on their Eastern border by celebrating Christmas on December 25th, the Western holiday, instead of January 7th, the Cyrillic calendar date. Jürgen Habermas (2008) might cite this as evidence of the postsecular, and Grace Davie (1994) or Paul Heelas and Linda Woodhead (2005) might call it shifting rather than declining religiousness, but these theories do not account for the governmentality of religion. Again in December 2015, a children's theatre in Crimea—recently annexed from Ukraine into Russian control—called Palace of Child and Youth Art was closed for promoting "Ukrainian nationalism and western symbols".[258] The play which attracted the attention of local authorities was called "Songs of the Amazon", written by Crimean author Viktor Stus to celebrate St. Nicholas Day. The story invokes the popular mythology of pre-Christian Ukrainian warrior women of the Steppes "battling evil and fighting for freedom and the independence of their native land".[259] The theatre owner Oleksandr Polchenko reported that officials took "particular offence at the costume of a young girl wearing a golden crown and impersonating the sun, which he says they saw as a reference to New York's Statue of Liberty," despite the fact that all of the oldest churches in Ukraine have sun goddess symbols carved on them.[260] Polchenko notes that "[t]hey were indignant, they asked what kind of propaganda of western values we had staged for the holiday […] They also described the embroidered clothing and the Ukrainian-language scenario as brazen Ukrainian nationalism".[261] The banning of Ukrainian mythology, language and embroidery are chillingly reminiscent of the laws leading to the Soviet genocide in the region just a few generations before. These Soviet-era tactics of repression are troubling for the future of freedom of expression in Russian-annexed territories. Expressions of culture, nationalism and faith are in this context indistinguishable. As one protester at Maidan avowed, "Maidan was a singular experience, when everyone felt real unity, real patriotism, and felt the presence of God".[262]

Fedor Sivtsov's reflections of the Maidan experience cannot be expressed in terms of 'secular' or 'religious'. He wrote in his journal after the Berkut had attacked the protesters and failed to disperse the crowd when millions began to sing the national anthem:

> Three things happened to me today.
> 1. I began to believe in God. When the Berkut broke through the barricades and began to push people back, children were brought to the stage, and those who did not fit on the stage were put in the middle of the circle. And people were praying and trying with the last ounce of their strength not to cry out of helplessness and fear. And then suddenly the church bells began to peal in the night. And these bells brought hope. And at that moment I began to believe in God.
> 2. I became a nationalist.
> I saw, beyond Berkut, the soldiers of the interior ministry, my compatriots, people who were supposed to represent and defend the law in my country.

They were fulfilling an idiotic and monstrous order that was in the interest of only one person – the president of a neighbouring country, because our president is not recognized here by anyone any longer. These soldiers were pushing the peaceful demonstrators, children, women, older people, and they did not care what they were doing.

And then I heard a cry from the stage: "They heard us! People are coming to us from all over Kyiv!" And then I looked back and saw an endless stream of people, Ukrainians who care about the fate of their fellow citizens. Ordinary fellow citizens who came to protect peaceful people. At that moment I became a nationalist.

3. I freed myself from fear.

The police and soldiers encircled the square and started pushing us. But they were not strong enough, and we pushed back; and even if we could not move them we could at least hold back the flood of beasts. At that moment I freed myself from fear.

Believe me, I am far from being the most fearless person in this country. But today I will go to Maidan again. For this night, and for these people, for this feeling of pride in being a single and united people – and for the dignity that we defended.

(Snyder and Zhurzhenko 2014)

Sivtsov's experience on the Maidan is expressed through impassioned language invoking discourses of religion, nationalism and emotion. He speaks of his changed identity in the language of conversion. The pealing of church bells in the terrifying moments the night of the demonstration convert him into an ally of the church, and the oceanic feeling[y] of oneness at the sight of all the citizens joining the protest convert him to the cause of the nation which brought them all together. He speaks of this powerful moment in terms of faith, with faith in the church and the nation indistinguishable from one another.

---

[y] In 1927, Romain Rolland wrote a letter to Sigmund Freud describing what he called "spontaneous religious sentiment" as 'oceanic'. Freud addressed Rolland's comment in the book *Civilization and Its Discontents*. He argued that humans in the womb have no concept of ego, or conscious separation from their mother, as they are one living organism. He hypothesized that most of men's ego development stems from the separation of the man from his mother. For example, he writes: "the dwelling-house was a substitute for the mother's womb, the first lodging, for which in all likelihood man still longs, and in which he was safe and felt at ease" (18). Thus the 'oceanic feeling' of oneness occurs when men are reminded of the time when they were one living organism with their mother. Freud, Sigmund. *Civilization and Its Discontents*. (Vienna: Internationaler Psychoanalytischer Verlag Wien, 1930)

Foucault argues that the subject does not produce knowledge, but that the subject itself is created in discourse. Davies and Harre elaborate on this theory of the subject:

> A subject position incorporates both a conceptual repertoire and a location for persons within the structure of rights for those that use that repertoire. Once having taken up a particular position as one's own, a person inevitably sees the world from the vantage point of that position and in terms of the particular images, metaphors, storylines and concepts which are made relevant within the particular discursive practice in which they are positioned. At least a possibility of notional choice is inevitably involved because there are many and contradictory discursive practices that each person could engage in.
> (Davies and Harre 1990: 46)

The Durkheimian religious/secular binary generates subject positions which are measured in relation to culturally Christian notions of 'religion' and 'the secular'. When examining groups which occupy the margins of this framework of subject positioning, it is possible to see how women's bodies are marked as 'religious' ('obeying' patriarchal arrangements) or 'political' (articulating female power). The religious/secular binary classification limits their agency as subjects of what are called 'religious' identities. As evidenced by Daly, Christ, Starhawk and others, any assertion of 'religion' that reflects a divine female becomes a necessarily politically-loaded feminist gesture.

Queer theory takes apart the categories of masculinity and femininity, and Critical Religion deconstructs the categories of religious and secular, moving the movements operating in the overlapping borderlands of 'religious' and 'secular' discursive territories into frameworks of visibility.[z] Movements like Femen, Native Faith, Hizmet, the Gezi Park protesters, and others which operate in these borderland spaces, are very often occupied by women. The subject positions created within the discursive boundaries of 'secular' and 'religious', or 'secular' and 'postsecular' limit women's expression in the three-fold way outlined by Merlin Stone: women's political and social rights in both the

---

[z] Naomi Goldenberg writes that "[b]y assuming that religion is an eternal and universal 'it' that identifies a bounded sphere of human life, distinct from what we term 'politics' or 'economics' or 'the secular,' we are doing more than hampering our understanding of epochs in the past. We are also obscuring our ability to see through the veils of ideologies that currently surround us. The task of lifting these veils, or, at least, of making them less opaque is one way to conceive of an objective for 'Critical Religion'."
Goldenberg, Naomi. "Some (Mainly) Very Appreciative Comments on Brent Nongbri's *Before Religion*." *The Critical Religion Association: Critical Approaches to the Study of Religion*. (May 6 2013. Retrieve at https://criticalreligion.org/2013/05/06/some-mainly-very-appreciative-comments-on-brent-nongbris-before-religion/)

church and state are actively denied, and women's self-fulfillment in inclusive theology which reflects female divine power is passively marginalized. Attempts within the field to theorize these marginal spaces fall short when they do not address the ways in which the religious/secular binary, the Christian ideology of religion and its own framework of dissent, has ruptured and been reconstituted in colonial contexts, and has moved and adjusted along with the concepts of the subject, the nation and the state.

Kristin Aune points out that according to a survey she conducted with Catherine Redfern, "feminists are much less likely to be religious".[263] In her article "Why Feminists Are Less Religious", she argues that first-wave feminist movements were heavily influenced by Enlightenment thinkers and Secularization Theory. Liberal feminist theory, then, and atheism have a structural kinship as movements.[264] Each measures itself in relation to a majority view. Atheism is defined by Richard Cimino as "oppositional identity in a culture of theism", and feminism is oppositional identity in a patriarchal culture.[265] The rise of 'the postsecular' in the field of Religious Studies has troubling implications for the subject position of feminists as secularized. While Secularization Theory is being disputed by Rosi Braidotti and others, 'the secular' as the categorical mirror of 'the religious' has not been deconstructed in writings on 'the postsecular'. These top-down frameworks do not reflect the realities on the ground where nuns protest arm-in-arm with Femen, Ukrainian muftis stand between protesters and the police at Maidan, and feminists pray in Gezi Park.

Mary Daly urged women to leave the Church en masse until it would recognize the Motherhood of God. The feminist task of honouring women's power in mythos requires making a space beyond a religious/secular divide where the conversation is possible. The 'feminist witchcraft' of Starhawk and others—like Femen and Goddess-worshipping pagans, as I argue—disavows the boundaries of the 'religion' category which reifies God the Father, and the 'secular' category, which still does not acknowledge the personhood of mothers. Christian fundamentalists have allied themselves with right-wing politicians in proclaiming the supremacy of God; where is the call to protect the sacred equality of the Goddess?

Feminisms, whether categorically 'religious' as tasfir, exegesis, or the Goddess Movement, or categorically 'secular' as civil society organizations, protest groups or state-involved service providers, are all concerned with telling the stories of women and ensuring that women's experiences are represented in the social and cultural imaginaire and mythos of the societies in which we work and live. Where particular ideologies may differ, tactics overlap when working in similar structural systems against structurally similar hegemonic forces.

To imagine a movement that is neither secular nor religious requires imagining a history where there is neither secular nor religious. The field of Critical Religion, and the works of Brent Nongbri and Timothy Fitzgerald in particular, re-tell the history of modernity before the concept of 'religious' and 'secular' develop, and then trace that development to contemporary articulations. Thus 'religious' and 'secular' can never be standalone categories; they always operate in a binary. The masked religious/secular binary in contemporary times allows the state to control what gets to be considered a religion and what does not, thus policing identity obliquely through religion as an Ideological State Apparatus.[aa]

RE-ORIENTATIONS OF IDENTITY

Identities—ethnicities, religions, or nations within a state—are conceptually bound by shared language, beliefs, and histories which differentiate from the majority, but this leads to what Iris Young calls "the 'essentialism' of cultural difference, where either participants or observers take a culture to be a coherent whole, relatively unchanging, and fully separate from other cultures".[266] This function of the identity category denies the diversity within identity groups, as well as syncretisms, or identity 'entanglements', to borrow Betlemidze's phrasing.[267] Essentialism erases the voices of dissent, the queers, the women, the feminists, and the deviants, or as Foucault puts it, the architects of "subjugated knowledges," so often present at protests.[268] Essentialism also mystifies and makes incomprehensible identities like Mormon feminist, Muslim atheist, or Conservative environmentalist. Globalization loosened the moorings of the hybrid-identity hypothesis,[269] so that the conventional categories of gender, race, sex, age, and religion as markers of difference are, to quote Jasbir Puar in *Terrorist Assemblages: Homonationalism in Queer Times*, "realigning in relation to contemporary forces of securitization, counterterrorism, and nationalism".[270] The implication of this idea is that

---

[aa] Louis Althusser theorized that there are at least eight (including religion, family, academia, etc.) Ideological State Apparatuses that support the supremacy of the State Ideology. The state maintains power through violence or the threat of violence, in the form of police, military, and law. According to Althusser, ISAs, on the other hand, are coercive institutions operating alongside the state to exert nonviolent pressure on citizens to obey the state. He writes that "certain elements of an ideology (the State Ideology) 'are realized in' or 'exist in' the corresponding institutions and their practices", meaning that while these institutions may seem to develop out of history, culture, or individual desire, they are formed in relation to the state and the state's ideological aims (1970: 77).
Althusser, Louis. *On the Reproduction of Capitalism: Ideology And Ideological State Apparatuses*. (1970). Trans. G. M. Goshgarian. London: Verso, 2014.

transnational forces, supranational, pan-religious, corporate movements, make use of the polemics of identity for war and money making. Self-conscious and taboo-shattering critique is necessary to transcend the boundaries of conventional categories.

Femen understands this darker side of identity-baiting. An image was posted on Femen International's Facebook page June 29, 2016, in red, white and black, drawn in the style of a wartime propaganda poster. Smoke rises from a black 'X' on a red backdrop where the Islamic State flag and the flag of the *front nationale*, the extreme right party of France, are draped. An angry topless woman, crowned with red flowers raises her fist in the foreground with a message scrawled across her chest: "JOIN FEMEN ANTIFASCIST FRONT".[271] The text accompanying the image read:

Because too much blood was shed, and in response, too much hate grows,
Because the superiority of some individuals over others based on arbitrary criteria is a spreading doctrine,
Because religious identity defines some people's lives,
Because security does not come from the re-assertion of borders nor from the exclusion of refugees,
Because our values of freedom are fought and betrayed,
And because today hatred has its icons, its names, its banners and its spokespeople:
FEMEN takes aim at modern fascisms: Islamism and extreme-right political parties internationally.[…] Islamists dream of a Caliphate based on a Sharia ruled by an almost unprecedented bloodthirsty patriarchal system. While this happens, extreme right political mafias, such as the National Front, take advantage of the climate of fear and gain voters seduced by their

manly speeches to counter Islamism. Armed with sexist, xenophobic, racist, homophobic ideals, promoting a fantasized Christian supremacy, they are the political representatives of the same totalitarianism, based on division in society and segregation, to ensure the superiority of a group of individuals over others.

The risk of an epidemic of fascist parties coming to power exists throughout Europe (Pegida movement in Germany, Golden Dawn in Greece…). Even the United-States of America are facing the growing popularity of Donald Trump on his racist anti-Black, anti-Hispanic, anti-Muslim, anti-woman crusade.

It is obvious that these two forms of fascism, religious and political, Islamism and traditional extreme right, are mutually reinforcing. As long as one exists and develops, the other will grow.

FEMEN has identified and targeted both totalitarian extremisms for several years already. […] Today, they are our two greatest enemies, toward whom as people we have no personal hatred, but as pernicious ideologies we have relentless determination to peacefully fight.

(Femen Movement 2016)

To paraphrase the comments of respondent Monica Miller on a presentation I gave at a feminist conference,[bb] the wealthy trans-national benefactors of the war machine do not care about the nuances of disagreement between interest groups, because the segregation created by the disagreement only makes it easier to control democratic processes.[272] Ideological divides between Catholics and Protestants, Christians and Muslims, white feminists and Muslim feminists, or Hispanics and lower-class whites are representative of the historical 'divide-and-conquer' tactic. In the passage above, Femen asserts that identity categories are manipulated by those who control "the productive power of recognition"[cc] to pit working-class people against one another.[273]

[bb] The presentation was titled "Between Sovereignties: Women between Church and State in Ukraine" and the conference was *Feminisms Beyond the Secular: Emerging Epistemologies and Politics in the 21st Century*, at Lehigh University, Bethlehem, Pennsylvania, March 21-23, 2016.

[cc] Birnbaum writes that "[R]ecognizing religion in the public sphere does not simply empower it, it does not pull it out of the closet of our privacy, but fixates that which is to be understood as religion. It draws boundaries around that which is supposed to be recognized under the label of religion. As I will show, Habermas recognizes a particular form of religion, one that fits his requirements for a liberal, deliberative democracy. But recognition is not simply productive, it is also conservative. Only those subjects are recognized that are, previous to the recognition, *recognizable*."

Birnbaum, Marla. "Exclusive Pluralism. The Problems of Habermas' Postsecular Argument and the Making of Religion." In *Religion as a Category of Governance and Sovereignty*. (Trevor Stack,

In terms of the field of Religious Studies, the categories of 'religion' and 'the secular' as silo terms are no longer adequate for coping with the complicated re-orientations of identity in the changing context of contemporary forces. In globalized society identities are increasingly fragmented, and in a global digital society of internet communities, identities are even disembodied. Contemporary methodologies need to address these social transformations.

Pamela Dickey Young writes that "method determines outcome… method is not separate from the data that give rise to a need for method". The lack of alternative method in the conceptual space between the categories of secularism and religion restricts examination of the radical contemporary shifts in religion, and understanding religious nationalist movements in particular.

"Poor Because of You" protest in Davos at the World Economic Forum Annual Meeting, where the richest people in the world, heads of state, monarchs, and CEOs of oil companies gather to discuss the future of our world. (Common Dreams 2012)

Naomi Goldenberg, Timothy Fitzgerald, eds. Leiden, Netherlands: Brill Publishing, 2015) p. 188.

SUPERNATIONAL ENTITIES AND SUBJUGATED KNOWLEDGES

As nations struggle through war and economic decline, the 'once-and-future-states' linger on the borders of the state's jurisdiction. They can participate in revolutions by leading anti-state protest movements or galvanizing support through populist politics, or they can wait for fiscally conservative governments to cede control of public services and bleed the state slowly. The nation-state is taxes and public service. As the cases of the Gülen Movement in Turkey and Yanukovich in Ukraine demonstrate, when all that is left of a privatized nation is an idea, sovereignty itself is threatened.

That said, ideas are not to be underestimated. While discussing the difference between violence and power, Hannah Arendt writes that violence is ultimately controlled by the state through police and the military, but power lies in the consent and consensus of groups. Power comes not from crazy individual citizens or dictators acting alone, but from networks of people energetically supportive of the solidarity of their movement. No matter how many men with guns are on the ground, drones are in the air, or bases are set up to colonize foreign territories, power cannot be killed with violence. Power rests in ideas. Governments that rely entirely on violence cease to have power. Arendt makes use of the example of the Russian invasion of Czechoslovakia to illustrate this point. No matter how much force Russia used, or how many implements they had at their disposal, the power of the idea of Czech and Slovakian ethnic sovereignty persisted against all odds, making the occupation ultimately unsustainable (and horrific for both sides).[274] The power of religious national movements lurks below the surface at the edges of the empire, dreaming of sovereignty.

If the nineteenth and twentieth centuries are marked by disillusionment with vestigial states called religions, Weber's *entzauberung*, then the twenty-first century is characterized by disenchantment with the state.[dd]

James Diamond writes:
> The dominant sensibility of our time, in intellectual and spiritual

---

[dd] I am calling this a disenchantment with the state because of increasingly disenchanted voters declining to participate in democratic elections, and the rise of leftist libertarian small-state communalist movements on one hand, and the success of big business conservative politicians canvassing against big government (for privatization) on the other. My analysis is an extension of Karl Polanyi's 1944 assessment of Late Capitalism.
Polanyi, Karl. *The Great Transformation: The Political and Economic Origins of Our Time.* (Boston: Beacon Press, 1944)

terms, is one of "coming after." In Western discourse, at least, we are clearly in an age of "post"s: post-modern, post-colonial, post-Communist, post-Christian. In Jewish circles it is fairly de rigueur to speak of this time as post-Holocaust, post-Zionist, post-denominational. Of late we are hearing in our culture a less familiar but no less important permutation of this "coming after" syndrome": the post-secular.

(James Diamond 2004)

The 'post's of James Diamond can add to their roster post-national on the crumbling fringes of colonial borders, and post-local as they are re-constituted internationally. American presidential candidate Donald Trump's call to "Make America Great Again" is the populist politics equivalent of the Postsecular— a call to imagine the resurrection of a vast spectre through its most grotesque characterizations of empire. Pan-Islamic movements, Brexit, neo-Ottoman politics, and the imperial aspirations of the modern Russian state are symptoms of the attending anxieties of Golden Age Thinking in a world of 'post's. As Polish theorist Agata Pyzik writes, "[i]f the Soviet Union 23 years into its existence wasn't called post-tsarist, why are we still defined as 'post-communist', and why is it relevant?".[275] New alternatives are yet to be theorized. So far, the 'Supernational Entities' which loom over contemporary international politics are international neo-imperial conservative movements. Perhaps, in the fray of the occupied square, collectives of peer-to-peer grassroots mobilizers will conceive of new ways of thinking and being that we cannot yet imagine.

The international rise of protests in public spaces, whether by feminists, environmentalists or others, signifies the disenfranchisement of citizens of these disenchanted nation states. Disen-franchisement is the failure of the state's essential democratic task of providing public mechanisms of critique and accountability. Citizens protesting with their bodies—putting their bodies at risk of ridicule, pain, and death—particularly in a digital age, should be of concern to governments invested in preserving democratic conventions. In an interview in 2016, Gayatri Chakravorty Spivak tells Steve Paulson about the death of her mother's aunt:

> I discovered that my mother's aunt hanged herself in 1926 when she was 17 because she was part of an anti-imperialist group. She was unable to kill, so therefore she killed herself. But she waited four days until she menstruated so that people would not think

that she was killing herself because of an illicit pregnancy. In her action she wanted to say that women do not just belong to men.

(Paulson 2016)

Spivak uses the story to explain the last resort of a subaltern woman, whose voice is so silenced that only perhaps in her martyrdom could she share a message. The darker side of disenfranchisement in the twenty-first century, the consort of disenchantment with the state, is the return of terrorism to the international arena. Hannah Arendt's 1948 work on twentieth century revolutions points to the need for avenues of expression for marginal members of society. She writes:

> What proved so attractive was that terrorism had become a kind of philosophy through which to express frustration, resentment, and blind hatred, a kind of political expressionism which used bombs to express oneself, which watched delightedly the publicity given to resounding deeds and was absolutely willing to pay the price of life for having succeeded in forcing the recognition of one's existence on the normal strata of society.

(Arendt 1948: 30)

A democratic state government's purpose as an institution is to provide and maintain stability. This goal is achieved through orchestrating the distribution of wealth, and minimizing corruption. When corruption is rampant and the system of wealth distribution needs revision, people feel disenfranchised and distrustful of government, leading to protest. As Maidan protester Andrij Bondar reflected: "[t]he Maidan today is a laboratory of the social contract. The social contract is what the broad masses of Ukrainian society have not had for so many years. We do not need a Father or a Leader. We need liberty".[276]

Every program and project of the democratic state should reflect the aim of reducing corruption and facilitating wealth distribution. When the country's wealth centralizes more and more in the few hands of the rich, and the poor become poorer, democracy itself is threatened. Democracy relies on the strength of a powerfully stable state. The social contract, the exchange of taxes for social services like healthcare, police and education, ensures safety, security and prosperity. When a democracy becomes corrupt, the rich avoid having their wealth taxed through loopholes and exceptions, while the poor fall below the tax line. This means that the middle class holds up the entire institution of democracy on their backs. It is the task of great leaders to build up the middle class.

During a Femen action against a right-wing rally in France, a Vice reporter spoke with a participant who had this to say: "Feminists have betrayed the cause of nationalism. Feminists are paid to disturb the nationalist movements of every country".[277] In both Turkey and Ukraine, countries sandwiched precariously between Imperial movements, challenging and changing government corruption is essential for creating a nation capable of withstanding the coercive pressures of the old empire. Further, socialist measures to expand the middle class creates the class which champions the democratic state and ensures its survival through times of social upheaval.

The tottering divide between Ukraine's millionaires who profited from the collapse of the Soviet Union and the impoverished masses, pushed to further extremes by economic turmoil and state corruption, all but depleted the middle class in Ukraine. As Russia advances on the eastern border in the War in Donbass, annexing the territories of Crimea, and the oblasts of Donetsk and Luhansk, the sovereignty of Ukraine as a state is in jeopardy. Femen demands closer political and economic ties between Ukraine and the European Union, and distance from Eastern alliances, for the anti-corruption assurances that democracy promises, and for the threat of violence against invaders that membership in the European Union would provide. Evidenced by the non-interference of the European Union and the United Nations in the war on Ukraine's eastern border with democratic Russia, Ukraine is a borderland for the taking, as it was for the Roman Empire and for Hitler from the west, and as it was for Imperial Russia and the Soviet Union from the east. The international rise in religious nationalist movements, both socialist and conservative, is inextricably linked to the jurisdictions of nation states and their colonial histories.

The notion of secularism as a universal ideology which societies move toward and away from, in opposition to religion as a universal ideology that societies move toward and away from is simplistic and does not encapsulate the relationship of tension between empires felt by Ukraine, north of the Black Sea, and Turkey, to the south of it, as the borderland territories between Europe and Asia. This is all the more obvious in the visual microcosm of the protest space.

'Religion', or identity groups categorized within the 'religious' umbrella of movements, has historically been a space to challenge the state. Canadian First Nations and ecological groups are working together to challenge the state's jurisdiction over unindustrialized territories; as in

Ukraine, these movements could also be described as Native Faith Movements, eco-paganism, neo-paganism, or Religion of the Ancestors. However, the particularly mystifying construction of the religion category depoliticizes these movements in ways which undermine their sovereignty and political aims.[ee] Examining the category of religion in relation to categories of governance moves 'private' religious practice into the realm of public evaluation and understanding. Thus, the feminist slogan "the personal is political" can be borrowed and remixed here to read, "the religious is political"[ff].[278]

When imperial systems collapse or decline into gradual collapse, religions and other identity groups fill the spaces. This erosion by postcolonial identity groups in contemporary times is exciting because it leaves spaces for feminist reinventions of sovereignty; it is also terrifying, because the cautionary tale of history warns that the vacuum will be filled with new dictators. Let us not forget that when the subjects of Imperial Russia were sick of war and the bourgeoisie in 1917, and the Tsar was away fighting wars on the Western front, every woman rose up from her seat in the factories fueling the war effort. They walked out into the street, fifty thousand women whom the army would not shoot, and the Empire fell. And just sixteen years later, Stalin declared Freedom of Religion, along with criminalizing homosexuality and abortion. These women were promised a voice in the new order, and once that new order was established, they were cast aside in favour of the oldest old boys club, the Russian Orthodox Church.

[ee] See Michael Ruecker, "Dances With 'Religion': A Critical History of the Strategic Uses of the Category of Religion by the Government of Canada and First Nations, 1885 to 1951", for a more detailed examination of Canadian depoliticization of First Nations sovereignty. Suzanne Owen also briefly discusses how political recognition is denied or made invisible by the application of the World Religions Paradigm to First Nations. She gives the example of how the Canadian census shows that a majority of Mi'kmaq in Newfoundland and Labrador are Catholics, with only 50 respondents checking the 'traditional spirituality' box, but that studying community practices tells a different story (2011: 260).
Ruecker, Michael. "Dances With 'Religion': A Critical History of the Strategic Uses of the Category of Religion by the Government of Canada and First Nations, 1885 to 1951." *Unpublished thesis*. (Ottawa: University of Ottawa, 2015)
Owen, Suzanne. "The World Religions Paradigm: Time For a Change." *Arts and Humanities in Higher Education*. (vol. 10 no. 3 (2011): 253-268. Retrieve online at http://ahh.sagepub.com/content/10/3/253.full.pdf+html)
[ff] The phrase "the religious is political" was used by Naomi Goldenberg in a Women in Religion course at the University of Ottawa.
Goldenberg, Naomi. "The Religious is Political." *Women in Religion*. Ottawa. University of Ottawa, 2015.

When asked, "What was your experience of the Orange Revolution of 2004/5?" Inna Shevchenko responded:

> I was 15 or 16, studying in the school in the small town where I was born in the south part of Ukraine. For me, it was a revolution that you could see everywhere. You would go out on the street and you hear people, like the neighbours you've known for 15 years of your life, talking about something they never talked about before. You look at your mother and she is watching news that she never was interested in... I believe revolution isn't physical. It's in the mind. One of the main goals in any revolution is to change the minds of people. The Orange Revolution brought completely new ideas to my society.

(Macnab 2014)

Shevchenko splashes her message across social media by any means necessary, even by flashing her eye-grabbing breasts to the world, because in the age of mass media, she knows that people must see it and share it to make the movement grow. The most eloquent and properly formatted essay in the world would not get more headlines than a bright image of Shevchenko lowering her panties and urinating on a poster of a man's face—in this case, Viktor Yanukovych—or a video of her screaming triumphantly about Joseph Ratzinger's resignation from the Papacy. These tactics, called Sextremism, are spreading Femen's ideas around the world.

Whether targeting the state or the church, Femen is taking aim at systemic power. This characteristic of their movement is shared with the Gezi Park protesters, who felt pushed to their limits by the tightening strictures of the ruling class, both ecclesiastic and civilian. Shevchenko's description of her childhood reflections on the Orange Revolution describes 'normal' people who are stirred into otherwise uncharacteristic mobilization. This is mirrored in the story of the Woman in Red at Gezi Park, who was not a masked hooligan, but a sensible academic roused into involvement by the conditions of the time in which she was living.

Stalin allied with the Russian Orthodox Church to build a mega-state wielding both violence and power. Today, Russian President Vladmir Putin is emulating this model and renewing ties with the Moscow Patriarchate. Like Stalin, he is criminalizing homosexuality[gg] and annexing Ukraine. Ukrainian women are hardly interested in whether this is a religious project or a secular project; the nativists are desperate to build a national identity separate from Russian settlers, and Femen, participants in the 2014

[gg] See The Council for Global Equality website for a list of the measures taken recently to restrict the free movement and choices of lesbian, gay, bisexual and trans Russians.
"The Facts on LGBT Rights in Russia." *The Council for Global Equality.* Accessed February 15 2017. Retrieve at http://www.globalequality.org/newsroom/latest-news/1-in-the-news/186-the-facts-on-lgbt-rights-in-russia

Ukrainian Revolution of Dignity, are fighting for the support of NATO to oust the Russians from their eastern provinces. When the time comes and sovereignties are reconstituted, will the women whose labours and love built the empire and also the women whose labours and love bolstered the religious nationalist movements be left behind again?

Women are intimately involved members of the anti-imperial resistance; this is evident cross-culturally and historically, from the February Revolution, to the Orange Revolution, to the Woman in Red, to the little girl dressed as a sun goddess at the Crimean Palace of Child and Youth Art. To their dismay, when the Empire loosens its iron hooks and independence is declared, the new state, with the help of the church, is thoroughly patriarchal. Inna Shevchenko was impelled into action with Femen when Ukraine's 2010 conservative government appointed an all-male presidential administration, mirroring the administration of the Orthodox Church. Femen are not calculating their resistance by the measurement system of religion versus the state, and they are not respecting the categorical boundaries between Ukrainian rulemakers in the Church or in the legislature. To Femen, women unrepresented by the church as well as the state, these institutions are part of the same patriarchal brotherhood which excludes them.

Where twentieth century scholars hypothesized the evolution of religion into nationalism, and indeed leaders like Ataturk and Lenin orchestrated such projects on a megalithic scale, the category of religion includes a universalizing valence which goes beyond the carefully patrolled borders of territorial sovereignty. The ideological jurisdiction and once-and-future valence of both states and religions and their twin histories map the slippages between the colonial and evangelical intentions of world leaders in contemporary times. In an age of globalization, identities are fragmented by the convergence of a mass of information and mass pluralism beyond the 19th and 20th century post-war configurations of the nation state. From these splinters of multiplicitous identity, multinational organizations emerge in a great reordering: NATO, the European Union, Facebook.com. Supernational identities emerge as well: pan-Islamism, feminism, 'Western culture'—these ideologies are mobilized through online networks beyond national lines. What comes after the age of 'post's?

Foucault examines the history of l'hôpital de la Salpêtrière, the French institution that was built to address the diseased, the mentally ill, and the poor in the 18th century, developing a theory of subjugated knowledges. He writes:

> Subjugated knowledges are those blocs of historical knowledge which were present but disguised within the body of functionalist and systematising theory

and which criticism - which obviously draws upon scholarship - has been able to reveal[...] It is through the re-emergence of these low-ranking knowledges, these unqualified, even directly disqualified knowledges (such as that of the psychiatric patient, of the ill person, the delinquent), and which involve what I would call a popular knowledge (*le savoir des gens*) though it is far from being a general commonsense knowledge, but is on the contrary a particular, local, regional knowledge, a differential knowledge incapable of unanimity and which owes its force only to the harshness with which it is opposed by everything surrounding it - that it is through the re-appearance of this knowledge, of these local popular knowledges, these disqualified knowledges, that criticism performs its work. (Foucault 1980: 82)

Where better to find the subjugated knowledges of a nation or a religion than amongst its protesters, terrorists and dissidents? Femen members counter-performing powerful social taboos against women's bodily autonomy were considered so radical that people described them as both mentally ill and delinquent. Their life experiences created a need to express themselves this way, and many observers with different life experiences were unable to relate to the subjugated knowledges of these "poor but sexy" women and their particular circumstances.[279] These 'disqualified' women operationalized taboo-breaking as a way to claim power.

Healthy identity formation is important both for the individual, and for the collective. The classical twentieth century identities of nationalism, race, gender, and religion are shifting in a digitally connected age. These categories no longer satisfy the needs of contemporary people, who crave new frameworks of self-definition and relationship with one another and the world we live in. The fallout is social unrest and instability; it will be interesting to see what all of this eschatological angst produces in the coming years.

Oksana Shachko painting, by Gleb Garanich.

Femen activist Oksana Shachko sits on a train to the city, contemplating the future. She says:

I'm not prepared to accept society as it is and the rules it imposes on us. I am prepared to fight to the bitter end even though I know that it won't lead to huge changes in my generation. I know that it's a start, and we are part of a long tradition of people who have fought and protested… There have been so many beautiful grand ideas which aimed to liberate the people and help them realize their ambitions. In the end, capitalism corrupted a lot of these ideas so now we see them in a distorted light and not as they really are. But I think our organization, our ideology, our outlook on the world will not crack under that pressure.

(Je Suis Femen 2014: 1:25:05)

CONCLUDING STATEMENT

  Oksana Shachko, the girl from a small town in Ukraine who once wanted to become a nun, traveled to the famous city of Paris to participate in a Free Amina demonstration. While in the city, she visited museums, marvelling at the paintings featuring breasty women carrying banners above armies, muses of the French Revolution, beside angels in heaven and Mary, mother of God, also topless.[280] These beautiful figures of cultural mythos were all sources of inspiration for her art and activism, undivided by categories of 'sacred' and 'profane'.

  When we see these brazen women in colourful editorials in the international news, standing tall, waving banners held high, beautifully and outrageously nude, their bodies emblazoned with shocking messages, sometimes it is difficult to imagine their journeys to that place. The smiling, nature-loving youths linking arms and putting their bodies between the trees in Gezi Park and city bulldozers did not spend their lives planning their martyrdom for environmentalism; a series of events and circumstances called life took them there. Whether or not we support their causes, and whether or not we support their tactics, the world can benefit from a little solidarity, and a little understanding. I have come to appreciate these earnest people, and getting to know them through my research has helped me to understand that we are all people, and our rights are sacred.

Alexandre Cernec 'edited' the 1878 painting by Félicien Rops, *The Temptation of St. Anthony* to reflect a Femen theme. The tagline of this image on Femen International's Facebook group states that "[n]ous sommes en France, pays laïque depuis plus de 100 ans. Blasphémer est notre droit… [w]e are in France, which have been a secular state for more than 100 years. Blasphemy is our right".
Thanks to Alexandre Cernec for his generous permission to use this image. Explore Cernec's work at www.cernec.fr.

[1] Panayiv, Oleksa. "Gods of Slavic Mythology." *Welcome to Ukraine*. Accessed January 2016.
[2] Lyubitseva, Olga. "Research on the Geography of Religion in Ukraine." *Peregrinus Cracoviensis, vol. 25 no. 3* (2014): 91.
[3] Lyubitseva 2014: 95.
[4] Krushynska, Olena. "Ancient wooden churches in the Land of Zakarpattya." *Welcome to Ukraine*. Accessed January 2016.
[5] Panayiv 2016.
[6] Rybakov, Boris. Moskva. *Le paganisme des anciens slaves* (1982). trans. Lise Gruel Apert 1994. Paris: Presses universitaires de France, 1994: 12.
[7] Rybakov 1982: 397.
[8] Rybakov 1982: 396.
[9] "Under the Protection of Our Lady." *Russian Museum*. Accessed February 2016.
[10] Krushynska 2016.
[11] Rybakov, Boris. "Iazychestvo drevnikh slavia [Old Russian Snake Amulets]." *Palaeoslavica, vol. 14 no. 2* (2006): 36.
[12] Karatnycky, Adrian. "Ukraine's Orange Revolution." *Council on Foreign Relations: Foreign Affairs, vol. 84 no. 2* (2005): 40.
[13] Yanowitz, Jason. "February's Forgotten Vanguard: The Myth of Russia's Spontaneous Revolution." *History: Features. International Socialist Review, no. 75* (2016).
[14] Burdzhalov, Édourd. *Russia's Second Revolution: The February 1917 Uprising in Petrograd*. Indianapolis: Indiana University Press, 1987.
[15] Snyder, Timothy. *Bloodlands: Europe Between Hitler and Stalin*. New York: Basic Books, 2010: 48.
[16] Melnyczuk, Lesa. *Silent Memories, Traumatic Lives: Ukrainian Migrant Refugees in Western Australia*. Welshpool, Australia: Western Australian Museum, 2012: 253.
[17] Snyder 2010.
[18] Snyder 2010: viii.
[19] Zakharov, Yevhen. "History of Dissent in Ukraine." *Virtual Museum of the Dissident Movement in Ukraine*. Ukrainian Helsinki Human Rights Union, 2005.
[20] Vasyl, Markus. *Religion and Nationalism in Soviet Ukraine after 1945*. Cambridge, Massachusetts: Harvard Ukrainian Studies Fund, 1985.
[21] Zakharov 2005.
[22] Ivakhiv, Adrian. "In Search of Deeper Identities: Neopaganism and 'Native Faith' in Contemporary Ukraine." *Nova Religio: The Journal of Alternative and Emergent Religions, vol. 8 no. 3*. University of California Press, 2005: 16.
[23] Hanovs, Deniss, and Valdis Tēraudkalns. *Ultimate Freedom - No Choice: The Culture of Authoritarianism in Latvia from 1934-1940*. Leiden, Netherlands: Brill Publishing, 2013: 66.
[24] Batalden, Stephen K. and Sandra L. Batalden. *The Newly Independent States of Eurasia: Handbook of Former Soviet Republics*. Phoenix, Arizona: The Oryx Press, 1997: 146.
[25] Ivakhiv 2005: 10.
[26] Rudnytsky, Ivan L. "The Political Thought of Soviet Ukrainian Dissidents." *Essays in Modern Ukrainian History*. 1987.
[27] Monaghan, Patricia. *Goddesses in World Culture, Volume 1: Asia and Africa*. Santa Barbara: Praeger, 2011: 199.
[28] Swatos, William H. Jr. *Politics and Religion in Central and Eastern Europe: Traditions and Transitions*. Westport, Connecticut: Greenwood Publishing Group Inc., 1994: 25.
[29] Wawrzonek, Michal. *Religion and Politics in Ukraine: The Orthodox and Greek Catholic Churches as Elements of Ukraine's Political System*. Newcastle-Upon-Tyne: Cambridge Scholars Publishing, 2014: 160.
[30] Karatnycky, Adrian. "Ukraine's Orange Revolution." *Council on Foreign Relations: Foreign Affairs, vol. 84 no. 2* (2005): 39.

[31] Wawrzonek 2014: 173.
[32] Karatnycky 2005: 37.
[33] Karatnycky 2005: 43-44.
[34] Wawrzonek 2014: 191.
[35] Tayler, Jeffrey. "Topless Jihad: Why Femen Is Right: The radical feminist group has ignited human-rights debates we need to have." *The Atlantic*. May 1 2013.
[36] Charkiewcz, Ewa. "The Impact of the Crisis on Women in Eastern Europe." *Committee for the Abolition of Third World Debt*. 2010.
[37] *Je Suis Femen*. Director Alain Margot. Caravel Production, 2014. Film.
[38] *Je Suis Femen*, 2014: 31:05.
[39] Kishkovsky, Sophia. "Ukrainian Court Fines Feminist Protesters." *New York Times*. July 28 2013.
[40] Kishkovsky 2013.
[41] The Observers. "How they protest prostitution in Ukraine." *France 24*. August 28 2009.
[42] Trefle, Céline. "FEMEN, the feminists turning the oppressed woman's body back against the oppressors." *BlaqSwans*. September 2 2013.
[43] Trefle 2013.
[44] Tayler 2013.
[45] Gray, Carmen. "Femen firebrand Inna Shevchenko speaks: The Ukrainian activist on how she learned to stop worrying and fight the power." *Dazed & Confused Magazine*. February 2014.
[46] *Femen - Sextremism in Paris* 2013: 16:15.
[47] Cochrane, Kira. "Rise of the naked female warriors." *The Guardian*. March 20 2013.
[48] Tayler 2013.
[49] Agence France-Presse 2011.
[50] *Je Suis Femen* 2014: 41:48.
[51] Phillips, Graham. "The tragic case of Ukraine's Oksana Makar draws to a close: Pressure is on the Mykolaiv court to reach a verdict that will show progress." *New Statesman*. October 30 2012.
[52] Phillips 2012.
[53] *Je Suis Femen* 2014: 2:57.
[54] *Je Suis Femen* 2014: 4:19.
[55] Solonyna, Yevhen. Inna Kuznetsova. "Ukrainian Villagers Say Alleged Police-Rape Case Just Tip Of Iceberg." *Europe Radio Liberty*. July 9 2013.
[56] Maccaud, Jeremy and Genaro Bardy. "Anna Hutsol 'The Femen have shown the way' of Maidan." 2014. [Naro]Minded. Accessed April 2 2016.
[57] Solonyna and Kuznetsova 2013.
[58] *Femen - Sextremism in Paris*, 2013: 1:25-5:05.
[59] Gray 2014.
[60] Gray, Carmen. "Femen firebrand Inna Shevchenko speaks: The Ukrainian activist on how she learned to stop worrying and fight the power." *Dazed & Confused Magazine*. February 2014.
[61] Shevchenko, Inna. "Charlie Hebdo Paris massacre: Everyone says 'Je Suis Charlie' now, but where were they when my friends were alive?" *International Business Times*. January 12 2015.
[62] Shevchenko 2015.
[63] Trefle, Céline. "FEMEN, the feminists turning the oppressed woman's body back against the oppressors." *BlaqSwans*. September 2 2013.
[64] Adamson, Danial Silas. "100 Women 2015: Return of a topless rebel." *BBC World Service*. November 28 2015.
[65] Adamson 2015.
[66] Sboui, Mounir. "Tunisia: Amina's father proud of her, shares her views." *ANSAmed*. June 6 2013.

67 Crick, Matthew. *Power, Surveillance, and Culture in YouTube™'s Digital Sphere.* Hershey, Pennsylvania: IGI Global Publishing, 2016: 126.
68 *Je Suis Femen*, 2014: 36:50.
69 Namazie, Maryam. "Why An International Day to Defend Amina?" *Maryam Namazie, Nothing is Sacred: Freethought Blogs*. April 2 2013.
70 *Femen - Sextremism in Paris*, 2013: 7:55.
71 Nasreen, Taslima. "Crazy Catholics!" *No Country For Women: Freethoughblogs.com*. November 20 2012.
72 Ratzinger, Joseph. "Congregation for the Doctrine of the Faith: Letter to the Bishop of the Catholic Church on the Pastoral Care of Homosexual Persons." *Given At Rome*, October 1 1986.
73 Editors Online. ""In gay we trust" …Topless women celebrate Pope's resignation in Paris." *Osundefender.org*. February 13 2013.
74 'Christian Messenger.' *Anders Breivik: His Life and Mission*. Online: self-published, 2012: 205.
75 Messenger 2012: 151.
76 Messenger 2012: 179.
77 Messenger 2012.
78 *Femen - Sextremism in Paris,* 2013: 11:30.
79 *Je Suis Femen*, 2014: 40:19.
80 *Femen - Sextremism in Paris*, 2013: 14:00.
81 *Je Suis Femen*, 2014: 1:25:05.
82 *Winter On Fire: Ukraine's Fight For Freedom*. Director Evgeny Afineevsky. Tolmor Production, 2014: 3:05.
83 *Winter On Fire*, 2014: 4:02.
84 *Winter On Fire*, 2014: 4:19.
85 *Winter On Fire*, 2014: 5:20.
86 *Winter On Fire*, 2014: 5:28.
87 *Winter On Fire*, 2014: 6:48.
88 *Winter On Fire*, 2014: 10:10.
89 *Winter On Fire*, 2014: 12:55.
90 *Winter On Fire*, 2014: 16:37.
91 *Winter On Fire*, 2014: 36:24.
92 Snyder, Timothy. Tatiana Zhurzhenko. "Diaries and memoirs of the Maidan: Ukraine from November 2013 to February 2014." *Eurozine.com*. June 27 2014.
93 *Winter On Fire*, 2014: 18:04.
94 *Je Suis Femen* 2014: 11:04.
95 Now World News. "FEMEN urinates on Ukrainian president." *YouTube.com*. December 1 2013.
96 Metzel, Mikhail. "Femen Protest Photos." *Cryptome*. January 29 2012.
97 Bidder, Benjamin. "Kiev's Topless Protestors: 'The Entire Ukraine Is a Brothel'." *Spiegel Online International.* May 5 2011.
98 *Je Suis Femen*, 2014: 45:30.
99 Girgenty, Guido. "Ukrainians bring down Yanukovych regime, 2013-2014." *Global Nonviolent Action Database*. George Lakey, ed. April 21 2014.
100 Shore, Marci. "Reading Tony Judt in Wartime Ukraine." *New Yorker*. August 11 2015.
101 *Winter On Fire*, 2014: 29:48.
102 *Winter On Fire*, 2014: 39:00.
103 *Winter On Fire*, 2014: 31:18.
104 Greener, Sue, and Asher Rospigliosi. "The Proceedings of the European Conference on Social Media." *University of Brighton, 10-11 July 2014*. Brighton: Academic Conferences and Publishing Limited, 2014: 446.
105 Markovic, Olesia. "Ukraine: A New Island of Dictatorship in Europe." *Politics: Al Jazeera*. January 20 2014.

[106] *Winter On Fire* 2014: 41:39.
[107] Girgenty 2014.
[108] Girgenty 2014.
[109] *Winter On Fire*, 2014: 38:21.
[110] *Winter On Fire*, 2014: 39:06.
[111] *Winter On Fire*, 2014: 39:10.
[112] Charkiewcz, Ewa. "The Impact of the Crisis on Women in Eastern Europe." *Committee for the Abolition of Third World Debt.* 2010.
[113] Snyder, Timothy. Tatiana Zhurzhenko. "Diaries and memoirs of the Maidan: Ukraine from November 2013 to February 2014." *Eurozine.com*. June 27 2014.
[114] Snyder and Zhurzhenko 2014.
[115] *Winter On Fire*, 2014: 1:09:40.
[116] *Winter On Fire*, 2014: 45:25.
[117] Girgenty 2014.
[118] *Winter On Fire*, 2014: 1:04:30.
[119] Snyder and Zhurzhenko 2014.
[120] Snyder and Zhurzhenko 2014.
[121] Girgenty 2014.
[122] *Winter On Fire*, 2014: 1:25:49.
[123] *Winter On Fire*, 2014: 1:25:55.
[124] Zmicier, Lukashuk. "Femen: Our War is Somewhat Different From Maidan." *Euroradio*. December 12 2014.
[125] Pomerantsev, Peter. "The Revolution of Dignity." *Adbusters*. June 26 2015.
[126] "Putin reveals secrets of Russia's Crimea takeover plot." *BBC News*. March 9 2015. Retrieve at http://www.bbc.com/news/world-europe-31796226.
[127] *Je Suis Femen* 2014.
[128] Cochrane, Kira. "Rise of the naked female warriors." *The Guardian*. March 20 2013.
[129] Murphy, Meghan. "There is a wrong way to do feminism. And Femen is doing it wrong." Feminist Current. Oct 31 2012.
[130] goliathrk. "First topless protest in an Islamic state leads to 3 arrests." *Reddit: World News*. April 11 2013.
[131] Murphy 2012.
[132] Aitkenhead, Decca. "Femen Leader Inna Shevchenko: 'I'm For Any Form of Feminism'." *The Guardian*. November 8 2013.
[133] Cochrane 2013.
[134] Mulvey, Laura. "Visual Pleasure and Narrative Cinema." *Film Theory and Criticism: Introductory Readings.* Leo Braudy and Marshall Cohen, eds. New York: Oxford University Press, 1999: 833-44: 835.
[135] Mulvey 1999: 835.
[136] Mulvey 1999: 835.
[137] Mulvey 1999: 833.
[138] Jones, Reece. "We Spoke to Kitty Green about her FEMEN Documentary 'Ukraine is Not a Brothel'". *Vice News*. June 17 2014.
[139] Drimonis, Toula. "Why as a Feminist I Will Never Identify With Femen." *Head Space*. August 5 2015.
[140] Najumi, Mohadesa. "Op-Ed: Where Femen Has Gone Wrong." *Feminist Wire*. April 7 2013. Retrieve at http://www.thefeministwire.com/2013/04/op-ed-where-femen-have-gone-wrong/.
[141] Mulvey 1999: 834.
[142] Masterson, Orla. "It's FemiNIST not FemiNAZI." *Student Independent News: NUI Galways's Online Student Newspaper.* April 2017.

[143] McCall, Leslie. "The Complexity of Intersectionality." *Signs: Journal of Women in Culture and Society, vol. 30, no. 3*. Chicago: The University of Chicago, 2005.

[145] "Bulletpoint." *The Guardian*. March 2013.
[146] Tayler, Jeffrey. "Topless Jihad: Why Femen Is Right: The radical feminist group has ignited human-rights debates we need to have." *The Atlantic*. May 1 2013.
[147] Smith College 2016.
[148] 'Ilana Alazzeh.' Wikia. Accessed June 1 2016.
[149] Daly, Mary. *Beyond God the Father: Toward a Philosophy of Women's Liberation*. Boston: Beacon Press, 1973: 19
[150] Drimonis 2015.
[151] Frenkel, Sheera. "Femen Is Bringing Its Topless Protest To Bethlehem — What Could Possibly Go Wrong?" *BuzzFeed News*. Dec 3 2013.
[152] Schenk, Christine. "Is religion the biggest problem facing feminism today?" *National Catholic*. March 6 2014.
[153] Schenk 2014.
[154] *Je Suis Femen*, 2014: 22:22.
[155] Matta, Xuan. "Feminists Against Femen." *Facebook.com*. October 20 2013.
[156] Raven, Charlotte. "Femen – the Beauty Fascist Fauminists." *Feminist Times*. Nov 1 2013.
[157] Shore, Marci. "Reading Tony Judt in Wartime Ukraine." *New Yorker*. August 11 2015.
[158] *Femen - Sextremism in Paris*, 2013: 4:28.
[159] Berlatsky, Noah. "Beyoncé Doesn't Perform for the Male Gaze." *Pacific Standard*. October 7 2014.
[160] Berlatsky 2014.
[161] Hennessy, Angela. "Meet the Topless Protester Who Stormed Parliament Hill Last Week." *Vice News*. May 14 2014.
[162] *Eye For Protest: From Body to Banner*. December 10 2015.
[163] Haidar, Ensaf. "Raif Badawi: Humanitarian, Freethinker, Writer." *Raif Badawi Foundation*. Accessed June 2016.
[164] Haidar 2016.
[165] Haidar 2016.
[166] Haidar 2016.
[167] "'I am not a slave': Nude Protester Calls for Solidarity." *Iranwire.com*. April 12 2016.
[168] Iranwire 2016.
[169] Dedorson, Emma Sofia. "She Fights With Breast and Words. Inna's Interview." *Femen Official Blog*. March 29 2016.
[170] Future Quest. "A Summer Experience for Youth." *School of Religion: Queen's University*. Kingston: School of Religion, 2012.
[171] Pollitt, Kathlyn. "Sexism and Religion: Can the Knot be Untied?" *Women in Secularism II Conference*. Washington D.C. March 2013.
[172] Nicolson, Nigel. "Virginia Woolf." *Books: The New York Times on the Web*. 2000.
[173] Gagne, Laura. "Athens, Persia Sparta." *University of Ottawa Lecture*, March 2013.
[174] *300*. Director Zack Snyder. Legendary Studios, 2006. Film.
[175] Robinson, Andrew. "Roland Barthes: The War Against Myth." *An A to Z of Theory. Ceasefire Magazine*. October 2011.
[176] Stone, Merlin. "The Great Goddess." *Heresies: A Feminist Publication on Art and Politics*. New York: Heresies Collective Inc., vol. 2 no. 1 (1978): 365.
[177] Daly 1973.
[178] Goldenberg, Naomi. "Some (Mainly) Very Appreciative Comments on Brent Nongbri's Before Religion." *The Critical Religion Association: Critical Approaches to the Study of Religion*. May 6 2013.
[179] Jakobsen, Janet, Ann Pellegrini. *Secularisms*. Durham: Duke University Press, 2008.

[180] Nongbri, Brent. *Before Religion: The History of a Modern Concept*. New Haven, United States: Yale University Press, 2013.
[181] Nawaz, Maajid. "I'm a Muslim reformer who is being smeared as an 'anti-Muslim extremist' by angry white liberals." *Voices: The Independent*.
[182] Hidayatullah, Aysha. *Feminist Edges of the Qur'an*. Oxford: Oxford University Press, 2014: 45.
[183] Hassan 1979.
[184] Hidayatullah 2014: 66.
[185] Hidayatullah 2014: 110.
[186] Gross, Rita M. *Feminism and Religion: An Introduction*. Boston: Beacon Press, 1996: 72.
[187] Bruns, J. Edgar. *God As Woman, Woman As God*. New York: Paulist Press, 1973: 74.
[188] Bruns 1973: 74.
[189] Daly 1973: 159.
[190] Ruether, Rosemary. *Liberation Theology: Human Hope Confronts Christian History and American Power*. New York: Paulist Press, 1972: 164.
[191] Gadon, Elinor. *The Once and Future Goddess: A Sweeping Visual Chronicle of the Sacred Female and Her Re-emergence in the Cult*. New York: HarperCollins, 1989: xv.
[192] Daly 1973: 11.
[193] Christ in Christ, Carol P. and Judith Plaskow. *Womanspirit Rising: A Feminist Reader in Religion*. San Francisco: Harper and Row, 1979: 364.
[194] de Beauvoir, Simone, trans. H. M. Parshley. *The Second Sex*. New York: Bantam Books, 1952: 267.
[195] Daly, Mary. *Gyn/ecology: The Metaethics of Radical Feminism*. Boston: Beacon Press, 1978: 56.
[196] Christ in Christ and Plaskow 1979: 368.
[197] Christ in Christ and Plaskow 1979: 365.
[198] Christ in Christ and Plaskow 1979: 369.
[199] Christ in Christ and Plaskow 1979: 371.
[200] Goldenberg, Naomi. "What is this Slouching Toward Bethlehem?: Is it a New Feminist Defense of Religion?" Presented at *Feminisms Beyond the Secular: Epistemologies and Politics for the 21st Century*, Lehigh University, Bethlehem Pennsylvania. March 22 2016.
[201] Varol, Onur, Emilio Ferrara, Christine L. Ogan, Filippo Menczer, and Alessandro Flammini. "Evolution of Online User Behavior During a Social Upheaval." *arXiv.org*. Center for Complex Networks and Systems Research School of Informatics and Computing, Indiana University, Bloomington, USA. 2014: 3.
[202] de Bellaigue, Christopher. "Turkey: 'Surreal, Menacing...Pompous'". *New York Review of Books*. December 19 2013.
[203] Watt, Montgomery. *The Cambridge History of Islam*. Cambridge: Cambridge University Press, 1970: 36.
[204] Latif, Iqbal. "How does one assume the title of Caliph?" March 17 2015.
[205] Pitman, Paul M. "The Rise of the Turks and the Ottoman Empire." in *Turkey: A Country Study*. Helen Chapin Metz, ed. Washington, DC: Federal Research Division of the Library of Congress, 1987.
[206] Pitman 1987.
[207] Pitman 1987.
[208] Alkhateeb, Firas. *Lost Islamic History: Reclaiming Muslim Civilisation from the Past*. London: Hurst & Company, 2014: 162.
[209] Vogt, Kari, Lena Larsen, Christian Moe. *New Directions in Islamic Thought: Exploring Reform and Muslim Tradition*. London: I. B. Tauris & Co. Ltd., 2009.
[210] Mango, Andrew. *Atatürk*. London: John Murray Publishers, 1999: 11.
[211] "Atatürk, Mustafa Kemal." *Ana Britannica Volume 2: Ami – Avr*. London: Funk & Wagnalls, 1987: 490.
[212] Mango, Andrew. Atatürk. London: John Murray Publishers, 1999: 1.
[213] Al-Rasheed, Kersten, and Shterin (2012: 46)

[214] Alkhateeb 2014.
[215] Mango 1999.
[216] Al-Rasheed, Madawi, Carool Kersten, and Marat Shterin, eds. *Demystifying the Caliphate: Historical Memory and Contemporary Contexts.* Oxford: Oxford University Press, 2015: 44.
[217] Vogt, Larsen, and Moe 2009.
[218] Nas, Tevfik F. *Economics and Politics of Turkish Liberalization.* Bethlehem, Pennsylvania: Lehigh University Press, 1992: 12.
[219] Mango 1999: 10.
[220] Ibrahim, Osman Rifat. "AKP and the great neo-Ottoman travesty." *Al Jazeera.* May 23 2014.
[221] Mango 1999.
[222] Mango 1999: 303.
[223] Ahmed, Leila. *A Quiet Revolution: The Veil's Resurgence, from the Middle East to America.* New Haven: Yale University Press, 2011: 68.
[224] Bulliet, Richard W. "Are the Turkish Leader Erdogan's claims of terrorist coup plotting to be believed?" *fgulen.com.* August 15 2016.
[225] *Love is a Verb.* Directors Terry Spencer Hesser and Stephan Mazurek. Global Vision Productions, 2014. Film.
[226] Bulliet 2016.
[227] Karaağaç, Barış. "Turkey in Crisis: Understanding the Erdogan/ Gulen Split." *The Real News Network.* January 13 2014.
[228] Karaağaç 2014.
[229] "Islamic scholar Gülen criticizes Turkish gov't response to Gezi protests." *Hürriyet Daily News.* March 20 2014.
[230] Agence France-Presse in Ankara. "Turkish court rejects Erdoğan's ban on his enemy's schools." *The Guardian.* July 14 2015.
[231] Karaağaç 2014.
[232] Arango, Tim, Ceylan Yeginsu. "Turkey to Release Tens of Thousands of Prisoners to Make Room for Coup Suspects." *New York Times.* August 17 2016.
[233] Agence France-Presse. "Turkey police fire rubber bullets at banned Gay Pride parade." *The Telegraph.* June 27 2016.
[234] "Turkey: Istanbul gay pride march banned over 'security' concern." *BBC.* June 17 2016.
[235] Agence France-Presse. "Turkey police fire rubber bullets at banned Gay Pride parade." *The Telegraph.* June 27 2016.
[236] Varol, Ferrara, Ogan et al. 2014: 1.
[237] Varol, Ferrara, Ogan et al. 2014: 1.
[238] Durkheim, Emile. *The Elementary Forms of the Religious Life* (1912). Trans. Karen E. Fields. New York: The Free Press, 1995: 208, 225.
[239] Taylor, Charles. *A Secular Age.* Cambridge: Harvard University Press, 2007: 5.
[240] McGuire, Meredith B. *Lived Religion: Faith and Practice in Everyday Life.* New York: Oxford University Press, 2008.
[241] Stack, Trevor, Naomi Goldenberg, Timothy Fitzgerald. *Religion as a Category of Governance and Sovereignty: Supplements to Method & Theory in the Study of Religion.* Leiden, Netherlands: Brill Publishing, 2015.
[242] Goldenberg, Naomi. "There is No Religion in the Bible." Unpublished manuscript. 2016b.
[243] Goldenberg 2016b.
[244] Owen, Suzanne and Teemu Tara. "The Category of 'Religion' in Public Classification: Charity Registration of The Druid Network in England and Wales." In *Religion as a Category of Governance and Sovereignty.* Trevor Stack, Naomi Goldenberg, and Timothy Fitzgerald, eds. Leiden, Netherlands: Brill Publishing, 2015: 5.
[245] Fitzgerald, Timothy. *Ideology of Religious Studies.* Oxford: Oxford University Press, 2005: 53.

[246] Goldenberg, Naomi. "The Category of Religion in the Technology of Governance: An Argument for Understanding Religions as Vestigial States." In *Religion as a Category of Governance and Sovereignty*. Trevor Stack, Naomi Goldenberg and Timothy Fitzgerald, eds. Leiden, Netherlands: Brill Publishing, 2015: 22-23.
[247] Jeffreys, Sheila. *Man's Dominion: The Rise of Religion and the Eclipse of Women's Rights*. Wiltshire: Routledge, 2012.
[248] Adamson, Danial Silas. "100 Women 2015: Return of a topless rebel." *BBC World Service*. November 28 2015.
[249] Namazie, Maryam. "Why An International Day to Defend Amina?" *Maryam Namazie, Nothing is Sacred: Freethought Blogs*. April 2 2013.
[250] "How the Lateran Treaty made the Catholic Church into a state." *Concordat Watch*. Accessed July 24 2016
[251] Concordat 2016.
[252] Juergensmeyer, Mark, Dinah Griego, and John Soboslai. *God in the Tumult of the Global Square: Religion in Global Civil Society.* California: University of California Press, 2015: 25.
[253] Mango 1999: 4.
[254] Diamond, James S. "The Post-secular: A Jewish Perspective." *Cross Currents: Association for Religion & Intellectual Life, vol. 53 no. 4* (Winter 2004).
[255] "Adana Çiftçileriyle Konuşma."March 16 1923, quoted in *The Turkish Times*, December 1 1995.
[256] MacKinnon, Mark. "How Vladimir Putin Helped Resurrect the Russian Orthodox Church." *The Globe and Mail*. January 15 2014.
[257] MacKinnon 2014.
[258] Kolokoltsev, Andrei. "Crimea children's theatre forced to shut for 'promoting western propaganda: Popular drama school complains of harassment from local officials who accused them of championing Ukrainian nationalism." *The Guardian: New East Network*. January 6 2016.
[259] Kolokoltsev 2016.
[260] Kolokoltsev 2016.
[261] Kolokoltsev 2016.
[262] *Winter on Fire* 1:32:54.
[263] Aune, Kristin. "Why Feminists Are Less Religious." *The Guardian*. March 29 2011.
[264] Aune 2011.
[265] Cimino, Richard. "Secular Rituals and Atheist Solidarity". *Atheist Identities Workshop: University of Ottawa*. November 22-24 2012.
[266] Young, Iris Marion. "Structural Injustice and the Politics of Difference," paper for the *AHRC Centre for Law, Gender, and Sexuality Intersectionality Workshop*. United Kingdom: Keele University, 2005: 28.
[267] Betlemidze, Mariam. "Mediatized Controversies of Feminist Protest: FEMEN and Bodies as Affective Events." *Women's Studies in Communication, vol. 38 no. 4* (2015): 374-379: 377.
[268] Foucault, Michel. *Power/Knowledge: Selected Interviews and Other Writings 1972-1977*. Trans. C. Gordon. New York: Pantheon Books, 1980: 82.
[269] Smith, Keri E. Iyall. Patricia Leavy. *Hybrid Identities: Theoretical and Empirical Examinations*. Leiden, Netherlands: Brill Publishing, 2008.
[270] Puar, Jasbir. *Terrorist Assemblages: Homonationalism in Queer Times*. Durham, United States: Duke University Press, 2007: 342.
[271] Femen.org 2016.
[272] Miller, Monica. Comments on Cameron Montgomery's presentation "Between Sovereignties: Women between Church and State in Ukraine" at *Feminisms Beyond the Secular: Emerging Epistemologies and Politics in the 21st Century,* Lehigh University, Bethlehem, PA. March 21-23 2016.
[273] Birnbaum, Maria. unpublished thesis. "Becoming Recognizable: Postcolonial Independence and the Reification of Religion." *European University Institute, Department of Social and Political Science*. Florence: 2015: 188.
[274] Arendt, Hannah. *On Violence*. New York: Harcourt, Brace and World, 1970: 83-90.

[275] Pyzik, Agata. *Poor But Sexy: Culture Clashes in Europe East and West*. Croydon, England: John Hunt Publishing, 2014.
[276] Snyder, Timothy. Tatiana Zhurzhenko. "Diaries and memoirs of the Maidan: Ukraine from November 2013 to February 2014." *Eurozine.com*. June 27 2014.
[277] *Femen - Sextremism in Paris* 2013: 16:15.
[278] Hanisch, Carol. "The Personal Is Political." *Notes from the Second Year: Women's Liberation*. New York: New York Radical Women, 1970.
[279] Pyzik 2014: 1.
[280] *Je Suis Femen* 2014: 37:41.

IMAGE CREDITS

Cover: Remixed by Studio Dreamshare, www.studiodreamshare.com. Samples courtesy of The Riahi Brothers, Arash T. Riahi, Arman T. Riahi, at www.everyday rebellion.net, the glorious *vinok* crown handmade by Nataliya Martynets at Etsy shop **NeedleworkUkraine**, and FEMEN Women's Movement's Flickr account for the image "Azarov pursued by Bloody Tits 'Krovosisi'." Special thanks to the incredible Moujan Taher for her picture "I'd rather be a rebel not a slave." **P8:** Yaroslav Debelyi. "100 Days." *Flickr*. June 3 2010. **P12:** Courtesy of the State Russian Museum. Retrieve at http://www.svyatayarus.ru/data/archeology/20_zmeevik/index.php?lang=en. **P13: Top:** Courtesy of the State Russian Museum. Retrieve at http://www.svyatayarus.ru/data/archeology/21_zmeevik/index.php?lang=en. **Bottom:** Courtesy of the State Historical Museum. Retrieve at http://www.svyatayarus.ru/data/ archeology/19_zmeevik/index.php?lang=en **P14: Left:** "Ukrainian Lullaby." Artist not named. Retrieve at slavput.ru. **Right:** "Mokosh Embroidery." Creator not named. Retrieve at kpecmuk.ru. **P15:** Martiskainen, Marppa. "Classic Embroidery in Karelia." *Elder Mountain Dreaming*. 1920s. Retrieve at eldermountaindreaming.com. **P16: Left:** Razsvit, Kiev, Ukraine. "Postcard printed in 1916." *Wikimedia Commons*. 1916. **Right:** Paris, Joseph. "Alexandra Shevchenko." *Wikimedia Commons*. March 31 2012. **P17:** "The Majority Language by City, Town, and Village Councils." *Ukrainian Census*. 2001. **P20:** Marchenko, Nina. "The Road of Sorrow." 2000. Attempts made in 2016 and 2017 to get permission from the gallery, no response. Many thanks to Marchenko for this incredible work. **P25:** Panayiv, Oleksa. "Masnytsya." *Welcome to Ukraine*. Retrieve at http://www.wumag.kiev.ua/-index2.php?param=pgs20092/50. **P26:** "Ancient Wooden Churches." Artist not named. Retrieve at slavput.ru. **P32:** Kishkovsky, Sophia. "Ukrainian Court Fines Feminist Protesters." *New York Times*. July 28 2013. Retrieve at http://www.nytimes.com/2013/07/29/world/ europe/ukrainian-court-fines-feministprotesters.html?_r=1. **P33:** Хамам - бой!. "Alexandra Shevchenko and Oles Buzina." *Wikimedia Commons*. 21 March 2009. **P34:** Хамам - бой!. "Alexandra Shevchenko and Oles Buzina." *Wikimedia Commons*. 21 March 2009. **P35:** The Observers. "How they protest prostitution in Ukraine." *France 24*. August 28 2009. Retrieve at http://observers.france24.com/en/20090828-how-they-protest-prostitution-ukraine-femen-sex-tourism. **P36:** Treti Pivni. "A wedding photo from the Carpathian mountains, circa 1930s." *Instagram: @third_roosters*. Posted 2016. 1930s. **P37:** Treti Pivni. "Beautiful Hutsul bridal headdress from the Carpathian village of Kornych, West Ucraine, made by copying old photographs." *Instagram: @third_roosters*. July 2016. **P38:** FEMEN Women's Movement. "Inna Shevchenko." *Wikimedia Commons*. July 15 2013. **P39:** FEMEN.org. "Femen Logo." Retrieve at Femen.org. **P40: Top:** Photo courtesy of Camilla Lobo. 2013. **Bottom:** Photo courtesy of Jacob Khrist. 2014. **P41:** Hutsol, Anna. "Anna Hutsol." Retrieve at Femen.org. **P42:** Photo generously shared by Alexander Nemenov. **P42:** "Quatre militantes de Femen anti-Poutine interpellées à Bruxelles." *La capitale*. 21 December 2012. Retrieve at http://www.lacapitale.be/628141/article/regions/bruxelles/actualite/2012-12-21/quatre-militantes-de-femen-anti-poutine-interpellees-a-bruxelles-photos. **P43:** Toxaby. "Femen in Minsk, Belarus." *Live Journal*. 2011. Retrieve at http://toxaby.livejournal.com/540303.html. **P45:** Phillips, Graham. "The tragic case of Ukraine's Oksana Makar draws to a close: Pressure is on the Mykolaiv court to reach a verdict that will show progress." *NewStatesman*. October 30 2012. Retrieve at http://www.newstatesman.com/world-affairs/2012/10/tragic-case-ukraines-oksana-makar-draws-close. **P45:** Katrandjian, Olivia. "Topless Women Protest Rampant Sex Trade and Violence Against Women in Ukraine." *ABC News*. March 18 2012. Retrieve at http://abcnews.go.com/International/topless-women-protest-rampant-sex-trade-ukraine/story?id=15468367. **P46: Left:** "Irina Krashkova refused counsel." *Donbass.UA*. October 30 2013. Retrieve at http://donbass.ua/news/ukraine/2013/10/30/progulivajuschaja-zasedanija-suda-krashkova-otkazalas-ot-advokata.html. **Right:** Solonyna, Yevhen. Inna Kuznetsova. "Ukrainian Villagers Say Alleged Police-Rape Case Just Tip Of Iceberg." *Europe Radio Liberty*. July 9 2013. Retrieve at http://www.rferl.org/content/ukraine-police-rape-case/25041179.html. **P48:** "Femen: violente altercation avec les manifestants contre le mariage gay."

Cercle de Vie. 20 November 2012. Retrieve online at http://cercledesconnaissances.blogspot.ca/2012/11/femen-violente-altercation-avec-les.html. **P49: Top:** "Femen: violente altercation avec les manifestants contre le mariage gay." *Cercle de Vie.* 20 November 2012. Retrieve online at http://cercledesconnaissances.blogspot.ca/2012/11/femen-violente-altercation-avec-les.html. **Bottom:** "Topless Women Celebrate Pope's Resignation." *Nigeria Today*. February 13 2013. Retrieve at http://www.nigeriatoday-ed234.com/2013/02/topless-women-celebrate-his-resignation.html. **P51:** "Amnesty Calls for Release of Activist." *Trumpet Media Group*. July 31 2013. Retrieve at http://trumpetmedia group.com/africa/tunisia/amnesty-calls-for-release-of-activist/. **P54:** Chamseddine, Roqayah. "'FEMEN' and the suppression of native voices." *Mondoweiss.* April 6 2013. Retrieve at http://mondoweiss.net/2013/04/suppression-native-voices/. **P55:** Shevchenko, Inna. "Memen in Morocco :) #Femen #FemenFrance #FemenTunisia." *Twitter: @femeninna*. June 29 2013. **P57:** Starbride. "Basta Berlusconi!" *Voices in the Wind: sweetnet.org.* February 25 2013. Retrieve at https://sweetnet.org/tag/femen/. **P60:** Montgomery, Cameron. "Antisemitism on the Rise in Europe: Some Photos." *Willful and Wayward*. March 4 2015. Retrieve at https://willfulandwayward.wordpress.com/tag/swastika/. **P62:** nasdaf. "Before & After - Kiev's Independence Square – Ukraine." *Reddit.* 2014. Retrieve at https://www.reddit.com/r/pics/comments/1ydjc9/before_after_kievs_independence_square_ukraine/. **P71:** Photo courtesy of Anna Hutsol. Personal correspondence. **P72:** Paris, Joseph. "Femen Against Euro 2012." *Wikimedia Commons*. June 8 2012. **P74:** Vocativ. "'Breasts as Bombs' - FEMEN Says They'll Turn to Guns if Necessary." *Youtube.com*. January 29 2013. Retrieve at https://www.youtube.com/watch?v=ZJpavnxbGJI. **P79:** Jordystories. "It's FemiNIST not FemiNAZI." *Redbubble*. (https://wanelo.co/ search? query=jordystories. **P80:** Mock, Janet. "Beyonce is a FEMINIST. In case y'all forgot. #BowDown #BeyMA." *Twitter: Janet Mock*. Retrieve at https://twitter.com/janetmock/status/503741635684237312?lang=en. **P89:** FEMEN Women's Movement. "Azarov pursued by Bloody Tits 'Krovosisi'." *Flickr.* June 5 2010. **P90:** @femenmovement. "Victoria Sendón." *Facebook.com.* 2014. Retrieve at www.Facebook.com/femenmovement. **P91: Top:** "Cinco activistas de Femen interrumpen la marcha 'Por la vida' en el centro de Madrid." *20 Minutos: Madrid*. March 23 2014. Retrieve at http://www.20minutos.es/ noticia/2093084/0/cinco-activistas-femen/interrumpen/marcha-vida/. **Bottom:** @femenmovement. "Sweden." *Facebook.com*. 2014. Retrieve at www.Facebook.com/femenmovement. **P92:** Paris, Joseph. "Femen à Paris 31 mars 2012." *Wikimedia Commons*. March 31 2012. **P93:** @FEMENCanada. "Décrucifions nous." *Facebook.com*. 2013. Retrieve at www.facebook.com/FEMENCanada. **P94: Top:** @FEMENCanada. "Dieu est féministe." *Facebook.com*. 2014. Retrieve at www.facebook.com/FEMENCanada. **Bottom:** @FEMENCanada. "Neda Topaloski." Facebook.com. 2014. Retrieve at www.facebook.com/FEMENCanada. **P96:** "Letter of Can Dündar." *Eye For Protest: From Body to Banner.* December 10 2015. Retrieve at http://eye4protest.blogspot.ca/2015/12/femen-turkey.html?view=sidebar. **P97:** "Femen Turkey." *Eye For Protest: From Body to Banner.* December 10 2015. Retrieve at http://eye4protest.blog-spot.ca/2015/12/femen-turkey.html?view=sidebar. **P98:** "Canadian Solidarity." *Eye For Protest: From Body to Banner.* December 10 2015. Retrieve at http://eye4protest.blogspot.ca/2015/12/femen-turkey.html?view=sidebar. **P99:** "Shevchenko supporting imprisoned Turkish journalists." *Eye For Protest: From Body to Banner.* December 10 2015. Retrieve at http://eye4protest.blogspot.ca/2015/12/femen-turkey.html?view= sidebar. **P101:** Iranian artist Moujan Taher. Personal correspondence 2017. **P103:** Western Fiasco. "Bare Breasts, a Femen Hymn." *Belong,* Independent, 2013. Retrieve at https://www.facebook.com/westernfiasco/. **P104:** Image courtesy of Anna Hutsol. **P107:** @femenmovement. "Sweden." Facebook.com. 2013. Retrieve at www.Facebook.com/femenmovement. **P119:** Lubunya. "Türkçe: XXII. İstanbul Onur Haftası etkinliklerinde kapsamında geleneksel olarak yapılan İstanbul Onur Yürüyüşü'nden görünüm." *Wikimedia Commons*. July 15 2014. **P121:** Katie J. M. Baker. "Brutally Tear-Gassed 'Woman in Red' Is Symbol of Turkey's Occupy Gezi." *Jezebel.* June 4 2013. Retrieve online at http://jezebel.com/brutally-tear-gassed-woman-in-red-is-symbol-of-turkey-511187628. **P122: Top:** Ari Alpert. *Lady in Red*. Stencil. September 1 2013. Retrieve online at http://triangleproject.blogspot.ca/2013/09/the-triangle-project-part-10-istanbul.html. **Bottom:** Christiane Gruber (photo). *Lady in Red*. Anonymous stencil. 4 June 2013.

Retrieve at http://jadaliyya1.rssing.com/chan-6965379/all_p59.html. **P123: Top:** Turgut, Pelin. "Live from 'Occupied' Gezi Park: In Istanbul, a New Turkish Protest Movement Is Born." *Time*. June 5 2013. Retrieve at http://world.time.com/2013/06/05/live-from-occupied-gezi-park-in-istanbul-a-new-turkish-protest-movement-is-born/. **Bottom:** EsraFurtana. "Gezi.. Ne diyim? Güzelsin... #WeAreGezi #direngeziparkı #occupygezi @edihvet." *Twitter: EsraFurtana*. June 8 2013. Retrieve at https://twitter.com/EsraFurtana. **P124: Top:** Turgut, Pelin. "Live from 'Occupied' Gezi Park: In Istanbul, a New Turkish Protest Movement Is Born." *Time*. June 5 2013. Retrieve at http://world.time.com/2013/06/05/live-from-occupied-gezi-park-in-istanbul-a-new-turkish-protest-movement-is-born/. **Bottom:** Sevim, Emine Gozde. From the series *Homeland Delirium*, 2013, on Ilariagenovesio. "Gezi Park Art and Activism in Turkey: #OccupyGezi Movement Through the Eyes of Contemporary Turkish Art." *Tumblr.com*. Retrieve at http://ilariagenovesio.tumblr.com/. **P131:** "Bare-breasted Protest of the Prime Minister of Turkey." *The Iranian Online Community in Belgium*. March 31 2014. Retrieve at http://www.iranian.be/news/2014/03/008116.htm. **P136:** Alizex786. (Alyshea Cummins). "@dreamshare supporting the feminist society of Turkey <3." *Instagram: Alize786*. July 15 2016. **P137:** Dreamshare. (Cameron Montgomery). "Excuse me, what are they chanting? "Where is my lover? Here I am." A tear in my eye at Istanbul Pride 2014." *Instagram: Dreamshare*. July 3 2014. Retrieve at https://www.instagram.com/p/p2KiE3Io89/. **P140:** FEMEN.org. "Religion Kills." Retrieve at Femen.org. **P152:** "1000s Pray For Russian Church Mired in Punk Controversy." *CTV News*. April 15 2012. Retrieve at http://www.ctvnews.ca/1000s-pray-for-russian-church-mired-in-punk-controversy-1.799748. **P143:** Paris, Joseph. "Manifestation des FEMEN devant le Ministère de la Justice français." *Wikimedia Commons*. October 15 2012. **P159:** @femenmovement. "AntiFascist Front." *Facebook.com*. 2016. Retrieve at www.Facebook.com/femenmovement. **P162:** Common Dreams Staff. "Women of FEMEN Crash 'Gangsters Party in Davos'." *Common Dreams: Breaking News and Views for the Progressive Community*. January 28 2012. Retrieve at http://www.commondreams.org/news/2012/01/28/women-femen-crash-gangsters-party-davos. **P171:** Garanich, Gleb. "Women in Femen." *Hindustan Times*. March 3 2012. Retrieve at http://www.hindustantimes.com/photos/world/women-in-femen/photo-gvzP9TppsQYxvQEk2a9YcO.html. **P173:** Cernec, Alexandre. Remix of Félicien Rops, *The Temptation of St. Anthony 1878*. April 16 2013. See Cernec's work at his website: www.cernec.fr.

BIBLIOGRAPHY

300. Director Zack Snyder. Legendary Studios, 2006. Film.
Adamson, Danial Silas. "100 Women 2015: Return of a topless rebel." *BBC World Service*. November 28 2015. Retrieve online at http://www.bbc.com/news/magazine-34949413
"Adana Çiftçileriyle Konuşma." March 16 1923, quoted in *The Turkish Times,* December 1 1995.
Agence France-Presse. "Turkey police fire rubber bullets at banned Gay Pride parade." *The Telegraph*. June 27 2016. Retrieve at http://www.telegraph.co.uk/news/2016/06/27/turkey-police-fire-rubber-bullets-at-banned-gay-pride-parade/
Agence France-Presse in Ankara. "Turkish court rejects Erdoğan's ban on his enemy's schools." *The Guardian*. July 14 2015. Retrieve at https://www.theguardian.com/world/2015/jul/14/turkish-court-throws-out-erdogans-ban-on-fethullah-gulen-schools-dershanes.
Ahmed, Loila. *A Quiet Revolution: The Veil's Resurgence, from the Middle East to America*. New Haven: Yale University Press, 2011.

Aitamurto, Kaarina, and Scott Simpson. *Modern Pagan and Native Faith Movements in Central and Eastern Europe*. New York: Routledge, 2014.

Aitkenhead, Decca. "Femen Leader Inna Shevchenko: 'I'm For Any Form of Feminism'." *The Guardian.* November 8 2013. Retrieve at https://www.theguardian.com/world/2013/nov/08/femen-leader-inna-shevchenko-interview

Alkhateeb, Firas. *Lost Islamic History: Reclaiming Muslim Civilisation from the Past*. London: Hurst & Company, 2014.

Al-Rasheed, Madawi, Carool Kersten, and Marat Shterin, eds. *Demystifying the Caliphate: Historical Memory and Contemporary Contexts.* Oxford: Oxford University Press, 2015.

Althusser, Louis. *On the Reproduction of Capitalism: Ideology And Ideological State Apparatuses.* (1970). Trans. G. M. Goshgarian. London: Verso, 2014.

Arango, Tim, Ceylan Yeginsu. "Turkey to Release Tens of Thousands of Prisoners to Make Room for Coup Suspects." *New York Times.* August 17 2016. Retrieve at http://www.nytimes.com/2016/08/18/world/europe/turkey-prisoners-erdogan.html

Arendt, Hannah. *On Violence*. New York: Harcourt, Brace and World, 1970.

Arendt, Hannah. *The Life of Mind - Thinking – Willing.* New York: Harcourt, Brace and World. 1978.

Arendt, Hannah. *The Origins of Totalitarianism.* San Diego: Harcourt Inc., 1948.

Argyle, M. and Beit-Hallahmi, B. *The Social Psychology of Religion.* Abingdon-on-Thames: Routledge, 1975.

"Atatürk, Mustafa Kemal." *Ana Britannica Volume 2: Ami – Avr.* London: Funk & Wagnalls, 1987.

Aune, Kristin. "Why Feminists Are Less Religious." *The Guardian.* March 29 2011. Accessed December 10 2016. Retrieve at https://www.theguardian.com/commentisfree/belief/2011/mar/29/why-feminists-less-religious-survey

Barlas, Asma. *"Believing Women" in Islam: Unreading Patriarchal Interpretations of the Qur'an*. Austin: University of Texas Press, 2002.

Barthes, Roland. Trans. Annette Lavers. *Mythologies.* London: Paladin, 1972.

Batalden, Stephen K. and Sandra L. Batalden. *The Newly Independent States of Eurasia: Handbook of Former Soviet Republics.* Phoenix, Arizona: The Oryx Press, 1997.

Beardsley, Eleanor. "With Topless Protests, 'Sextremists' March In Paris." *NPR Radio.* October 19 2012. Accessed February 13 2017. Retrieve at http://www.npr.org/2012/10/19/163257726/with-topless-protests-sextremists-march-in-paris

Bennett, Jessica. "How to Reclaim the F-Word? Just Call Beyoncé." *Time Magazine Online.* Aug 26 2014. Retrieve at http://time.com/3181644/beyonce-reclaim-feminism-pop-star/

Berlatsky, Noah. "Beyoncé Doesn't Perform for the Male Gaze." *Pacific Standard*. October 7 2014. Retrieve at https://psmag.com/social-justice/beyonce-91908.

Betlemidze, Mariam. "Mediatized Controversies of Feminist Protest: FEMEN and Bodies as Affective Events." *Women's Studies in Communication*, vol. 38 no. 4 (2015): 374-379. Retrieve at http://www.tandfonline.com/doi/full/10.1080/07491409.2015.1089103

Bidder, Benjamin. "Kiev's Topless Protestors: 'The Entire Ukraine Is a Brothel'." *Spiegel Online International.* May 5 2011. Retrieve online at http://www.spiegel.de/international/europe/kiev-s-topless-protestors-the-entire-ukraine-is-a-brothel-a-760697.html

Birnbaum, Maria. "Exclusive Pluralism: The Problems of Habermas' Postsecular Argument and the Making of Religion." In *Religion as a Category of Governance and Sovereignty*. Trevor Stack, Naomi Goldenberg and Timothy Fitzgerald, eds. Leiden, Netherlands: Brill Publishing, 2015. p. 182-196.

Birnbaum, Maria. unpublished thesis. "Becoming Recognizable: Postcolonial Independence and the Reification of Religion." *European University Institute, Department of Social and Political Science.* Florence: 2015.

Braidotti, Rosi. "In Spite of the Times: The Postsecular Turn in Feminism." *Theory, Culture & Society,* vol. 25 no. 6 (2008): 1-24.

Brock, David C. *Understanding Moore's Law: Four Decades of Innovation.* Philadelphia: Chemical Heritage Press, 2006.

Bruns, J. Edgar. *God As Woman, Woman As God.* New York: Paulist Press, 1973.

"Bulletpoint." *The Guardian.* March 2013. Retrieve online at https://profile.theguardian.com/user/id/11668722

Bulliet, Richard W. "Are the Turkish Leader Erdogan's claims of terrorist coup plotting to be believed?" *fgulen.com.* August 15 2016. Retrieve online at http://fgulen.com/en/home/1324-fgulen-com-english/press/columns/25006-an-ottoman-empire-of-the-mind

Bunting, Annie. "Theorizing women's cultural diversity in feminist international human rights strategies." *Journal of Law and Society.* 1993. Retrieve at papers.ssrn.com.

Burdzhalov, Édourd. *Russia's Second Revolution: The February 1917 Uprising in Petrograd.* Indianapolis: Indiana University Press, 1987.

Carlyle, Thomas. *Heroes and Hero-Worship, The Hero as Divinity.* London: Chapman and Hall Limited, 1840.

Cassano, Jay. "Turkish Protests Are About Democracy, Not Religion: Western media are characterizing the demonstrations as a clash between Islamism and secularism—but it's government abuse of power that Turks are protesting." *The Nation.* June 5 2013. Retrieve at https://www.thenation.com/article/turkish-protests-are-about-democracy-not-religion/

Charkiewcz, Ewa. "The Impact of the Crisis on Women in Eastern Europe." *Committee for the Abolition of Third World Debt.* 2010. Retrieve at http://cadtm.org/The-Impact-of-the-Crisis-on-Women

Chatterjee, Partha. "Fasting for Bin Laden: The Politics of Secularization in Contemporary India." in Scott, David and Charles Hirschkind, eds, *Powers of the Secular Modern: Talal Asad and His Interlocutors.* Stanford: Stanford University Press, 2006.

Christ, Carol P. and Judith Plaskow. *Womanspirit Rising: A Feminist Reader in Religion.* San Francisco: Harper and Row, 1979.

Christ, Carol P. and Judith Plaskow. *Weaving the Visions: New Patterns in Feminist Spirituality.* San Francisco: Harper and Row, 1989.

'Christian Messenger.' *Anders Breivik: His Life and Mission.* Online: self-published, 2012.

"Christianization of Kievan Rus Commemorative Coins." *National Bank of Ukraine.* Accessed April 20 2014. Updated 2008.

Cimino, Richard. "Secular Rituals and Atheist Solidarity". *Atheist Identities Workshop: University of Ottawa.* November 22-24 2012.

Cochrane, Kira. "Rise of the naked female warriors." *The Guardian.* March 20 2013. Retrieve at https://www.theguardian.com/world/2013/mar/20/naked-female-warrior-femen-topless-protesters.

Connolly, William E. *Why I Am Not A Secularist.* Minneapolis: University of Minneapolis Press, 1999.

Crick, Matthew. *Power, Surveillance, and Culture in YouTube™'s Digital Sphere.* Hershey, Pennsylvania: IGI Global Publishing, 2016.

Daly, Mary. *The Church and the Second Sex.* Boston: Beacon Press, 1968.

Daly, Mary. *Beyond God the Father: Toward a Philosophy of Women's Liberation.* Boston: Beacon Press, 1973.

Daly, Mary. *Gyn/ecology: The Metaethics of Radical Feminism.* Boston: Beacon Press, 1978.

Davie, Grace. *Religion in Britain Since 1945: Believing Without Belonging.* Hoboken, New Jersey: Wiley Blackwell Publishers, 1994.

Davies, Bronwyn, Rom Harré. "Positioning: The Discursive Production of Selves." *Journal for the Theory of Social Behaviour,* vol. 20 no. 1. (March 1990): 43–63.

de Beauvoir, Simone, trans. H. M. Parshley. *The Second Sex.* New York: Bantam Books, 1952.

de Bellaigue, Christopher. "Turkey: 'Surreal, Menacing...Pompous'". *New York Review of Books.* December 19 2013.

Dedorson, Emma Sofia. "She Fights With Breast and Words. Inna's Interview." *Femen Official Blog.* March 29 2016. Accessed April 21 2016. Retrieve at http://femen.org/she-fights-with-breast-and-words-innas-interview/

Dhaliwal, Sukhwant, and Nira Yuval-Davis. *Women Against Fundamentalism*. London: London Lawrence & Wishart, 2014.

Diamond, James S. "The Post-secular: A Jewish Perspective." *Cross Currents: Association for Religion & Intellectual Life,* vol. 53 no. 4 (Winter 2004).

Dickey Young, Pamela. *Feminist Theology/Christian Theology: In Search of Method.* Minneapolis: Augsburg Fortress, 1990.

Dreamshare. (Cameron Montgomery). "Excuse me, what are they chanting? "Where is my lover? Here I am." A tear in my eye at Istanbul Pride 2014." *Instagram.* July 3 2014. Accessed February 23 2017. Retrieve at https://www.instagram.com/p/p2KiE3lo89/

Dressler, Markus and Arvind-Pal S. Mandair. *Secularism and Religion-Making*. Oxford: Oxford University Press, 2011.

Drimonis, Toula. "Why as a Feminist I Will Never Identify With Femen." *Head Space*. August 5 2015. Retrieve at http://headspacepress.com/feminist-doesnt-relate-femen/

Durkheim, Emile. "Introduction à la morale." *Revue Philosophique*, 1920.

Durkheim, Emile. *The Elementary Forms of the Religious Life* (1912). Trans. Karen E. Fields. New York: The Free Press, 1995.

Editors Online. ""In gay we trust" ...Topless women celebrate Pope's resignation in Paris." *Osundefender.org*. February 13 2013. Retrieve at http://www.osundefender.org/in-gay-we-trust-topless-women-celebrate-popes-resignation/

EsraFurtana. "Gezi.. Ne diyim? Güzelsin... #WeAreGezi #direngeziparkı #occupygezi @edihvet." *Twitter*. June 8 2013. Accessed February 22 2017. Retrieve at https://twitter.com/EsraFurtana

Fine, Cordelia. *Delusions of Gender: How Our Minds, Society, and Neurosexism Create Difference.* New York: W. W. Norton, 2010.

Finn, Geraldine. "On the Reification of Ideas —Of Man—and the Return of the Repressed." Presented March 9 2016 in *Gender and Religion.* Ottawa: University of Ottawa.

Fitzgerald, Timothy. *Ideology of Religious Studies*. Oxford: Oxford University Press, 2005.

Foucault, Michel. *Power/Knowledge: Selected Interviews and Other Writings 1972-1977*. Trans. C. Gordon. New York: Pantheon Books, 1980.

Foucault, Michel. *The Foucault Reader*. Paul Rabinow, ed. Toronto: Random House Ltd., 1984.

Frenkel, Sheera. "Femen Is Bringing Its Topless Protest To Bethlehem — What Could Possibly Go Wrong?" *BuzzFeed News*. Dec 3 2013. Retrieve at https://www.buzzfeed.com/sheerafrenkel/femen-are-bring-their-topless-protest-to-bethlehem-what-coul?utm_term=.jnpAjpk52#.bfpkal5NW

Freud, Sigmund. *Civilization and Its Discontents*. Vienna: Internationaler Psychoanalytischer Verlag Wien, 1930.

Frye, Bob, 2015 comment on Al Jazeera English. "The Future of Feminism?" *YouTube.com*. October 25 2012. Retrieve online at https://www.youtube.com/watch?v=TdaKVqIy0LE

Future Quest. "A Summer Experience for Youth." *School of Religion: Queen's University.* Kingston: School of Religion, 2012.

Gadon, Elinor. *The Once and Future Goddess: A Sweeping Visual Chronicle of the Sacred Female and Her Re-emergence in the Cult.* New York: HarperCollins, 1989.

Gagne, Laura. "Athens, Persia Sparta." *University of Ottawa Lecture*, March 2013.

Gaylor, Annie Laurie. *Women Without Superstition: 'No Gods, No Masters'*. Madison, Wisconsin: Freedom from Religion Foundation, 1997.

Gaylor, Annie Laurie. "The History of Women in Freethought." *Women in Secularism Conference: Center for Inquiry*. August 16-18 2012.

Gimbutas, Marija. *The Language of the Goddess: Unearthing the Hidden Symbols of Western Civilization*. San Francisco: Harper & Row, 1989.

Girgenty, Guido. "Ukrainians bring down Yanukovych regime, 2013-2014." in *Global Nonviolent Action Database*. George Lakey, ed. April 21 2014. Retrieve online at nvdatabase.swarthmore.edu

Goldenberg, Naomi. "Some (Mainly) Very Appreciative Comments on Brent Nongbri's *Before Religion*." *The Critical Religion Association: Critical Approaches to the Study of Religion*. May 6 2013. Retrieve at https://criticalreligion.org/2013/05/06/some-mainly-very-appreciative-comments-on-brent-nongbris-before-religion/

Goldenberg, Naomi. "The Category of Religion in the Technology of Governance: An Argument for Understanding Religions as Vestigial States." In *Religion as a Category of Governance and Sovereignty*. Trevor Stack, Naomi Goldenberg and Timothy Fitzgerald, eds. Leiden, Netherlands: Brill Publishing, 2015.

Goldenberg, Naomi. "The Religious is Political." *SRS 2112: Women in Religion*. Ottawa: University of Ottawa, 2015.

Goldenberg, Naomi. "What is this Slouching Toward Bethlehem?: Is it a New Feminist Defense of Religion?" Presented at *Feminisms Beyond the Secular: Epistemologies and Politics for the 21st Century*, Lehigh University, Bethlehem Pennsylvania. March 22 2016.

Goldenberg, Naomi. "There is No Religion in the Bible." Unpublished manuscript. 2016.

goliathrk. "First topless protest in an Islamic state leads to 3 arrests." *Reddit: World News*. April 11 2013. Retrieve at https://www.reddit.com/r/worldnews/comments/1fbm3a/first_topless_protest_in_an_islamic_state_leads/#ca8q3cq.

Gray, Carmen. "Femen firebrand Inna Shevchenko speaks: The Ukrainian activist on how she learned to stop worrying and fight the power." *Dazed & Confused Magazine*. February 2014. Retrieve at http://www.dazeddigital.com/artsandculture/article/18444/1/femens-firebrand-inna-shevchenko

Greener, Sue, and Asher Rospigliosi. "The Proceedings of the European Conference on Social Media." *University of Brighton*, 10-11 July 2014. Brighton: Academic Conferences and Publishing Limited, 2014. https://books.google.ca/books?id=OVkTBAAAQBAJ&pg=PA442&dq=how+many+protesters+occupied+maidan+square&hl=en&sa=X&ved=0ahUKEwjc5JzVnJfMAhUHvYMKHYwbDdkQ6AEIGzAA#v=onepage&q=how%20many%20protesters%20occupied%20maidan%20square&f=false

Gross, Rita M. *Feminism and Religion: An Introduction*. Boston: Beacon Press, 1996.

Gupta, Raadhika. *Religion, Gender and Body Politics: Post-Secular, Post-Colonial and Queer Perspectives*, Feb 12-14 2015. Utrecht University.

Habermas, Jürgen. "Secularism's Crisis of Faith: Notes on Post-Secular Society". *New Perspectives Quarterly*, vol. 25 (2008): 17-29.

Habermas, Jürgen. *Between Naturalism and Religion*. Cambridge: Polity Press, 2008.

Haidar, Ensaf. "Raif Badawi: Humanitarian, Freethinker, Writer." *Raif Badawi Foundation*. Accessed June 2016. http://www.raifbadawi.org/about-raif-badawi/all-about-raif-badawi.html

Hanisch, Carol. "The Personal Is Political." *Notes from the Second Year: Women's Liberation*. New York: New York Radical Women, 1970.

Hanovs, Deniss, and Valdis Tēraudkalns. *Ultimate Freedom - No Choice: The Culture of Authoritarianism in Latvia from 1934-1940*. Leiden, Netherlands: Brill Publishing, 2013.

Hasegawa, Tsuyoshi. *The February Revolution, Petrograd, 1917*. Washington: University of Washington Press, 1981.

Heelas, Paul, and Linda Woodhead. *The Spiritual Revolution: Why Religion is Giving Way to Spirituality*. Oxford: Blackwell Publishing Ltd., 2005.

Hennessy, Angela. "Meet the Topless Protester Who Stormed Parliament Hill Last Week." *Vice News*. May 14 2014. Retrieve at https://www.vice.com/en_ca/read/meet-the-topless-protestor-who-stormed-parliament-hill-last-week

Hidayatullah, Aysha. *Feminist Edges of the Qur'an*. Oxford: Oxford University Press, 2014.

"How the Lateran Treaty made the Catholic Church into a state." *Concordat Watch*. Accessed July 24 2016. Retrieve online at http://www.concordatwatch.eu/topic-841.843

Hutchinson, Sikivu. *Moral Combat: Black Atheists, Gender Politics, and the Values Wars.* Los Angeles: Infidel Books, 2011.

"'I am not a slave': Nude Protester Calls for Solidarity." *Iranwire.com.* April 12 2016. Retrieve at https://iranwire.com/en/features/1750

Ibrahim, Osman Rifat. "AKP and the great neo-Ottoman travesty." *Al Jazeera.* May 23 2014. Retrieve at http://www.aljazeera.com/indepth/opinion/2014/05/akp-great-neo-ottoman-travesty-201451974314589207.html.

'Ilana Alazzeh.' *Wikia.* Accessed June 1 2016. Retrieve at http://genchange.wikia.com/wiki/Ilana_Alazzeh

Ilariagenovesio. "Gezi Park Art and Activism in Turkey: #OccupyGezi Movement Through the Eyes of Contemporary Turkish Art." *Tumblr.com.* Accessed February 22 2017. Retrieve at http://ilariagenovesio.tumblr.com/

"Irina Krashkova refused counsel." *Donbass.UA.* October 30 2013. Retrieve at http://donbass.ua/news/ukraine/2013/10/30/progulivajuschaja-zasedanija-suda-krashkova-otkazalas-ot-advokata.html

"Islamic scholar Gülen criticizes Turkish gov't response to Gezi protests." *Hürriyet Daily News.* March 20 2014. Retrieve at http://www.hurriyetdailynews.com/islamic-scholar-gulen-criticizes-turkish-govt-response-to-gezi-protests.aspx?pageID=238&nID=63849&NewsCatID=338

Ivakhiv, Adrian. "In Search of Deeper Identities: Neopaganism and 'Native Faith' in Contemporary Ukraine." *Nova Religio: The Journal of Alternative and Emergent Religions*, vol. 8 no. 3. University of California Press, (2005): 7–38.

Jacobs, Jonathan D. "The Ineffable, Inconceivable, and Incomprehensible God Fundamentality and Apophatic Theology." *Oxford Studies in Philosophy of Religion.* Oxford: Oxford University Press, 2015.

Jacoby, Susan. "A Woman's Place? The Dearth of Women in the Secular Movement." *The Humanist: A Magazine of Critical Inquiry and Social Concern,* (Fall 2012). Retrieved from http://thehumanist.org/september-october-2012/a-woman%E2%80%99s-place-the-dearth-of-women-in-the-secular-movement/

Jakobsen, Janet, Ann Pellegrini. *Love the Sin: Sexual Regulation and the Limits of Religious Tolerance.* Beacon Press, 2004.

Jeffreys, Sheila. *Man's Dominion: The Rise of Religion and the Eclipse of Women's Rights.* Wiltshire: Routledge, 2012.

Je Suis Femen. Director Alain Margot. Caravel Production, 2014. Film.

Joas, Hans. *Do We Need Religion? On the Experience of Self-Transcendence.* Boulder, Colorado: Paradigm Publishers, 2008a.

Joas, Hans. "Antisecularism: Jürgen Habermas." *European Journal of Sociology*, 49 (2008b): 467-471.

Jonas, Silvia. *Ineffability and its Metaphysics: The Unspeakable in Art, Religion, and Philosophy.* London: Palgrave Macmillan, 2016.

Jones, Reece. "We Spoke to Kitty Green about her FEMEN Documentary 'Ukraine is Not a Brothel'". *Vice News.* June 17 2014. http://www.vice.com/read/we-spoke-to-kitty-green-about-her-femen-documentary-ukraine-is-not-a-brothel

Juergensmeyer, Mark, Dinah Griego, and John Soboslai. *God in the Tumult of the Global Square: Religion in Global Civil Society.* California: University of California Press, 2015.

Julian, Hana Levi. "Neo-Nazi Parties Win Seats in 2 European Parliament Elections: An anti-EU trend is sweeping Europe; the other ominous trend is a rapidly rising anti-Semitism." *The Jewish Press.* May 26 2014. http://www.jewishpress.com/news/breaking-news/neo-nazi-parties-win-seats-in-2-european-parliament-elections/2014/05/26/ Accessed April 2, 2016.

Karaağaç, Barış. "Turkey in Crisis: Understanding the Erdogan/ Gulen Split." *The Real News Network.* January 13 2014. Retrieve at http://therealnews.com/t2/index.php?option=com_content&task=view&id=31&jumival=11318

Karatnycky, Adrian. "Ukraine's Orange Revolution." *Council on Foreign Relations: Foreign Affairs,* vol. 84 no. 2 (2005): 35-52.

Kehrer, Günther. "Religion." in Cancik, Hubert, Burkhard Gladigow, Karl-Heinz Kohl, eds. *Handbuch religionswissenschaftlicher Grundbegriffe*. Stuttgart: Kohlhammer, vol. 4 (1998): 418-425.

King, Karen L. *The Gospel of Mary of Magdala: Jesus and the First Woman Apostle*. Santa Rosa, California: Polebridge Press, 2003.

Kolluoglu, Poyraz. "The Gezi Park Events: Affective Intensities and Communal Ties." *Unravelling Religion Conference*, May 13-14. Kingston: Queen's University, 2013.

Kolluoglu, Poyraz. "The Postmodern Sacred in a Belated Modernity: Environmentalism, Motivations and Meanings in the Gezi Movement." *Unravelling Religion III Conference*, March 1. Kingston: Queen's University, 2016.

Kolokoltsev, Andrei. "Crimea children's theatre forced to shut for 'promoting western propaganda: Popular drama school complains of harassment from local officials who accused them of championing Ukrainian nationalism." *The Guardian: New East Network*. January 6 2016. Retrieve at http://www.theguardian.com/world/2016/jan/06/crimea-children-theatre-forced-to-shut-western-propaganda

Krindatch, Alexei D. "Religion in Postsoviet Ukraine as a Factor in Regional, Ethno-Cultural and Political Diversity." *Religion, State & Society,* vol. 31 no. 1 (2003).

Krushynska, Olena. "Ancient wooden churches in the Land of Zakarpattya." *Welcome to Ukraine.* Accessed January 2016. Retrieve at http://www.wumag.kiev.ua/index2.php?param=pgs20092/56

Kuzio, Taras. *Independent Ukraine: Nation-state Building and Post-communist Transition*. New York: Routledge, 2015.

Larsson, Milène. "Femen - Sextremism in Paris." *Vice Media News.* June 11 2013. http://www.vice.com/en_ca/video/femen-sextremism-in-paris

Latif, Iqbal. "How does one assume the title of Caliph?" March 17 2015. Retrieve at http://iqballatif.newsvine.com/_news/2015/03/17/31048154-how-does-one-assume-the-title-of-caliph

Lesiv, Mariya. *The Return of Ancestral Gods: Modern Ukrainian Paganism as an Alternative Vision for a Nation*. Kingston: Queen's University Press, 2013.

Love is a Verb. Directors Terry Spencer Hesser and Stephan Mazurek. Global Vision Productions, 2014. Film.

Lyubitseva, Olga. "Research on the Geography of Religion in Ukraine." *Peregrinus Cracoviensis*, vol. 25 no. 3 (2014): 91-100.

Maccaud, Jeremy and Genaro Bardy. "Anna Hutsol 'The Femen have shown the way' of Maidan." 2014. *[Naro]Minded*. Accessed April 2 2016. Retrieve at http://www.narominded.com/2014/11/anna-hutsol-les-femen-ont-montre-la-voie-de-maidan/

MacKinnon, Mark. "How Vladimir Putin Helped Resurrect the Russian Orthodox Church." *The Globe and Mail.* January 15 2014. Accessed March 10 2014. Retrieve at http://www.theglobeandmail.com/news/world/how-vladimir-putin-helped-resurrect-the-russian-orthodox-church/article16361650/

Macnab, Geoffrey. "'I Don't Want to be Liked': Inna Shevchenko, Leader of Women's Rights Group Femen, Talks Dictators, Documentaries and Death Threats." *Independent.* January 17 2014. Retrieve at http://www.independent.co.uk/news/people/profiles/i-dont-want-to-be-liked-inna-shevchenko-leader-of-womens-rights-group-femen-talks-dictators-9062734.html#gallery

Mango, Andrew. *Atatürk*. London: John Murray Publishers, 1999.

Markovic, Olesia. "Ukraine: A New Island of Dictatorship in Europe." Politics: Al Jazeera. January 20 2014. Retrieve at http://www.aljazeera.com/indepth/opinion/2014/01/ukraine-new-island-dictatorship-europe-201412010435224893.html

Masuzawa, Tomoko. *The Invention of World Religions: How European Universalism was Preserved in the Language of Pluralism.* Chicago: University of Chicago Press, 2005.

Masterson, Orla. "It's FemiNIST not FemiNAZI*." Student Independent News: NUI Galways's Online Student Newspaper.* April 2017. Retrieve at http://www.sin.ie/2017/04/18/its-feminist-not-feminazi/

Matta, Xuan. "Feminists Against Femen." *Facebook.com*. October 20 2013. Retrieve at https://www.facebook.com/EXit-FEMEN-The-truth-about-Femen-272316346234582/)

McCall, Leslie. "The Complexity of Intersectionality." *Signs: Journal of Women in Culture and Society*, vol. 30, no. 3. Chicago: The University of Chicago, 2005.

McGuire, Meredith B. *Lived Religion: Faith and Practice in Everyday Life*. New York: Oxford University Press, 2008.

Melnyczuk, Lesa. *Silent Memories, Traumatic Lives: Ukrainian Migrant Refugees in Western Australia*. Welshpool, Australia: Western Australian Museum, 2012.

Metzel, Mikhail. "Femen Protest Photos." *Cryptome*. January 29 2012. Retrieve at https://cryptome.org/info/femen/femen-protest.htm

Miller, Monica. Comments on Cameron Montgomery's presentation "Between Sovereignties: Women between Church and State in Ukraine" at *Feminisms Beyond the Secular: Emerging Epistemologies and Politics in the 21st Century*, Lehigh University, Bethlehem, PA. March 21-23 2016.

Mitchell, Joni. "Big Yellow Taxi." *Ladies of the Canyon*, Reprise, 1970.

Monaghan, Patricia. *Goddesses in World Culture, Volume 1: Asia and Africa*. Santa Barbara: Praeger, 2011.

Montgomery, Cameron. "Antisemitism on the Rise in Europe: Some Photos." *Willful and Wayward.* March 4 2015. Accessed February 20 2017. Retrieve at https://willfulandwayward.wordpress.com/tag/swastika/

Mulvey, Laura. "Visual Pleasure and Narrative Cinema." *Film Theory and Criticism: Introductory Readings*. Leo Braudy and Marshall Cohen, eds. New York: Oxford University Press, 1999: 833-44.

Murphy, Meghan. "There is a wrong way to do feminism. And Femen is doing it wrong." *Feminist Current*. Oct 31 2012. Accessed May 12 2016. Retrieve at http://www.feministcurrent.com/2012/10/31/there-is-a-wrong-way-to-do-feminism-and-femen-is-doing-it-wrong/

Najumi, Mohadesa. "Op-Ed: Where Femen Has Gone Wrong." *Feminist Wire*. April 7 2013. Retrieve at http://www.thefeministwire.com/2013/04/op-ed-where-femen-have-gone-wrong/.

Namazie, Maryam. "Why An International Day to Defend Amina?" *Maryam Namazie, Nothing is Sacred: Freethought Blogs.* April 2 2013. http://freethoughtblogs.com/maryamnamazie/2013/04/02/why-an-international-day-to-defend-amina/

Nas, Tevfik F. *Economics and Politics of Turkish Liberalization*. Bethlehem, Pennsylvania: Lehigh University Press, 1992.

Nasreen, Taslima. "Crazy Catholics!" *No Country For Women: Freethoughblogs.com*. November 20 2012. http://freethoughtblogs.com/taslima/2012/11/20/femen-protested-against-crazy-catholics/ Accessed January 10 2016.

Nawaz, Maajid. "I'm a Muslim reformer who is being smeared as an 'anti-Muslim extremist' by angry white liberals." *Voices: The Independent.* Accessed February 4 2017. Retrieve at http://www.independent.co.uk/voices/anti-extremism-muslim-far-left-politics-quilliam-social-reform-a7388931.html

Nicolson, Nigel. "Virginia Woolf." *Books: The New York Times on the Web*. 2000. Accessed February 1 2017. Retrieve at http://www.nytimes.com/books/first/n/nicolson-woolf.html

Nongbri, Brent. *Before Religion: The History of a Modern Concept*. New Haven, United States: Yale University Press, 2013.

Now World News. "FEMEN urinates on Ukrainian president." *YouTube.com*. December 1 2013. Retrieve online at https://www.youtube.com/watch?v=IkzaDGKXMZo Nongbri, Brent. *Before Religion: A History of a Modern Concept*. New Haven: Yale, 2012.

Orwell, George. *1984*. London: Secker and Warburg, 1949.

Owen, Suzanne. "The World Religions Paradigm: Time For a Change." *Arts and Humanities in Higher Education,* vol. 10 no. 3 (2011): 253-268. Retrieve at http://ahh.sagepub.com/content/10/3/253.full.pdf+html

Owen, Suzanne and Teemu Tara. "The Category of 'Religion' in Public Classification: Charity Registration of The Druid Network in England and Wales." In *Religion as a Category of Governance and Sovereignty*. Trevor Stack, Naomi Goldenberg, and Timothy Fitzgerald, eds. Leiden, Netherlands: Brill Publishing, 2015. p. 90-114.

Paulson, Steve. "Critical Intimacy: An Interview with Gayatri Chakravorty Spivak." *Los Angeles Review of Books.* July 29 2016. Retrieve at https://lareviewofbooks.org/article/critical-intimacy-interview-gayatri-chakravorty-spivak/

Pollitt, Kathlyn. "Sexism and Religion: Can the Knot be Untied?" *Women in Secularism II Conference*. Washington D.C. March 2013.

Pamuk, Şevket. *A Monetary History of the Ottoman Empire*. Cambridge: Cambridge University Press, 2000.

Panayiv, Oleksa. "Gods of Slavic Mythology." *Welcome to Ukraine.* Accessed January 2016. Retrieve online at http://www.wumag.kiev.ua/index2.php?param=pgs20092/50

Pitman, Paul M. "The Rise of the Turks and the Ottoman Empire." in *Turkey: A Country Study*. Helen Chapin Metz, ed. Washington, DC: Federal Research Division of the Library of Congress, 1987. Retrieve at https://www.loc.gov/item/95049612/

Polanyi, Karl. *The Great Transformation: The Political and Economic Origins of Our Time*. Boston: Beacon Press, 1944.

Pomerantsev, Peter. "The Revolution of Dignity." *Adbusters.* June 26 2015. Retrieve at http://www.adbusters.org/article/the-revolution-of-dignity/

Proshak, Vitaliy. "Paganism in Ukraine: Its Beliefs, Encounter with Christianity, and Survival." *Theological Reflection,* 7 (2006): 140-148.

Puar, Jasbir. *Terrorist Assemblages: Homonationalism in Queer Times*. Durham, United States: Duke University Press, 2007.

"Putin reveals secrets of Russia's Crimea takeover plot." *BBC News*. March 9 2015. Retrieve at http://www.bbc.com/news/world-europe-31796226.

Pyzik, Agata. *Poor But Sexy: Culture Clashes in Europe East and West*. Croydon, England: John Hunt Publishing, 2014.

Rahman, Fazlur. *Islam and Modernity: Transformation of an Intellectual Tradition*. Chicago: University Of Chicago Press, 1984.

Rahman, Fazlur. *Islam.* Chicago: University Of Chicago Press, 2002.

Ratzinger, Joseph. "Congregation for the Doctrine of the Faith: Letter to the Bishop of the Catholic Church on the Pastoral Care of Homosexual Persons." *Given At Rome*, October 1 1986. Retrieve at http://www.vatican.va/roman_curia/congregations/cfaith/documents/rc_con_cfaith_doc_19861001_homosexual-persons_en.html

Raven, Charlotte. "Femen – the Beauty Fascist Fauminists." *Feminist Times.* Nov 1 2013. Retrieve at http://www.feministtimes.com/femen-the-beauty-fascist-fauminists/

Reed, Betsy, ed. *Nothing Sacred: Women Respond to Religious Fundamentalism and Terror*. New York: Nation's Books, 2002.

Robinson, Andrew. "Roland Barthes: The War Against Myth." *An A to Z of Theory. Ceasefire Magazine.* October 2011. Retrieved at: http://ceasefiremagazine.co.uk/in-theory-barthes-5/

Rudnytsky, Ivan L. "The Political Thought of Soviet Ukrainian Dissidents." *Essays in Modern Ukrainian History*. 1987. Retrieve at http://www.ditext.com/rudnytsky/history/diss.html

Ruecker, Michael. "Dances With 'Religion': A Critical History of the Strategic Uses of the Category of Religion by the Government of Canada and First Nations, 1885 to 1951." *Unpublished thesis*. Ottawa: University of Ottawa, 2015.

Ruether, Rosemary. *Liberation Theology: Human Hope Confronts Christian History and American Power*. New York: Paulist Press, 1972.

Ruether, Rosemary. *To Change the World: Christology and Cultural Criticism*. Eugene, Oregon: Wipf and Stock Publishers, 1981.

Rybakov, Boris. "Iazychestvo drevnikh slavia [Old Russian Snake Amulets]." *Palaeoslavica*, vol. 14 no. 2 (2006).

Rybakov, Boris. Moskva. *Le paganisme des anciens slaves* (1982). trans. Lise Gruel Apert 1994. Paris: Presses universitaires de France, 1994.

Saint-Cyr, Yosie. "Defining Religion Under the Charter—Church of the Universe Case." *Slaw: Canada's Online Legal Magazine.* April 15 2010. Accessed February 15 2016. Retrieve at http://www.slaw.ca/2010/04/15/defining-religion-under-the-charter%E2%80%95church-of-the-universe-case/

Sanna. "Paganism." *Hagstone*. Accessed March 16 2016. Retrieve at http://hagstone.blogspot.ca/p/paganism.html

Sboui, Mounir. "Tunisia: Amina's father proud of her, shares her views." *ANSAmed*. June 6 2013. Retrieve at http://www.ansamed.info/ansamed/en/news/nations/tunisia/2013/06/06/Tunisia-Amina-father-proud-her-shares-her-views_8828268.html

Scharfstein, Ben-Ami. *Ineffability: The Failure of Words in Philosophy and Religion*. Albany New York: State University of New York Press, 1993.

Schenk, Christine. "Is religion the biggest problem facing feminism today?" *National Catholic.* March 6 2014. Retrieve at http://ncronline.org/blogs/simply-spirit/religion-biggest-problem-facing-feminism-today

Schüssler Fiorenza, Elisabeth. *Jesus: Miriam's Son, Sophia's Prophet*. New York: Continuum, 1994.

Schüssler Fiorenza, Elisabeth. *In Memory of Her: A Feminist Theological Reconstruction of Christian Origins*. New York: Crossroad, 1995.

Shaikh, Sa'diyya. "Exegetical Violence: Nushuz in Quranic Gender Ideology." *Journal for Islamic Studies,* vol. 17 no. 1 (1997): 49-73.

"Shepherdess FEMEN." *Vmir.su*. January 30 2014. Retrieve at http://www.vmir.su/67628-pastushki-femen.html

Shevchenko, Inna. "Sextremism: The New Way for Feminism to Be!" *Huffpost Lifestyle: United Kingdom.* February 7 2013. Accessed July 8 2015. Retrieve at http://www.huffingtonpost.co.uk/inna-shevchenko/sextremism-the-new-way-for-feminism_b_2634064.html

Shevchenko, Inna. "Charlie Hebdo Paris massacre: Everyone says 'Je Suis Charlie' now, but where were they when my friends were alive?" *International Business Times.* January 12 2015. http://www.ibtimes.co.uk/charlie-hebdo-paris-massacre-je-suis-charlie-demos-are-too-late-save-my-friends-1483003 Accessed January 30 2015.

Shevchenko, Inna. "Inna Shevchenko: Charlie Hebdo and the Godless Witch." *International Business Times.* January 30 2015. http://www.ibtimes.co.uk/inna-shevchenko-charlie-hebdo-godless-witch-1485921 Accessed January 30 2015

Shore, Marci. "Reading Tony Judt in Wartime Ukraine." *New Yorker*. August 11 2015. Retrieve at http://www.newyorker.com/books/page-turner/reading-tony-judt-in-wartime-ukraine

Smith, Keri E. Iyall. Patricia Leavy. *Hybrid Identities: Theoretical and Empirical Examinations*. Leiden, Netherlands: Brill Publishing, 2008.

Smith College. 2016. http://www.smith.edu/sfs/accounts_tuition.php

Snyder, Timothy. *Bloodlands: Europe Between Hitler and Stalin.* New York: Basic Books, 2010.

Snyder, Timothy. Tatiana Zhurzhenko. "Diaries and memoirs of the Maidan: Ukraine from November 2013 to February 2014." *Eurozine.com.* June 27 2014. Retrieve at http://www.eurozine.com/diaries-and-memoirs-of-the-maidan/.

Solonyna, Yevhen. Inna Kuznetsova. "Ukrainian Villagers Say Alleged Police-Rape Case Just Tip Of Iceberg." *Europe Radio Liberty*. July 9 2013. Retrieve at http://www.rferl.org/content/ukraine-police-rape-case/25041179.html

Solzhenitsyn, Aleksandr. *The Gulag Archipelago*. France: Éditions du Seuil, 1973.

Stack, Trevor, Naomi Goldenberg, Timothy Fitzgerald. *Religion as a Category of Governance and Sovereignty: Supplements to Method & Theory in the Study of Religion*. Leiden, Netherlands: Brill Publishing, 2015.

Stanton, Elizabeth Cady. *The Woman's Bible* (1895). New York: Dover Publications Inc., 2002.

Steinmetz, Katy. "Ukraine, Not the Ukraine: The Significance of Three Little Letters." *Time Magazine Online*. March 5 2014. Retrieve at: http://time.com/12597/the-ukraine-or-ukraine/

Stone, Merlin. "The Great Goddess." *Heresies: A Feminist Publication on Art and Politics*. New York: Heresies Collective Inc., vol. 2 no. 1 (1978).

Swatos, William H. Jr. *Politics and Religion in Central and Eastern Europe: Traditions and Transitions*. Westport, Connecticut: Greenwood Publishing Group Inc., 1994.

Tayler, Jeffrey. "Topless Jihad: Why Femen Is Right: The radical feminist group has ignited human-rights debates we need to have." *The Atlantic*. May 1 2013. Retrieve at http://www.theatlantic.com/international/archive/2013/05/topless-jihad-why-femen-is-right/275471/

Taylor, Charles. *A Secular Age*. Cambridge: Harvard University Press, 2007.

"The Facts on LGBT Rights in Russia." *The Council for Global Equality*. Accessed February 15 2017. Retrieve at http://www.globalequality.org/newsroom/latest-news/1-in-the-news/186-the-facts-on-lgbt-rights-in-russia

Toksvig, Sandi. "Sandi Toksvig's Top 10 Unsung Heroines." *The Guardian: Culture*. October 28 2009. Accessed April 17 2014. Retrieved at: http://www.theguardian.com/books/2009/oct/28/sandi-toksvig-unsung-heroines

Trefle, Céline. "FEMEN, the feminists turning the oppressed woman's body back against the oppressors." *BlaqSwans*. September 2 2013. http://blaqswans.org/en/2013/09/feminisme-aux-seins-nus/#comment-193655 Accessed March 2014.

Turgut, Pelin. "Live from 'Occupied' Gezi Park: In Istanbul, a New Turkish Protest Movement Is Born." *Time*. June 5 2013. Accessed January 12 2015. Retrieve at http://world.time.com/2013/06/05/live-from-occupied-gezi-park-in-istanbul-a-new-turkish-protest-movement-is-born/

"Turkey: Istanbul gay pride march banned over 'security' concern." *BBC*. June 17 2016. Retrieve at http://www.bbc.com/news/world-europe-36561731

"Ukraine agrees tough austerity package to gain $17.5bn IMF bailout." *RT News*. March 3 2015. Accessed April 30 2016. Retrieve at https://www.rt.com/business/237157-ukraine-cuts-budget-imf/

Ukraine. "How They Protest Prostitution in Ukraine." *The Observer: France 24*. August 28 2009. Retrieve at http://observers.france24.com/en/20090828-how-they-protest-prostitution-ukraine-femen-sex-tourism

Varol, Onur, Emilio Ferrara, Christine L. Ogan, Filippo Menczer, and Alessandro Flammini. "Evolution of Online User Behavior During a Social Upheaval." *arXiv.org*. Center for Complex Networks and Systems Research School of Informatics and Computing, Indiana University, Bloomington, USA. 2014. Retrieve at https://arxiv.org/pdf/1406.7197.pdf#cite.Tufekci2012

Vasyl, Markus. *Religion and Nationalism in Soviet Ukraine after 1945*. Cambridge, Massachusetts: Harvard Ukrainian Studies Fund, 1985.

Vogt, Kari, Lena Larsen, Christian Moe. *New Directions in Islamic Thought: Exploring Reform and Muslim Tradition*. London: I. B. Tauris & Co. Ltd., 2009.

Wadud, Amina. *Qur'an and Woman: Rereading the Sacred Text from a Woman's Perspective*. Oxford: Oxford University Press, 1992.

Watt, Montgomery. *The Cambridge History of Islam*. Cambridge: Cambridge University Press, 1970.

Wawrzonek, Michal. *Religion and Politics in Ukraine: The Orthodox and Greek Catholic Churches as Elements of Ukraine's Political System*. Newcastle-Upon-Tyne: Cambridge Scholars Publishing, 2014.

Western Fiasco. "Bare Breasts, a Femen Hymn." *Belong*, Independent, 2013.
Weber, Max. *The Protestant Ethic and the Spirit of Capitalism* (1905). New York: Routledge, 1992.
Winter On Fire: Ukraine's Fight For Freedom. Director Evgeny Afineevsky. Tolmor Production, 2014. Film.
Yanowitz, Jason. "February's Forgotten Vanguard: The Myth of Russia's Spontaneous Revolution." *History: Features. International Socialist Review*, no. 75 (2016). Retrieve at http://isreview.org/issue/75/februarys-forgotten-vanguard Accessed April 10 2016.
Young, Iris Marion. "Structural Injustice and the Politics of Difference," paper for the *AHRC Centre for Law, Gender, and Sexuality Intersectionality Workshop*. United Kingdom: Keele University, 2005. Retrieve at https://www.kent.ac.uk/clgs/documents/word-files/events/young.paper.doc
Yushchenko, Viktor. "Resources on Ethics, Faith and Public Life." *Berkeley Centre for Religion, Peace and World Affairs*. July 26 2008. Retrieve at: http://berkleycenter.georgetown.edu/resources/quotes/viktor-yushchenko-on-the-prospect-of-a-ukrainian-national-church-at-a-meeting-with-bartholomew-i
Zakharov, Yevhen. "History of Dissent in Ukraine." *Virtual Museum of the Dissident Movement in Ukraine.* Ukrainian Helsinki Human Rights Union, 2005. Retrieve at http://museum.khpg.org/eng/index.php?id=1127288239 Accessed April 16 2016.
Zetkin, Clara. *Lenin on the Woman Question*. New York: International Publishers Co., 1934.
Zmicier, Lukashuk. "Femen: Our War is Somewhat Different From Maidan." *Euroradio*. December 12 2014. http://euroradio.fm/en/femen-our-war-somewhat-different-maidan. Accessed March 20 2016.

www.ingramcontent.com/pod-product-compliance
Lightning Source LLC
Chambersburg PA
CBHW041127300426
44113CB00003B/87